Advance Praise for *Transnational Social Protection*

"This book is an essential reference point in academic and policy debates on transnational social protection and the need to rethink the structures for the provision of social welfare and access to rights across borders given the realities of human mobility in a global context of neoliberalism, inequality, deindustrialization, and austerity."

—**Alexandra Délano Alonso**, Associate Professor of Global Studies, The New School

"More and more people are citizens of one country but live and work in another. How do they obtain social protections? How do they manage the vagaries of work, health, and the law? What roles are played by governments, communities, non-profits, families, and friends? In *Transnational Social Protection*, Levitt, Dobbs, Sun, and Paul provide deeply researched answers to these questions. They develop the idea of Hybrid Transnational Social Protections (HTSP) and, via case studies and data, offer new and compelling insights on migration from the perspective of families struggling to make do in a complicated world."

—**Paul Osterman**, NTU Professor, MIT Sloan School

"This book is a must-read for scholars and practitioners struggling to make sense of the 'triple-win' migration and development discourse. It offers a transnational multi-sectoral approach to thinking afresh about the roles of states, markets, the third sector, and social networks and families in securing migrant rights and protections in a world fragmented by the power of economic nationalism."

—**Brenda Yeoh**, National University of Singapore

"This book moves the field forward in several ways. First, it asks important central questions: how do people gain access to social protections within the context of migration? How do they negotiate such protections for themselves and their families as they reside in places offering markedly different levels of or exclusion from state-provided social protection? How does this change as they move through the life course? Second, it uses but also notes how much prior research on transnationalism or state-centered social protections cannot fully describe how migrants and their families seek to access such social protections. Finally, and critically, the authors use empirical fieldwork-based evidence to describe and analyze how migrant families create resource environments to get access to social protections. They effectively ground and develop their theoretical arguments with data and cases. An important contribution."

—**Rob Smith**, Professor of Public and International Affairs, Marxe School, Baruch College, and Sociology Department, Graduate Center, CUNY

Transnational Social Protection

Social Welfare Across National Borders

PEGGY LEVITT, ERICA DOBBS,
KEN CHIH-YAN SUN, AND RUXANDRA PAUL

OXFORD
UNIVERSITY PRESS

Oxford University Press is a department of the University of Oxford. It furthers the University's objective of excellence in research, scholarship, and education by publishing worldwide. Oxford is a registered trade mark of Oxford University Press in the UK and certain other countries.

Published in the United States of America by Oxford University Press
198 Madison Avenue, New York, NY 10016, United States of America.

Library of Congress Cataloging-in-Publication Data
Names: Levitt, Peggy, 1957– author. | Dobbs, Erica, author. |
Chih-Yan Sun, Ken, author. | Paul, Ruxandra, author.
Title: Transnational social protection : social welfare across national
borders / Peggy Levitt, Erica Dobbs, Ken Chih-Yan Sun, Ruxandra Paul.
Description: 1 Edition. | New York, NY : Oxford University Press, [2023] |
Includes bibliographical references and index.
Identifiers: LCCN 2022034966 (print) | LCCN 2022034967 (ebook) |
ISBN 9780197666838 (paperback) | ISBN 9780197666821 (Hardback) | ISBN 9780197666852 (epub)
Subjects: LCSH: Transnationalism. | Migration, Internal. |
Public welfare. | Social problems. | Social justice.
Classification: LCC HM1271 .L485 2023 (print) | LCC HM1271 (ebook) |
DDC 305.8—dc23/eng/20220722
LC record available at https://lccn.loc.gov/2022034966
LC ebook record available at https://lccn.loc.gov/2022034967

DOI: 10.1093/oso/9780197666821.001.0001

To migrants, refugees, and their loved ones, who manage risks, get ahead, and confront hardship by living lives that transcend borders and who deserve generous and reliable social protections wherever they are.

Contents

Acknowledgments

Books are always written in community and this one involved an especially large number of friends and colleagues who made important contributions along the way. The idea for this research grew out of our conversations with our wonderful colleague, the late Prof. Sarah Van Walsum, who cared deeply about protecting the rights of domestic workers. We developed the idea of "resource environments" with Charlotte Lloyd, Armin Mueller, and Jocelyn Viterna. Valentina Mazzucato, Breda Gray, Paolo Boccagni, Jean Michel Lafleur, Thomas Faist, Basak Bilecen, Beth Simmons, Rey Koslowski, Sarah Lockhart, Shannon Gleeson, Xochitl Bada, Rubén Hernández-León, Robert C. Smith, Jackie Hagan, Eric Fong, Gina Lai, Yao-tai Li, Adam Cheung, Hon Chu Leung, Denise Tang, Lake Lui, Sara Curran, Helen Marrow, Tiffany Joseph, Brenda Yeoh, Shirlena Huang, Elaine Ho, Ningning Chen, and Kenneth Dean offered us constructive suggestions at various stages along our way. So did participants at various conferences and seminars where we presented our work including an Exploratory Seminar at the Radcliffe Institute at Harvard University, the American Sociological Association, the Eastern Sociological Society, the American Political Science Association, the Sociology Department of Hong Kong Baptist University, and at the Asia Research Institute at the National University of Singapore. We especially appreciate David Weil's careful reading of our chapter on labor rights.

Oxford University Press has been supportive of this project from the outset. We are indebted to James Cook for his clear instruction and guidance throughout the process. We also thank the three anonymous reviewers for their insightful feedback which strengthened the manuscript. Their input was foundational to this project.

Several editors also helped us to polish our writing. Kate Epstein, Jill Smith, and the late Debra Osnowitz went over our work with a fine-toothed comb and thus merit a special thank-you. Bai-yu Su and Naomi Tilles helped us format and fact-check the manuscript multiple times. Robert Levers deserves great thanks for his wonderful graphics. We sincerely acknowledge all of this meticulous work. The responsibility for any errors or mistakes is our own.

This book would not have been possible without institutional support. We thank Pomona College, Villanova University, Amherst College, Wellesley College, Harvard University, and Hong Kong Baptist University for supporting this project. In particular, we gratefully acknowledge the generous funding from the Subvention of Publication Program at Villanova University, the 2021 National Science and Technology Council Taiwanese Overseas Pioneers Grants (TOP Grants), and the Chiang Ching-kuo Foundation. We also sincerely thank the administrators at our former and current institutions who helped us navigate the bureaucratic hurdles in our paths. While their hard work is often invisible, it was central to ensuring that this book saw the light of day.

Finally, and most importantly, we thank the many migrants and refugees we have collaborated with in our individual work whose experiences found their way into these pages. We also deeply thank our families for their support, encouragement, and for generously tolerating the time we took away from them while writing this book.

Introduction

Transnationalizing Social Protection: A Proposed Framework

In June 2020, the *New York Times* reported that Northwestern Memorial Hospital in Chicago had conducted "the first known lung transplant in the United States for Covid-19" (Grady 2020). Dr. Ankit Bharat, the director of the lung transplant program, performed the surgery. Born in India, Dr. Bharat attended medical school there before emigrating to the United States, following a well-worn path laid down by many of his colleagues—one in every seven doctors in the United States is of Indian origin. India sends more doctors to the United States than any other country. In fact, the COVID-19 crisis has thrown the United States's dependence on immigrant health care workers into sharp relief: 16 percent of registered nurses, 29 percent of physicians, and 38 percent of home health aides in the United States are foreign born (Gelatt 2020).

While many stories tell of foreign-trained medical staff who emigrate to work in US hospitals, a less familiar narrative is how these same hospitals establish outposts and partnerships overseas. Johns Hopkins University, for example, works in collaboration with multiple partners abroad, including two in the United Arab Emirates (UAE). Again, Indian workers are central to the success of these endeavors: 3.5 million Indian citizens live and work in the UAE, making it the top destination for Indian emigrants (Connor 2017). In this case, though, Indians are less likely to be working in hospitals and more likely to be building them. They come as laborers rather than highly skilled physicians. And unlike the life of a surgeon in Chicago, these workers face deplorable conditions: pay is meager and living and working conditions are difficult. Any attempt to improve them meets with severe reprisals, including mass deportations (Mauk 2014). Yet every year, thousands of laborers from across the subcontinent join thousands of workers from other poor countries to work abroad because their families back home cannot afford food, medicine, or school fees without it.

Transnational Social Protection. Peggy Levitt, Erica Dobbs, Ken Chih-Yan Sun, and Ruxandra Paul,
Oxford University Press. © Oxford University Press 2023. DOI: 10.1093/oso/9780197666821.003.0001

Moving abroad to support one's family is a common but risky strategy. Chittam Malaya was one of the 10,000 residents from the southeastern Indian state of Telangana who go to work in the Persian Gulf every year. Unfortunately, he is also one of the nearly 450 migrant workers who have died on the job in Dubai since 2014 (Reuters 2017). But although rural Telangana suffers from water shortages that make it almost impossible for farmers to stay afloat, Hyderabad, its capital, is a thriving hub for global tech companies and hospital centers. Apollo Hospitals, a national chain with an international reputation, established Asia's first "health city" there more than thirty years ago. It offers centers of excellence across a number of clinical departments (Apollo Hospitals 2019). In fact, many private hospitals in India have become international health care providers. They are magnets for Indian doctors who want to return home and wealthy patients from across the globe who seek lower cost, readily available, high-quality care (Block 2018; Mathai 2015). Given that medical expenses are now the leading cause of personal bankruptcy in the United States, it is not surprising that an increasing number of Americans look outside the country's borders to get the attention they need.

These experiences bring to light how an array of actors—states, corporations, nonprofit organizations, communities, and households—mitigate risk in a world on the move. They challenge traditional narratives about social welfare as something provided by states to their citizens in a single place. They show how illness and poverty in one part of the world are deeply connected to another part (Gingrich and Kongeter 2017). They also drive home that individuals face very different levels of risk. To emigrate as a doctor is not nearly as perilous as emigrating as a day laborer. Working in a liberal democracy like the United States or the United Kingdom brings with it different opportunities and challenges from working in an authoritarian state like the UAE (A. Paul 2017; Parreñas et al. 2019). Moving capital to invest in a health care partnership is often easier than moving people. Gender, age, education, socioeconomic status, and nationality all mediate risks and rewards and shape access to social protection, giving rise to an extraordinarily stratified set of opportunities and vulnerabilities for migrants and nonmigrants alike (Constable 2014; Mingot and Mazzucato 2018b; Fitzgerald 2019).

To not connect what happens in the places to which migrants travel with the places they leave behind is to miss a key piece of this picture. Dr. Bharat is clearly an asset to his patients, but he is no longer an asset to India. What does it mean for the Indian public health system when so many of its skilled physicians work abroad? And what does it say about the US health care system when it employs some of the world's most skilled physicians but millions of its own citizens cannot afford their care? Hospitals in the United States and the UAE are built and staffed by immigrants. But half a world away—in Mexico, or India, or the Philippines—who is taking care of these workers' children and parents? Private urban hospital centers in India, Thailand, and the Gulf states that cater to global patient flows may keep domestic medical staff from emigrating abroad and may even entice expats home (Cohen 2015; Johnston et al. 2010). But what are the implications of these kinds of resource allocations for basic health services, especially in rural areas? How do we square the fact that, as we write, many countries in the Global North have made remarkable progress toward vaccinating their citizens against COVID-19 while a shortage of vaccines throughout the Global South is keeping morbidity and mortality at all-time highs?

Traditional answers to questions about managing risk and precarity generally focus on the state. These top-down narratives only partially explain how social protection regimes are being reconfigured to respond to today's widespread migration and mobility. In the absence of the state, the family must step in, especially when it comes to the care of children or the elderly. Some families also have the financial means to purchase services via the market or the opportunity to access free or subsidized alternatives through nonprofit community organizations. Which ever way individuals and households piece together social protection, the underlying assumption is that access is limited by proximity: membership in the nation-state via citizenship, geographic proximity to the distribution of services within a given territory, and embeddedness in specific local family or social networks all place natural limits on the availability of social protection.

We believe this conventional wisdom is sorely out of date. How and where people earn their livelihoods, the communities with which they identify, and where the rights and responsibilities of citizenship get fulfilled have changed dramatically (Smith 2006; Levitt 2007; Ho 2019). Societies are increasingly diverse—racially, ethnically, and religiously, but also in terms of membership and rights (Vertovec 2007; Wessendorf 2014; Shams 2020). There are increasing numbers of long-term *residents without membership* who live for extended periods in a host country without full rights or representation. There are also more and more long-term *members without residence* who live outside the countries where they are citizens but continue to participate in the economic and political lives of their homelands. There are professional-class migrants who carry two passports and know how to make claims and raise their voices in multiple settings, but there are many more poor, low-skilled, and undocumented migrants who are marginalized in both their home and host countries.

Our goal in these pages is to analyze how these changes are transforming social welfare as we know it. How do individuals and families protect and provide for themselves when they are born in one country, and then study, work, and become legal residents of multiple countries over the course of their lives? What happens when they do so at a time when many states are stepping back from the social welfare functions they traditionally provided?

What our opening anecdotes suggest—and what our book argues—is that a new set of social welfare arrangements has emerged that we call hybrid transnational social protection (HTSP). We find that HTSP sometimes complements and sometimes substitutes for traditional modes of social welfare provision. Migrants and their families unevenly and unequally piece together *resource environments* across borders from multiple sources, including the state, the market, nongovernmental organizations (NGOs), and their social networks. Local, subnational (i.e., states and provinces), national, and supranational (i.e., regional and international governance bodies) actors are all potential providers of some level of care. Changing understandings of how and where rights are granted that go beyond national citizenship will aid migrants and nonmigrants in their efforts to protect themselves across borders. In fact, we suggest four logics upon which rights are based: the logic of citizenship, the logic of personhood/humanity, the logic of the market, and the logic of community. Each brings with it a different set of assumptions about the sources, scope, and rationales behind HTSP. Indeed, as the state steps back, the burden is increasingly on individuals to navigate their way through this complex set of opportunities and constraints. Variations in their ability to do so is another major source of inequality.

Let us briefly clarify our terminology before we proceed. Our use of the term *transnational* extends far beyond a simple back-and-forth dynamic between two states. Rather, it includes all the possible sites and scales from which social protections are accessed and aggregated. We use the term *hybrid* to capture how mixed, fluid, and contingent these configurations can be. Hybrid transnational social protections are the policies, programs, people, organizations, and institutions that provide for and protect individual migrants and their families across borders—whether these are voluntary, forced, settled, short-term, or circular movements. We include grounded actors that provide for and protect people who move transnationally; transnational actors that provide for and protect grounded individuals; and transnational actors that provide for and protect transnational individuals (Levitt et al. 2017). Our definition of social protection is in line with that of the Organisation for Economic Co-operation and Development (OECD) with an expanded focus on education and labor rights.[1]

We see migration as a form of social protection and as a catalyst for transforming how and where protection is provided. We also see clearly that hybrid transnational social protection redistributes inequalities but does not eliminate them. It enhances vulnerability for some and empowers others by offering them more meaningful, achievable choices about how and where to provide for themselves. The stories we tell in these pages are about the messy overlap between empowerment and exploitation and about the new winners and losers that arise as a result. Our intention is to provide a comprehensive, big-picture view of these changes—across the stages of life, social protection sectors, and the world. We do not offer a state-of-the-art, all-inclusive discussion of developments in each of the sectors we cover. Instead, we provide a broad overview of changes affecting people as workers, learners, health care seekers, caregivers and members of their families and communities, and highlight the connections between them. We hope that this book will inspire policymakers and researchers alike to dig deeper into each.

The New Context of Social Protection

The considerable changes in the *where* and *by whom* in social protection we describe result from equally dramatic changes in patterns of migration and in the social contract between citizen and state.

Ever larger numbers of people are on the move, either by force or by choice, temporarily or for extended periods, and with great success or great struggle. Deepening global economic interdependence, declining birth rates and aging populations that leave industrialized economies dependent on migrant labor to function, and structural underdevelopment that excludes the highly educated and lower skilled from viable employment in many poor countries are just some of the root causes of these flows. In 2020, there were 281 million people living "voluntarily" outside their countries of origin, up from 173 million in 2000. The number of refugees and asylum-seekers who fled conflict, persecution, violence, or human rights violations also doubled from 17 to 34 million between 2000 and 2020 (The United Nations 2021). Paradoxically, 80 percent of the countries that host refugees and asylum-seekers are low- and middle-income countries rather than high-income societies in the Global North (The United Nations 2021; FitzGerald 2019). This does not include the large numbers of people who move temporarily or circulate regularly to work or study, for short or lengthy stays, without the intention or ability to settle permanently.

A second factor driving changes in social protection is the decline of the welfare state. For much of the twentieth century, citizens in most industrialized countries relied on services offered by national and local governments for social protection. They held the state responsible for the benefits they received as citizens or workers. Even in countries where workers received benefits based on their employment, the state played an active role in regulating the market and costs.

Today, deindustrialization, neoliberalism, and austerity mean that, in many cases, both expectations about the state and its actual role as a guarantor of basic protections have radically changed. Around the world, supranational financial institutions like the International Monetary Fund and the World Bank require countries needing loans to slash government spending and implement austerity measures to reduce budget deficits. Deindustrialization swept across much of the Global North from the 1970s onward, driven by shifts in production to lower cost countries in Asia and Latin America and technological changes that made a large industrial workforce obsolete (Gough and Wood 2004; Sassen 2006; Kubalcíková and Havlíkovâ 2016). With the loss of industry came the decline of the industrial unions that had been key guarantors of safe working conditions and decent health and retirement benefits. Deindustrialization and offshoring went hand in hand with—and were often facilitated by—the emergence of neoliberalism, which emphasized deregulation, privatization, and reduced government spending. After 1989, in the post–Cold War era, the collapse of communism in Central and Eastern Europe meant that jobs and social protections previously guaranteed by the state were limited or done away with. As the state stepped back and the market became a more important site of social protection provision, socioeconomic rather than citizenship status became a more important determinant of access to social welfare. Even in cases where the state still provides social protection, albeit limited, benefits are often restricted to citizens living inside its borders. This ever-narrower scope of social protections increases stratification and deepens risk.

What happens, then, when the welfare state in decline meets a world of mobility and migration? We see three major ongoing shifts that cause and are consequences of HTSP.

The Disaggregation of Citizenship and Social Rights

One of the most influential takes on the idea of social rights as a function of citizenship was T. H. Marshall's *Citizenship and Social Class* (Marshall 1950). Using the United Kingdom as his example, Marshall mapped the long march toward social protection from the eighteenth to the twentieth century. This period witnessed three key stages in the evolution of citizenship: the development of civil rights, political rights, and social rights, respectively—social protection in the form of the welfare state that emerged as the working class gained the right to vote. Here, citizenship is a status, a state's legally binding recognition of an individual's full membership. But membership is only open to a relatively exclusive club. Indeed, Marshall himself acknowledged that his analysis was "by definition, national" (Marshall 1950, 9).

Legal citizenship, however, does not guarantee social or political rights. Marshall, after all, based his analysis on relatively wealthy liberal democracies. In poor countries, in spite of voter demands, states often lack the capacity to offer extensive social protections or implement the protections they promise because their institutions are too weak and their coffers too empty. In authoritarian states, social rights may be on offer while political rights are not. As a result, what political philosopher Seyla Benhabib (2004) calls "disaggregation," or the decoupling of rights from citizenship status, is increasingly common. Even affluent, liberal democracies are backing away from the generous social rights previously afforded to their citizens. The latest trend in welfare state retrenchment is "flexicurity," a model that combines flexibility (in the labor market) and security through state-sponsored social protection (European Commission 2021).

Today, the everyday lives of ordinary people are out of sync with this linear model of citizenship and social rights. National policies vary but, in some places, noncitizens without political rights do have access to some social rights (Cuadra 2012). Anyone who can show proof of residency in Spain, for example, is eligible for care through the national health service (Parella Rubio et al. 2019). After six months in the country, Argentina also offers all residents access to its public health system, regardless of citizenship.

Any student can enroll in the Mexican public school system. Similarly, unauthorized immigrants in some United States cities and states, such as San Francisco and Massachusetts, are entitled to limited health care even though they lack political voice (Marrow and Joseph 2015). In the context of liberal democracies, the degree to which noncitizens are eligible for social rights generally depends upon the type of welfare state in place, the relative political power of progressive political actors, and how key state agents see their roles and missions as social services providers (Sainsbury 2012; Marrow 2009).

Not only are states extending limited social rights to non-citizens, they also sometimes offer political rights as well. Increasing numbers of countries allow noncitizen voting in city and provincial elections. This is particularly the case in Europe. According to EU law, EU nationals who live in another EU member state have the right to vote in local elections, as well as for the European Parliament (Groenedijk 2008). In countries like Denmark, Norway, Portugal, Sweden, and the United Kingdom, nonnationals can vote in elections for regional or national representative bodies. Immigrants resident in Chile for more than five years are eligible to vote in national elections (Finn 2020). In Ireland, the state not only allows all noncitizens who are of age to vote in local elections, but has also invested in ensuring they know they have this right (Dobbs 2017). Some countries extend noncitizen voting rights for legal residents as part of reciprocal voting agreements. They exchange the right of their citizens to vote in the countries where they are living for migrants' right to vote (Arrighi and Bauböck 2017). For example, Spain's decision to grant local voting rights to immigrants from South America depended upon those states extending the same rights to Spanish citizens living within their borders (Arango 2013). Subsequently, immigrant voting rights and immigrant access to the welfare state are increasingly related: expanding political rights to noncitizens leads to calls for more generous welfare provisions as politicians try to attract new immigrant voters through social spending (Ferwerda 2021). We must, therefore, examine the complex, changing interplay between citizenship and sociopolitical rights. Indeed, determining just how much rights and citizenship can be disaggregated is one of the key challenges to understanding who wins and who loses when social protection extends across borders.

That said, in most countries, opposition to granting noncitizens full access to social rights is quite common. Citizens also disagree over what rights legal versus undocumented migrants should be eligible for. In their research on public attitudes toward the social rights of migrants in the United States, for example, sociologist Irene Bloemraad and her colleagues found most respondents were against allowing immigrants without documents "access to public elementary and high schools, in-state tuition to public colleges and universities, social security for workers and their families, emergency health care, Medicare and Medicaid, food stamps, or welfare benefits" (2016, 1662). While misconceptions are rampant about how much noncitizens actually access the welfare state, the perceived threat these immigrants represent fuel the fires of far-right populism across Europe and the United States (Norris and Inglehart 2019; Schierup et al. 2006).

The De-territorialization of Social Protection

In a nationally bounded model, states offer social protection to their citizens within their borders and citizens who emigrate no longer receive social protection from their home countries. Nor is there an expectation that receiving states will extend significant protections to immigrants or to their citizens who live outside the country for extended periods. Eligibility for a nation-state's social protections therefore requires membership (i.e., citizenship) and residence within its territories (i.e., territoriality). Contemporary migration also strongly challenges this idea. Today, a wide range of countries of origin and destination routinely, if grudgingly, provide social services to the noncitizens within their borders or to their citizens living abroad.

While source countries have always assisted their emigrant citizens through consular relations, in recent years they have significantly expanded their migrant engagement policies (Iskander 2013; Cano and Délano 2007; Cook-Martin 2013). Indeed, over half the countries in the world now have some sort of diaspora policies in place (Gamlen et al. 2019). More than thirty countries have gone so far as to create a special government ministry dedicated to their diasporas (Gamlen 2019). These efforts add up to a kind of "state-led transnationalism" that extends the reach of the state to citizens living beyond its borders (Margheritis 2007). Indeed, the vice minister for Salvadorans abroad reflected these sentiments when he characterized his mission as transcending "the exclusive protection of citizens within a specific territory. Protecting sovereignty also means protecting the human rights of Salvadorans, wherever they may be" (Délano Alonso 2018, 20).

There are many reasons for this. According to the World Bank, in 2019, remittances to low- and medium-income countries reached a record of

US$554 billion (World Bank 2020). Many countries now depend upon these revenues, not just for the well-being of individual households but to subsidize infrastructure, education, and health care (World Bank Group 2019). They want to make sure that these monies keep flowing. Some emigrants have also become politically powerful enough that they can favorably sway receiving-country foreign policy toward their homelands (Délano Alonso 2018; Levitt 2001; Lopez 2015). Both democratic and authoritarian states use a variety of tactics to engage, assist, surveil, and control their expatriate citizens to achieve their political and economic goals (Gamlen 2019; Tsourapas 2021).

Organizations like the World Bank, the International Organization for Migration, and the Global Forum on Migration and Development promote these policies as drivers of economic development and as potential tools of global governance. They recognize that states are remittance-dependent and that transnationally oriented migrants are potential investors, political lobbyists, or drivers of economic growth (De Haas 2010). These policies do not just address the needs of long-term migrants—they are also aimed at temporary migrants, students, and highly mobile citizens, who live aspects of their lives simultaneously in several countries. Citizens who emigrate, to paraphrase A.O. Hirschman (1970), therefore, are no longer choosing between exit and voice—rather, they are exiting *with* voice and states are carefully listening (Duquette-Rury 2019).

While these developments transform the geography where the social contract between citizen and state is fulfilled, national territory remains important. We do not mean to suggest that states are driven by altruism. In fact, countries of both origin and destination use social protection and immigration policies to *care for*, *coerce*, and/or *keep out* different groups, sometimes pursuing all three seemingly contradictory agendas at the same time.

Decentering the State

The third major shift in conventional wisdom about social welfare is that the nation-state is no longer the key purveyor of rights and protections. We see a state that is both *downsizing* and *supersizing* and that protects citizens and noncitizens alongside other actors. Its role in direct service provision is diminished by *re-familiarization*, or placing the responsibility for care back on the individual or family; *privatization*, or the shift away from the public sector; and *marketization*, or the use of for-profit market entities to deliver social services (Kubalcíková and Havlíková 2016). The rise of neoliberal economic policies, based on self-reliance and minimal intervention in the market, transformed the market into an ever more important source of social welfare.[2]

As the state downsizes, and health care, pension funds, and education are increasingly privatized, states also back away from regulating firms and labor markets. Offshoring and outsourcing are now key strategies for firms pursuing growth and precarious employment is a fact of life for many workers. The rise of the global "gig" economy, in which individuals lack benefits, wage guarantees, predictable work schedules, and the expectation of long-term employment with a single firm, is the latest way in which the state is exempting itself from the social welfare business (Thelen 2019). That said, we must remember the difference between the state as provider and the state as underwriter. As the political theorist Chiara Cordelli notes, "What the new era has delivered is not smaller governments, but rather bigger, yet privatized, ones" (2020, 1). In contrast, as the rise in diasporic institutions makes clear, the state is also supersizing. It expands its footprint beyond its borders by creating such institutions and by enhancing consular services, by entering into bilateral agreements to manage its workers abroad, and by directly intervening in the domestic politics of states where its citizens live and work (Délano Alonso 2018; Gamlen 2019).

The role of the nation-state in setting social policy is challenged not only from without but from within. Research reveals many examples in which national governments are purposefully or implicitly handing over responsibility for social welfare to subnational and nongovernmental actors. By doing so, they cede control over who gets access to what pieces of the social safety net. The "gray zones" created by disjunctures between urban, provincial, and national policies can be important windows of opportunity. They allow pro-immigrant state and local governments to provide when the national government refuses to do so. In Spain, for example, regional and local governments flatly rejected national policies that restricted access to health care for undocumented immigrants and continued to offer services (Dobbs and Levitt 2017). In North America, immigrant hometown associations partner with home-country governments to match and magnify remittances that fund expanded social policies in communities of origin (Duquette-Rury 2014). Civil society and subnational government actors can, to some degree, counteract the effects of national governments' downsizing efforts.

Perhaps the most powerful change neoliberalism has wrought is that it casts doubt on the state's legitimate right to intervene in the market as a provider of health care, education, or retirement services. By doing so, it accelerates the disaggregation of rights from citizenship. Individuals are no longer worthy of social protections by virtue of their membership but on the basis of their ability to pay. In this new demos, "All conduct is economic conduct; all spheres of existence are framed and measured by economic terms and metrics, even when those spheres are not directly monetized" (Brown 2015, 10). While the private sector always played some role in providing social welfare, in many countries, it now trumps the state in terms of power and legitimacy—with serious implications for the social protection of citizens and noncitizens alike.

The Multiple Scales of Social Protection

A continued focus on the nation-state also misses the many ways in which national policy is supplemented, complemented, and subverted not only by subnational arrangements but by international law and supranational organizations as well. To accommodate people on the move, governments often enter into bilateral and multilateral agreements, backed by global intergovernmental organizations like the United Nations (UN), the International Labor Organization (ILO), the OECD, and the World Bank. International policy instruments like the UN Migrant Workers Convention and the ILO Migration of Employment Convention also provide frameworks under international law for such types of cooperation. To date, social protection for international migrants focuses primarily on workers. Some legal migrants (about 23 percent) enjoy indiscriminate access to social services and social security benefits in host countries on the basis of bilateral and multilateral arrangements. These guarantee that benefits are paid overseas. Eligibility and level are jointly determined by countries of origin and destination (i.e., totalization of benefits) (Avato et al. 2010). But where do these rights come from? And are they truly enforceable? This is a topic for its own book, so we touch only briefly on it here.

After World War II, the Universal Declaration of Human Rights, which commits signatory states to its principles and obligations, included the right to social security and basic social rights such as food, clothing, housing, medical care, and necessary social services. In 1966, the International

Covenant on Economic, Social and Cultural Rights (ICESCR) also required its signatories to uphold certain social rights. At present, 162 states have signed. Special human rights treaties support and augment the ICESCR. For example, the Convention on the Elimination of All Forms of Discrimination against Women, the Convention on the Rights of the Child, the International Convention on the Protection of the Rights of All Migrant Workers and Members of Their Families, and the Convention on the Rights of Persons with Disabilities all contain the right to health care and the right to social security. These conventions guarantee rights on the basis of personhood rather than citizenship or residence. Under each treaty, a committee is charged with evaluating individual cases in which violations may have occurred (Kaltenborn 2015).

That the international community connects human rights to development also strengthens international cooperation around social rights. The right to an adequate standard of living (including access to food, water, and housing), health, and social security were at the core of the Post-2015 Development Agenda that was negotiated as the framework for achieving the Millennium Development Goals. The ILO also introduced the idea of a *social protection floor* that includes basic social security guarantees for all, across the life cycle. By 2012, the United Nations, the World Bank, and the G20 countries all endorsed this approach. The Social Protection Inter-Agency Cooperation Board was established in 2012 to coordinate efforts to put this in place across international agencies (Deacon 2013).

In 2015, the United Nations adopted the 2030 Agenda for Sustainable Development, which outlines plans to reduce poverty; provide social protection; protect the planet; and encourage peace, justice, and inclusivity—in short, a vision of social protection for all, including migrant workers and refugees. In 2016, the UN Development Group published the Social Protection Coordination Toolkit as a step toward implementing these international mechanisms of social protection. It also established the Joint Fund Window for Social Protection Floors to guide countries in combining national and international resources to pay for social protection floors.

Therefore, at least in theory, if a state fails to provide or protect, an individual can appeal to any one of these international institutions or conventions. In reality, however, their power is often more symbolic than real. Due to several difficult challenges, they do not translate into significant sources of protection in people's lives. For one thing, ratification numbers remain low. Too many states renege on fully complying with the commitments to which they sign. Some states are reluctant to see social rights as human rights. When the UN General Assembly adopted the International Convention on the Protection of the Rights of Migrant Workers and Members of their Families in 1990, only twenty-two countries ratified it. The convention took thirteen years to be fully implemented. While the ILO proposed various mechanisms to protect the rights of workers regardless of their citizenship status and argued for equal treatment of both native- and foreign-born populations, the principle of nondiscrimination did not gain much traction in practice (Vittin-Balima 2002; Olivier and Govindjee 2013). But although these efforts are uneven and often fall short of achieving their goals, they normalize the idea that international actors endow individuals with rights (Beckfield 2010; Buzan and Wæver 2003; R. Paul 2017). They also legitimize grassroots calls for greater cross-national coordination of social protections for footloose populations.

Changing Context, Changing Coverage

Although we start by acknowledging that we live in a world on the move, this is not to suggest, by any means, that free movement is easy. There is what political scientist Thomas Faist calls a "mobility paradox"—a mismatch between the desire of hundreds and millions of people around the world to move and their actual ability to do so (Faist 2018). We write at a moment when xenophobia and nationalism are on the rise. Native-born locals accuse migrants of overburdening the national social welfare system or taking jobs that they never wanted to begin with (Fujiwara 2008; Dreby 2015). Even in the context of perpetual cycles of populism and greater openness, however, we believe that the underlying institutional changes that drive forward the transnationalization of social protection will remain in place. They are an integral part of an ever more globalized economy and labor market and of the strategies used by more and more states to extend their boundaries to include members living outside them.

In sum, our book is about how these developments transform the ways in which individuals and families protect and provide for themselves. We investigate how the decoupling of social rights from citizenship has led to a reconfiguration of responsibility and a new division of labor among the actors engaged in risk management and basic care provisions. We identify how this reallocation of responsibility maps onto distinct logics of social rights and use the concept of *resource environment* to show how migrants and their families piece together packages of protections from multiple sources in multiple settings across time and place. We also examine the additional work done by social protection policies or the tensions between what actually functions as *social protection, social cooptation,* and *social repulsion* and how migrants navigate their way between the three. By social cooptation, we mean the ways in which actors offer social protection in exchange for compliance with or active support of their social and political agendas. By social repulsion, we mean how social protection is actively used to marginalize or keep out certain groups.

Our Argument and Contributions

We argue that state-driven, territorially limited, and nationally bounded systems of social protection are giving way to or, at least operating in tandem with, transnational modes of social protection. Rather than treating the national and the supranational as strongly connected but still separate and discrete, as many prior studies have done, we see individual migrants and nonmigrants, and the national, regional, and supranational institutions and policies that affect them, as embedded in the same transnational social field. They protect themselves and their families using resources derived from the multiple sites and sources within that field. While the state is still a crucial actor, it by no means acts alone in providing social protection. Beyond countries of origin and destination, we include the market, NGOs, and communities as sources of support. Individuals use these in countries of both origin and destination to create resource environments that heighten vulnerability and risk for some and liberate and empower others.

Our argument, therefore, moves the conversation about social protection forward in several important ways. First, we analyze national and supranational laws and policies and the lives of individuals and their families in the same breath. Second, we use a multi-scalar, multi-sited approach that brings to light how subnational, national, and transnational actors complement, supplement, or subvert one another (Dobbs and Levitt 2017; Dobbs et al. 2018). By doing so, we unsettle the static relationship between citizenship, protection, and space. Third, we expand upon the notion of resource environments, which takes us beyond state actors as the primary providers of social protection. Fourth, we trace how the different logics of *constitutional rights, human rights, commodities,* and *community* affect the social protections available to nonresident citizens and long-term residents without citizenship. Finally, our analysis incorporates understudied social protection sectors that are integral to this conversation. We look at social protections across the life cycle, including those for children and families, education, labor rights, health care, and senior care. We also discuss developments beyond Europe and the United States—an important corrective to discussions which, up until now, have been largely dominated by experiences in the Global North.

The next section expands upon the different logics underlying various approaches to HTSP and how they redefine what social protections are provided and who is responsible for providing them. The section that follows lays out our notion of resource environment in greater detail.

The Contrasting Logics of Rights and Their Consequences for Social Protection

Social and economic protection may be conceptualized as *constitutional rights, human rights, commodities,* or *community*. As Table I.1 lays out, these understandings operate simultaneously but combine and dominate debates differently across social and political contexts. Constitutional rights, together with the welfare state, build on national constitutions and other legislation that mandate the rights and opportunities available to all citizens. The international human rights regime relies on international law as a universal foundation and specifies governmental obligations toward all persons, regardless of citizenship status. Meanwhile, commodities, services, and social protection can be bought and made available to all who can afford to pay. As a set of community ties, social protection depends on individuals' ability to turn to family or friends and mobilize social networks, as well as activate connections with civil society organizations to manage risk and get ahead.

Our conceptual framework brings to light the ways in which HTSP actually functions as a layered structure. States continue to play an important role by providing direct social assistance; regulating the markets for education, health, and labor; setting rules governing benefits and working conditions; and making social insurance available. They specify constitutional rights that stipulate the state's responsibilities to its citizens, wherever they may be.

Table I.1 Foundations of Hybrid Transnational Social Protection

Foundation	Social Protections as Constitutional Rights	Social Protections as Human Rights	Social Protections as Commodities	Social Protections as Community
Source	National constitutions. The welfare state.	International law.	Global markets. Supply and demand.	Personal connections. Civil society.
State Role and Influence	Intervention. Supersizing to support citizens on national territory and abroad.	Intervention. Supersizing to protect all people on national territory.	Regulatory. Downsizing (welfare state retrenchment) where welfare state previously existed.	Non-intervention. Laissez-faire. In some cases: support to civil society organizations.
Logic/Rationale	National solidarity. Equal rights for all citizens. For nationals abroad: diaspora engagement.	Humanitarian. Nondiscrimination. Universal (though minimal) provision.	Economic. Marketization. Competition. Choice. Cost-effective: reduces welfare cost in national budget.	Communitarian. Libertarian. Allows flexibility for people who want to utilize social capital. Cost-effective: reduces welfare cost.
State–Citizen Relationship	High priority, politicized, a point of contention in electoral competition.	Irrelevant, in theory. In practice, highly contentious due to tension with national sovereignty.	Individual as consumer. Apolitical, in theory. States often intervene to secure better terms for their nationals.	Individual as community member. States urge all to find non-state solutions. Politicized: the left pushes back against welfare state erosion.
Resource Environment	Nationally bound or bound by (regional) labor market; transnational aspects cover citizens abroad, émigrés, and their descendants.	Destination-country dependent. In crises: international community and transnational civil society.	Market-bound. Transnational. Economic and political actors (states) compete for service providers and customers.	National or transnational. Personal-network dependent. Local-community dependent. Social-capital dependent.
Providers	State institutions at home and abroad: public administration, consulate network, embassies; sometimes in partnership with civil society.	State institutions, intergovernmental organizations, transnational civil society.	Migrant service providers. Private firms. State institutions acting in market actor capacity.	Informal networks. Family and friends. Charities and civil society organizations. Churches and religious organizations.

(*continued*)

Table I.1 Continued

Foundation	Social Protections as Constitutional Rights	Social Protections as Human Rights	Social Protections as Commodities	Social Protections as Community
Access	All citizens. Often excludes noncitizens.	Universal. Citizens and noncitizens. Prioritizes some noncitizens recognized as categories of vulnerable migrants (refugees).	Citizens and noncitizens. Universal, though conditioned on ability to pay. Favors resource-rich actors.	Highly dependent on individual connections and membership in various communities. Citizenship plays variable role.
Inequality as a Problem?	Yes. This seeks to solve it. Constitutions emphasize equal rights, equal opportunities. Welfare states seek to reduce inequality for citizens.	To some extent. The international community acknowledges states cannot provide at same level for all.	No. Inequality is natural and to be expected.	Yes and no. People have different abilities to construct and access community. Civil society intervenes.
Source of Inequality	Differences in welfare states' profiles and development; variation in state capacity; variation in civil society development and involvement.	Bi-/multilateral agreements. Non-enforceability. Selective application.	Differences between people's ability to pay for services or afford travel to provide/ access services.	Differences in social networks and civil society strength at home and abroad.
Individual-Level Solutions to Lack of Social Protection	Migration and naturalization to access better resources and welfare abroad; political participation for political change.	Migration and attainment of protected group status under international law. Limited advocacy for further monitoring.	Migration to earn money and afford better services. Migration to find better services for lower cost abroad.	Migration expands and diversifies social networks, allowing people to function in transnational communities.

Growing marketization and privatization reflect another understanding of social protection. Here, individuals are viewed not as citizens entitled to equal rights and opportunities but as consumers purchasing services in the global market. In this scenario, providers reach out to international clients. The state recedes, its role limited to regulating the business environment so that the market functions more efficiently and profitably. In the global market for health services, for example, inequality is expected and access to certain services and providers depends on a consumer's ability to pay. The wealthy, more than the poor, benefit from this social protection regime.

The state's retreat from direct welfare provision and adequate social supports often goes hand in hand with changes in cultural norms and expectations that place the onus for achieving well-being on the individual. In some cases, this stance grows out of the belief that the market, together with the freedom of choice it affords, produces better outcomes than the state can provide. It emerges in cases where the state lacks the capacity to provide adequate social welfare. When the state is barely present, poor people who cannot afford to purchase social protection from the market rely on informal networks of friends, family, charities, and religious organizations to manage risk and secure their livelihoods. Their success depends on their social capital—on how effectively they construct and mobilize community—irrespective of their citizenship status. For example, a noncitizen with strong ties to other immigrants and to immigrant community and religious organizations may be better able to secure childcare than a citizen who recently arrived in a new area and has few social connections.

Finally, international conventions and laws are the fourth logic of transnational social protection. Clearly, the number of international instruments that affirm generic human rights or the rights of particular groups such as workers or migrants is growing. While they often fail to deliver or lack the necessary teeth to punish noncompliance, they nevertheless institutionalize the idea that basic, universal standards of protection should be available to everyone, anywhere.

As Table I.1 shows, today's regime of hybrid transnational social protection contrasts with traditional social welfare systems, in which the role of the state is both central and legitimate. Here the state's involvement varies across each layer of the regime, from intervention and supersizing to downsizing. The logic driving actors in each layer also differs. Social protection under international law builds on a humanitarian logic, whereas constitutional rights stem from principles of national solidarity and equality for members of a political community.

In contrast, laissez-faire, or unregulated, approaches to social protection emerge among those who believe the state incapable of providing for human needs or not their most appropriate protector. This view sees individuals as better suited to make their own decisions about the variety of services available in the market. According to some logics (e.g., social protection as constitutional rights), the state-citizen relationship is at the core of the arrangement; for others (e.g., human rights and market-based social protection), citizenship status is largely irrelevant. Some logics take on inequality as a fundamental problem. Others deem it normal and therefore something to expect and get on with.

Resource Environments as a Response

But a central question remains: How do individuals and families actually get access to social protections in the context of migration and mobility? They do so by creating resource environments whose scope and effectiveness depend upon the distinct logics of social protection outlined above. These include services provided by the state; services purchased from the market; services accessed through nonprofit organizations such as churches, labor unions, and NGOs; and supports available through friends and family members (Levitt et al. 2017). The resource environment is what is actually available to an individual in their toolkit of care as opposed to what is theoretically or legally available.[3]

The cluster of protections an individual or family can assemble depends upon the nature of the market; the strength and capacity of countries of origin and destination; the third-sector organizational ecology (i.e., the number and types of organizations, what they do, and their capacity to provide); and the characteristics of individual migrants, families, and communities. These characteristics include migrants' country of origin; place of residence; and the breadth and depth of an individual's social networks, in addition to gender, race, ethnicity, religion, class, and education. In some cases, all four sources are available in the countries of origin and destination but, in other cases, they are not. Resource environments also change dramatically over time. By leaving some groups well protected and others increasingly vulnerable, different kinds of alliances and struggles continuously transform what is on offer. For instance, the fight for universal health coverage in the United States gave rise to cross-class coalitions that produced, at least temporarily, more favorable conditions for all, including documented and undocumented migrants.

Let us offer two illustrations to make this more concrete. The resource environment of a college-educated, employed Swedish citizen residing in South Korea might look something like Figure I.1 below. It shows each of the four sources of social protection from which she can access support from her home and host countries. The size of the arrow reflects the relative proportion of social protection coming from each source.

This particular individual has access to a wide array of social protections from the Swedish state, including affordable childcare, paid parental leave, excellent schools, old-age pensions, and so on. Given her education and employment, she is also probably able to buy additional protections from Swedish companies in the private market, to access benefits from third-sector organizations, and to avail herself of supports from her family and friends who have social and cultural capital to spare. On the Korean side, while she is only eligible for emergency care from the Korean state, the multinational corporation (or market) she works for in Seoul covers most of her needs including health insurance, pension contributions, and the cost of education for her future children. She also belongs to several nonprofit organizations

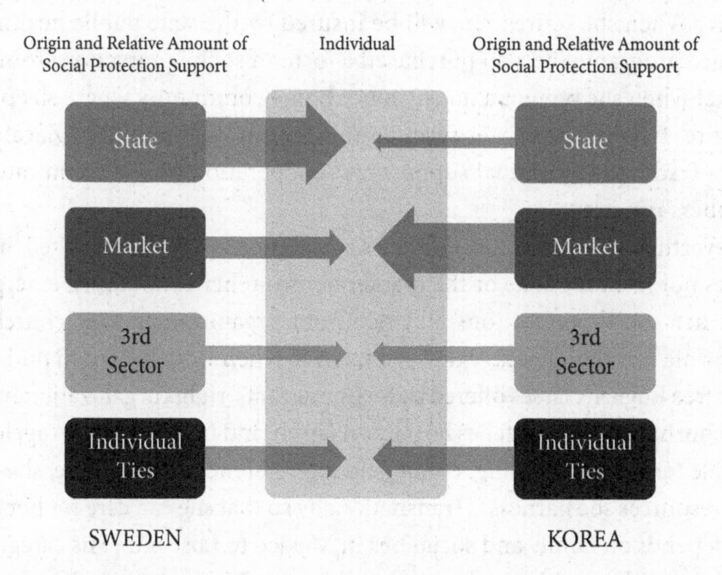

Figure I.1 College-educated, employed Swedish citizen living in South Korea

and is building a strong network of expatriate friends she can call upon if need be. She has little difficulty meeting her needs wherever she is.

Now, let's imagine the resource environment of a woman with little formal education and skills who is a citizen of Mexico but who currently lives in Los Angeles without documentation. She works in the informal economy, cleaning houses and preparing food to sell to construction workers at their work sites. Because of her status, she has no access to social protection provided by the federal government, nor does she make enough money to purchase protections from the market. California, however, offers public benefits to "nonqualified" (as determined by federal law) immigrants (Fortuny and Chaudry 2011). It stands out as a state that moved aggressively to extend publicly funded health coverage to immigrants with and without papers. Therefore, our hypothetical individual can apply for "Covered California," a health insurance program funded by the state. Even though undocumented immigrants are technically ineligible, when she applies, she may qualify for Medi-Cal, the state health care program for low-income residents that provides prenatal care, emergency services, and long-term care services (Dobbs and Levitt 2017).

Our hypothetical subject can also access some social protections from the Mexican government. Through the Instituto de los Mexicanos en el Exterior (Institute for Mexicans Abroad), she is eligible for an array of civic, health, education, and financial supports. Moreover, if she returns to Mexico when she retires, she will be insured by the state public health insurance program. She also purchased a form of social protection from the market when she bought a house in her home community where she plans to retire. Finally, she comes from an indigenous community in Zacatecas where traditions of mutual support and cooperation between community members run deep.

Nevertheless, most of this migrant's social protection in the United States comes not from the state or the market but from her community, emerging from her social connections and nonprofit organizations. Her church in California has a food pantry that she turns to when work is hard to find. She takes free English classes offered by an immigrants' rights organization in her neighborhood. And she relies heavily on family and friends in Los Angeles to provide temporary housing, credit, and job references. Meanwhile, she also uses resources she harnesses transnationally so that she can care for her son. She depends on family and social ties in Mexico to raise him. His caregivers supplement the health care he receives from the Mexican state with services they purchase from the market. They do so by using the remittances she sends. He also attends a preschool that is financed by a Dutch NGO.

Three things stand out about Figure I.2. First, rather than having most of her needs provided by one nationally bound source, the Mexican woman we describe must piece together social protection for herself and her family from a large number of *disparate, informal,* and *transnational* sources. Second, no single possible source of social protection covers all of her needs, as indicated by the relative thinness of each arrow. Third, the largely transnational sources on which she relies are in no way contractually guaranteed. They are, therefore, unreliable and sometimes disappear. While laws contractually obligate states to provide for citizens, and the market guarantees that most purchased services are provided, there are no such guarantees for people relying on social networks and third-sector organizations. Each can withdraw their support at any time and without recourse for the migrant (Levitt et al. 2017).

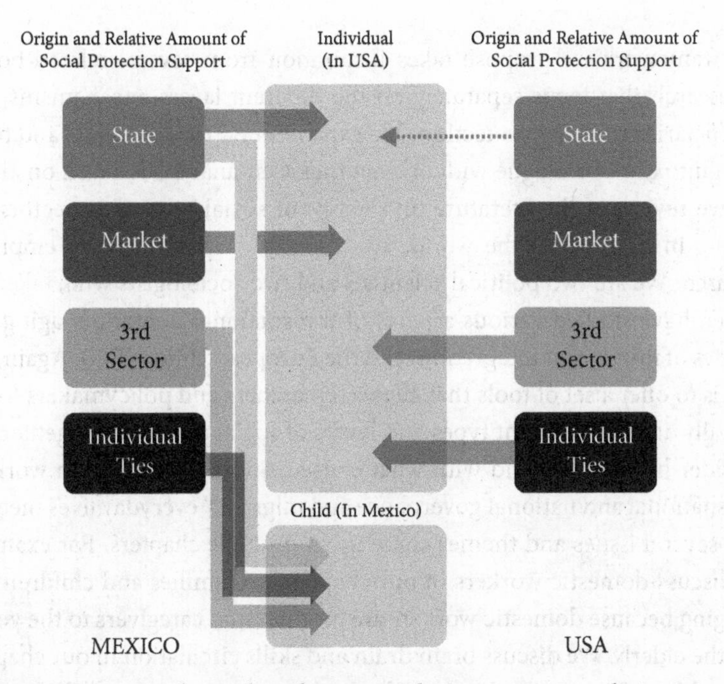

Figure I.2 Primary-educated, undocumented Mexican migrant living in California and working in the informal sector

We use a dotted line in the case of the social protections this individual receives from the U.S. state because while she is not eligible for any services from the federal government, she is eligible for certain basic services from the state government in California.

The resource environment of a woman with a similar legal and socioeconomic profile changes significantly depending upon where she moves. Let's compare the experiences of another undocumented Mexican woman with similar levels of education who moves from Puebla to Wyoming. Her resource environment looks different because of the very different benefits provided to migrants and nonmigrants by these cities and states. The NGO sector in Wyoming, a relatively new destination for immigrants, is much less established and more poorly funded than the network of providers in California. The strength of the labor market also varies, which affects how willing employers are to hire undocumented workers and to offer them benefits. Finally, since fewer migrants live in Wyoming than in California, they stand out more, which can make it more dangerous to seek care even when it is available (Sexsmith 2017; Schmalzbauer 2014).

The Research upon which We Build

The framework we propose takes inspiration from several related bodies of research that focus separately on the different layers, mechanisms, and beneficiaries of social protection. We expand upon these insights and bring them into direct dialogue with one another. Our analysis is based on an extensive review of the literature on a range of social protection sectors operating in all parts of the world. We also draw upon our own empirical research. We are two political scientists and two sociologists who, taken together, have studied various aspects of transnational migration, aging, the politics of immigrant integration, and the European Union (EU). Again, our goal is to offer a set of tools that allows researchers and policymakers to holistically analyze different types and layers of social protection together. We consider how, where, and with what consequences the top-down world of transnational and national governance and migrants' everyday lives meet. In fact, several issues and themes come up in multiple chapters. For example, we discuss domestic workers in our chapters on families and children and on aging because domestic workers are mothers and caregivers to the young and the elderly. We discuss brain drain and skills circulation in our chapters on health and education because the health-care workers and teachers are also students. Involuntary migrants, with or without documentation, come up frequently in these pages because they are parents, children, workers, and care seekers. This is another reason that understanding HTSP demands a multi-sectoral, multilayered approach.

A first body of research that we build upon concerns the everyday lives of individual migrants and families. A second body of work looks at institutions and policies. Together, they include scholarship on (1) transnational migration; (2) global social policy; (3) neo-institutionalist approaches to policy formation; (4) social welfare transformation through international agreements such as bi- and multilateral accords, state diasporic policies, and international conventions; and (5) scholarship on capabilities versus functionings.

Migration Scholarship and Its Corollaries

Mainstream migration scholarship still suffers from methodological nationalism, or the assumption that the world is and always will be organized into discrete, bounded nation-states. Because US and European research still focuses primarily on migrants' incorporation and assimilation into host countries, it tends to ignore how they protect and provide for themselves across borders. When we learn of transnational health or educational schemes, it is primarily from health and education researchers.

In contrast, strands of transnational migration scholarship, which take migrants' simultaneous embeddedness in multiple societies seriously, provide us with important foundations upon which to build (Glick-Schiller and Faist 2009; Levitt 2012; Mazzucato 2011). For example, research on transnational families, or on how families raise children and care for the elderly across borders using formal and informal networks and on the domestic workers who care for them, is well underway (Lutz 2008; Parreñas 2005; Van Walsum 2011; Acedera et al. 2018; Baldassar 2016; Bryceson 2019; Parreñas et al. 2020). One strand of this work deals with the treaties and institutions put in place to protect these workers (Piper 2017; Ford 2019; Bada and Gleeson 2015; Iskander 2017). The role of hometown associations is another well-developed thread (Lamba-Nieves 2017). Hometown associations are community organizations, with some combination of migrant and nonmigrant members, which provide transnational social protection by supporting schools, health clinics, or social services in communities of origin (Bada 2014; Duquette-Rury 2019).

The transnational social field approach these analyses employ knits together allegedly separate spaces in countries of origin and destination into a single, sometimes seamless, and sometimes deeply fractured, social, political, and emotional space. This allows researchers to productively rework categories such as class, race, gender, inequality, and development by elucidating how they are constituted across borders (Joseph 2015; Roth 2012; Levitt 2001; Glick-Schiller and Salazar 2013; Faist and Bilecen 2014). It also brings into sharp relief how being healthy, educated, and socially secure are simultaneously constructed within and beyond national borders.

To date, much of this work looks at a single aspect of social protection across borders without sufficiently exploring how transformations across sectors and in different parts of the world are remaking the social safety net as we know it. While an important step forward, we now need to bring these isolated case studies into a more fully integrated whole. While the scholarship on transnational families spells out how kinship and private sector providers influence the resources that migrants and nonmigrants can access, few studies link these family practices to the larger transnational social structures that enable and constrain them. In contrast, the framework we propose strongly connects the experiences of individuals and households to the meso- and macro-level contexts in which they take shape—not only the political economic context but the supranational institutions and policies that, in combination with national policies, strongly affect migrants' ability to protect themselves.

Policies and Institutions

A second broad but fragmented body of research we draw upon concerns the policies, policy-making institutions, and providers that legitimize and implement social protections across borders. They include many of the UN agencies and conventions we have described. Again, while these illuminate important pieces of the changes we describe, when taken separately, they do not provide a sufficiently complete picture of the foundational rearrangements underlying the emergence of HTSP.

Research on global social policy (Deacon 2013; Yeates 2006) examines how international actors' discourses and applications of social policy affect what nation-states provide. As countries grew more economically and politically interdependent, transnational organizations put increasing pressure on states to conform to their standards for social and human rights. The emergence of "a global society" amplified calls for "a new politics of global responsibility" and for global social redistribution, regulation, and provision that included cross-border social welfare arrangements (Deacon et al. 1997; Sabates-Wheeler et al. 2011). While these standards provided a language of inclusion and specified basic rights and mechanisms beyond the state for guaranteeing them, they often fall short when it comes to enforcement.

Neo-institutionalists see countries as embedded in a "world polity" led by a network of powerful international organizations that also set policies and create institutions that state actors then follow (Meyer et al. 1997). As these global norms and logics gain strength and acceptance, nation-states find the pressure to conform to them difficult to resist. That is why, these scholars say, we see similar approaches to human rights, environmental protections, or labor rights around the globe, including a shift away from rights as guaranteed by citizenship to something endowed by personhood (Boli 2005). Critics question the breadth and depth of global convergence, arguing that the global social structure is, in fact, fragmented, uneven, and regionalized (Beckfield 2010; Buzan and Wæver 2003). They take issue with how much "world society" norms actually influence local contexts. They remain unconvinced by the mechanisms of diffusion that are not adequately specified in much of this scholarship (Levitt and Merry 2009).

Versions of this approach to social welfare transformation take the region rather than the world as their unit of analysis. Regional blocks, it turns out, often develop their own standards, rules, and regulations when it comes to rights (R. Paul 2017). Much of this work draws on the European experience and the bilateral arrangements it enters into with nonmember states (LaFleur and Romero 2018; Mingot and Mazzucato 2018a; Faist et al. 2015; R. Paul 2017; Bilecen 2020; Boccagni 2011). Ruxandra Paul (2017), for example, notes the importance of regional economic integration projects—and bilateral/multilateral agreements concerning temporary workers—in influencing governments' inclination to extend social protection beyond their borders.

We also build on the research on diasporic policies and long-distance nationalism (Gamlen 2019; Délano Alonso 2018). This recalibration of the relationship between countries of origin and their expatriate citizens deterritorializes social protection. Countries of destination do this as well when they continue to provide benefits to migrants who have spent most of their working lives within their territories before eventually returning home. These policies also reflect and drive forward an expansion of the logics upon which HTSP is based. They generate the political will and institutions that social protections across borders rely on. Their sharp focus on the state, however, leaves out other actors—individuals, households, and many non-state actors—that are increasingly important players in welfare provision.

Capabilities and Functionings

Clearly, however, some migrants are better positioned to mobilize resources across borders than others. As Thomas Faist (2018, 142) observed, "The ability of migrants to take advantage of existing regulations between emigration and immigration states in transnational European social spaces is highly uneven . . . the linkages of social security systems across borders are tenuous at best for the majority of migrants from outside the EU." This is, in part, because turning potential resources into actual support requires concrete action. We find Sen's (1997) and Nussbaum's (2013) distinctions between capabilities and functionings useful here. While capabilities, or being able to do things like get married, become educated, or access health care, are things individuals choose to achieve and have access to, functionings are capabilities that have been realized or achieved. Migrants' ability to activate and assemble existing resources, or to translate capabilities into functionings, strongly influences how powerfully and effectively they are protected. There is, all too often, a disconnect between their desire to improve their life chances and mitigate risk and the strategies available to them with which to do so—between accurate knowledge about what is rightfully theirs and the need to seek out deeply distrusted state institutions to claim it (Mingot and Mazzucato 2018a; Mingot and Mazzucato 2018b; Marrow and Joseph 2015; FitzGerald 2019). One of the many uncomfortable truths in these pages is how much families differ in their ability to translate capabilities into functionings when they choose or are forced to move.

Implications

The world we describe is far from a world of "welfare without borders" (R. Paul 2017). Indeed, even the most generous, portable arrangements covering migrants and citizens abroad still face major challenges over inclusion, coverage, and differences in costs, access, and eligibility. As individuals juggle and negotiate commitments and responsibilities, so too researchers need to consider the changing constellation of factors that influence people's choices about risk management. Rather than thinking separately about getting a better job, educating children, or caring for aging parents, people take all of these challenges simultaneously into account and come up with a comprehensive strategy for moving forward.

Our views of *protection* and, in particular, the ways it is accessed transnationally, go far beyond mere survival. Transnational social protection not only provides a way to manage risk, but it is also an intergenerational mobility strategy—a tool for actualizing the individual's or household's life projects. Migrant workers from less-developed countries send remittances to protect family members from social and financial vulnerability (Dreby 2010; Yarris 2017). In contrast, middle-class parents in Hong Kong, Taiwan, and mainland China send their children to be educated abroad to protect the next generation from future risks such as political uncertainty and a changing global economy (Ong 1999; Waters 2011; Lan 2018b).

Writing this book has been a sobering experience. It confronts us with several uncomfortable truths. At best, we believe, rethinking the relationship between citizens and states, a process for which we advocate, will promote new policies and inform new institutions. We hope that these policies will enhance and expand the range of meaningful and accessible choices available to individuals; allow them to break free from corrupt, inefficient systems; and extend social protection to previously excluded groups. But HTSP offers no comprehensive cure. As these pages reveal over and over again, inequality is reshuffled, not eliminated. Enhanced protections for some result in greater vulnerability for others.

We are particularly concerned that migrants' political voices be heard and their demands for rights be respected as social welfare systems in countries of origin and destination rely on them more and more. This interdependence seriously affects the politics of migration. Governments in countries of destination cannot afford to shut out the nannies and nurses who care for their young and elderly even when populism is on the rise. Governments in countries of origin can no longer think of emigration as a safety valve because today's migrants, recalling the words of Hirschman, exit and maintain their voices (Hirschman 1970; Duquette-Rury 2019). Given the economic importance of remittances and the rising importance of the expatriate vote, governments of countries of origin are recognizing that emigrant citizens will no longer be satisfied with platitudes. They demand that their voices be heard.

We are also concerned that states are less and less accountable for the welfare of their citizens. Whereas professional, well-educated migrants have many places to turn for social protection, the state remains the provider of last resort for most of the world's poor. What, then, is an appropriate role for countries of origin in providing for their emigrants? Which institutions, located where, should be responsible for protecting and providing for the many long-term residents—in the destination country—with are without full membership? These individuals—so integral to the care of the young and the elderly and to the construction, gardening, and restaurant sectors—often live without access to basic services in the countries where they settle. Governments have to answer to the native-born who fear that immigrants will unravel the social fabric, but are they not also morally responsible to the people who keep their societies running?

Another uncomfortable truth involves tough questions of distributive justice. What constitutes a fair transnational allocation of resources, especially as the consequences of HTSP in one part of the world can have repercussions in others? The decision to seek social protection transnationally affects not only migrants and their families but the nonmigrants who stay behind. Doctors from less-developed societies like India or the Philippines may now be the backbone of health care systems in Europe or the United States, but their departure has left health care systems in their native countries seriously weakened. International clinics designed to attract medical tourists may benefit cash-strapped migrants wishing to bypass long waiting lists or expensive copayments for elective procedures in their homelands, but these institutions also worsen local disparities in access to care (Holdaway et al. 2015). Remittances can enable family members back home to purchase goods and services, but the rising cost of living deeply hurts families who do not receive this financial support. Senior citizens who move abroad for care fare well, but they displace locals who cannot afford the facilities opened to serve this new, more monied population.

Our work, then, is not just about migrants and their families. It is a response to widespread social injustice and inequality in today's global world. Our task in these pages is to tease out who is emancipated and empowered by HTSP and who is disempowered and even victimized. Which configurations of actors and institutions enable more individuals and families to move from capabilities to functioning? We hope that these pages provide tools for policymakers, researchers, and concerned citizens who are committed to making sure that people everywhere get the basic rights and protections to which every dignified human being is entitled.

1
Children and Families

People often say "it takes a village to raise a child" but in today's global world, it can take several villages, towns, cities, and countries. For some children, the resulting resource environment is plentiful. It provides all the social protection they need. For others, the available package of supports falls far short. In this chapter, we identify changes in the experiences of childhood, parenting, and family life in a world on the move. How does having children affect family migration strategies? How does migration help families protect and provide for their offspring? What patterns can we see in the resource environments constructed across borders? What are the costs and benefits of transnational migration as a strategy to deal with opportunities and risks?

We begin in the small village of Miraflores, on the southwest coast of the Dominican Republic. Residents of Miraflores have been moving to Boston for more than fifty years (Levitt 2001). Even today, because jobs are so hard to come by, any working-age adult—who can—migrates. They leave their children to be cared for by parents, aunts, and siblings, hoping to be quickly reunited once they settle in the United States. But reunions are rarely so simple, nor do they happen so fast.

The experiences of the Cárdenas family capture some of these complexities. Doña Teresa Cárdenas had six children. One passed away many years ago. Of the remaining five, Carmen and Hortensia live in the United States, Jaime and his wife go back and forth between Boston and the island, and Teresita and Carlos live in the Dominican Republic.[1]

Despite one major bump in the road, Carmen's experience is an immigrant success story. Soon after moving to Boston, she fell in love with Roberto, a college graduate who owned a children's clothing store. For many years, they ran that store together in what was then Boston's most important Latinx neighborhood. They bought a home and several rental properties. Roberto went on to work for the mayor as his liaison to immigrant communities. Both Carmen and Roberto are politically active in US and Dominican politics.

Transnational Social Protection. Peggy Levitt, Erica Dobbs, Ken Chih-Yan Sun, and Ruxandra Paul, Oxford University Press. © Oxford University Press 2023. DOI: 10.1093/oso/9780197666821.003.0002

Two of their four children are college graduates. Javier, Carmen's son from her first marriage, is the only sad part of this otherwise happy story.

Carmen left Javier with her mother and elder sister when she first went to Boston. By the time Javier joined her there, mother and son had grown apart. Life in Boston was not easy for Javier, who dropped out of high school, had three children, and could not find steady work. Eventually, he was deported after serving time in jail for a minor offense. While his wife and children remain in Boston, he is back in Miraflores with no job and no chance to legally return to the United States. In fact, Carmen still works to be able to send money back to support him.

Teresita, Carmen's older sister, tried migrating but did not make it. After that, she became the family caregiver, tending to her aging mother and her siblings' children. She does not like depending on Carmen and Hortensia for support. While her house now has running water, indoor plumbing, and many convenient appliances, Teresita still feels short changed. She always has to ask, and only her brothers and sisters get to answer. She sees their children climbing the socioeconomic ladder while her son, Eduardo, has only a part-time job at a pharmacy. When he wanted to take computer lessons and Carmen's children wanted to study dance, her nieces won out. With money extremely tight, Teresita often feels overwhelmed by the stress of assisting Eduardo, his wife, their three children, and Javier, who now lives with them.

As the story of the Cárdenas family makes clear, not all members benefit equally from migration as a risk management strategy. The contexts in which families piece together resource environments for raising children are highly stratified. The poorest of the poor usually cannot afford to migrate. They depend on the resources that are available within the boundaries of their nations and communities, even as these grow scarcer. Migrants' ability to provide for their children depends upon their social and economic status; their national contexts; and how well their citizenship, residence, and legal status entitles them access to their rights (Dreby 2010; Sun 2013). Social protection also depends on migrants' ability to mobilize personal connections, such as family, friends, and acquaintances, and social capital, including memberships in civil society organizations and churches. Life across borders, therefore, has profound, long-term, unanticipated consequences for children that go far beyond the individual child or the current generation (Berckmoes and Mazzucato 2018; Mazzucato et al. 2015).

This chapter lays out the broad contours of transnational social protections for five different groups of children affected by migration: (1) children left behind, (2) noncitizen children born or growing up in countries of destination, (3) children sent ahead, (4) children sent back, and (5) internationally adopted children. Each group comes from diverse backgrounds and has access to different types and levels of resources, legitimated by our four logics of rights. The boundaries between these groups are permeable. A child left behind may later become a child sent ahead who may later become a child sent back. The experiences of these children also underscore the importance of disaggregating citizenship and social rights (children may be underprotected by the state where they are citizens or residents); going beyond the nation to understand social protection strategies (the extent to which a child's well-being is a function of resources accumulated across borders); and decentering the state's role in the safety net (children may receive critical support from sources other than the government). In fact, for those children whose parents are detained or deported, who are themselves seeking asylum or who are undocumented, the state is simultaneously a provider of social protection and a source of uncertainty and risk.

Left-Behind Children

Lots of movies, songs, and novels tell of the hurt and vulnerability that left-behind children experience when their parents migrate to work abroad. In the Philippines, the widely acclaimed movie *Anak*[2] tells the story of a left-behind daughter who falls prey to a world of vices after her mother leaves for Hong Kong (Madianou 2016). In 2015, Romania competed in the Eurovision Song Contest with the song "De la capat" ("All Over Again") performed by Voltaj. The song and the accompanying video are a consciousness-raising manifesto about the costs and benefits of parents moving abroad to support their children.

The label "left behind," however, must be taken with a grain of salt. It conjures up images of abandoned children, an idea encouraged by sensationalist media or governments seeking to demonize migrants. But while left-behind children may spend long periods with just one parent or with friends or family members, they are hardly abandoned. Rather, their parents decide that they will be able to provide for their children better by migrating than by staying home and relying on family or community members to provide support in their absence.

Global Care Chain and Transnational Resource Flow

Sociologist Arlie Hochschild (2000) coined the term "global care chains" to describe the ways in which international migration restructures the distribution of reproductive labor across borders (also see Parreñas 2000; A. Paul 2017). Many migrant women entrust their own children to their female relatives, following the logic of social protection as community, or paid caregivers in the homeland, accessing social protection as commodity, while taking care of their employers' children in host societies (Carling et al. 2012). This phenomenon points to the hybrid and stratified nature of transnational social protection, reinforcing the divide between the Global North and the Global South. Privileged parents in wealthier societies transfer caregiving responsibilities to migrant workers from poorer countries to be able to cope better with the competing demands of personal and professional life. For these parents, migrants constitute an essential part of the resource environment they rely on to fulfill their parenting responsibilities and obligation.

Providing care for parents in the North, however, often comes with harsh daily challenges for migrant workers. As we discuss in Chapter 3, migrant domestic workers typically receive less legal protection than paid caregivers who are citizens. It is difficult to live and work under one's employer's roof. Many workers live socially isolated lives, face risks of labor abuse, and are denied pathways to citizenship in the societies (Parreñas et al. 2020). Taking care of other people's children is also challenging. In many cases, migrant workers develop deep emotional attachments to the children under their care but must cope with the anxiety, jealousy, and even competitiveness that biological parents feel toward them (Hondagneu-Stelo 2007). They must constantly remind themselves that they are not truly members of the family.

Gender shapes the ways in which migrant workers fulfill their parenting responsibilities and obligations across borders. While migrant men can rationalize their absence by regularly sending money home, most migrant women who provide economically for their families are still expected to be emotionally and socially available to their children left back home.

Pei-chia Lan (2006), for example, found that in addition to their monetary contributions, many of the migrant women employed as domestic workers in Taiwan regularly wrote letters, sent texts, had expensive gifts delivered, planned family menus, and supervised their children's daily activities. These migrant mothers believed that such gestures allowed them to be a steady presence in their children's everyday lives and to sustain emotional connections to the next generation. However, studies have consistently found that children left behind, especially young children and teenagers, are more inclined to blame migrant mothers than fathers for not "being there" (Dreby 2010; Parreñas 2005).

Like their parents, children who are left behind struggle to make sense of the transnational separation they face. The story of Juan, a young Honduran interviewed by sociologist Leah Schmalzbauer (2008), reveals the challenges of negotiating physical and emotional separation. Juan's father and siblings left Honduras because they could not make ends meet. Before they migrated, Juan never knew where his next meal would come from. Now, there is plenty of food in the refrigerator, he has a new bed and computer, and he attends a school that many of his neighbors cannot afford. Because they talk regularly by phone, Juan still feels close to his dad, who is part of his life. He admires his father's sacrifices and is grateful to him.

Money, however, divides as well as unites. Juan's father scolds him for being wasteful and spoiled. He wants Juan to have everything he needs but to not take his good fortune for granted. From Juan's perspective, his father is too cautious and even stingy. He knows nothing about his father's earnings and the difficulties he faces at work. "Don't people in the United States and Canada make lots of money?" he asks himself. Arguments about money and how to spend it are frequent.

Juan's musings speak to the trade-offs involved in transnational family life: physical separation in exchange for greater security and better prospects. For well-off families, with many opportunities, the decision to parent across borders is a choice. The primary breadwinner gets a better job, or a child gets to study at a better school. But for most of the migrants we describe, migration means family survival. Without it, basic needs like food, housing, utilities, and education will go unmet. While parents of left-behind children may miss birthdays, first communions, or graduation celebrations, they still provide basic care (Parreñas 2005; Schmalzbauer 2008; Carling 2008; Carling et al. 2012; Horst et al. 2014; A. Paul 2017). In many cases, the remittances they send also support the broader extended family (Thai 2014). But while remittances improve children's chances of achieving financial security and social mobility, they often come at great social and emotional cost.

Remittances, Protections, and New Risks

Migrant parents use money to maintain ties to their children. Since they cannot be present, they send material goods to make up for the emotional loss (Coe 2011; Waters 1999; Schmalzbauer 2005; Hoang and Yeoh 2015; Dreby 2010). Sociologist Mary Waters (1999), for example, learned the expression "barrel children" when she studied West Indian families. It referred to the barrels filled with goods from America that parents sent back to their children. But just as families feel they have arrived on more solid ground, conditions in the country of settlement may worsen. Remittances grow smaller and less reliable, causing confusion and stress. As Juan's story suggests, nonmigrants, who generally know little about migrants' lives or romanticize them, blame family members for not sending enough money back home (Cohen 2011; Carling 2008; Thai 2014).

When parents migrate, it also disrupts the power hierarchy in the family. The once all-powerful parent, who is now older and remains behind, becomes dependent on her migrant children. The father becomes dependent on his daughter. The grandmother who is raising her granddaughter becomes beholden to her charge because the granddaughter might complain to her breadwinning parent that she does not like the way her grandmother gets things done (Levitt 2001). Children left behind quickly learn to exploit the disparity between real and surrogate parental authority, which undermines caregivers' efforts to impose discipline.

By creating new inequalities within and across countries, these challenges transform the lives of all family members (Hoang and Yeoh 2015). When consumerism serves as a proxy for love, community expectations about consumption and success also change. Children want to eat the manufactured, processed foods their relatives bring home when they visit. Because these are imported, they are much more expensive than traditional staples (Thai 2014). Nonmigrants also develop a taste for the status-symbol luxury goods they cannot afford. Resentment arises between the haves and have-nots, as social protection for some families intensifies the sense of deprivation for others. Consumerism, in turn, can be a hard habit to break. As those with means become accustomed to a lifestyle that is only sustainable if remittances continue, living transnationally becomes a necessary norm. As Leah Schmalzbauer (2008, 344) writes, "the partnering of lofty expectations with the belief that remaining in Honduras is a viable way of reaching their goals may set youths and their families up for disappointment."

Parenting across Borders: Redefining Kinship

Most migrant parents abroad turn to family networks to provide care for their children (Sun 2013; Gamburd 2000; Dreby 2010; Boccagni 2015). Their strategies depend on which parent migrates. Migrant mothers from the Philippines (Parreñas 2008), Sri Lanka (Gamburd 2000), Indonesia (Silvey 2006), and Mexico (Dreby 2010) often leave their husbands, parents, and siblings in charge. Stay-at-home dads may become primary caretakers, or they may delegate care so they can continue to work for pay. International studies scholar Kristin Yarris (2017) discovered that grandmothers in Nicaragua generally became the primary caregivers. "Grandmother care," she writes, "is both a form of social reproduction (everyday caregiving labor necessary for children and families' well-being) and a means of social regeneration (a moral practice that embodies cultural values of solidarity and sacrifice in response to global migration)" (Yarris 2017, 24).

Clearly, not all caregivers are alike. The energy and emotion of caregiving, coupled with its time demands, take their toll, especially on older adults. Grandparents do not have the same stamina or authority they had when raising their own children. When their grandchildren reach adolescence and want more independence, the techniques they used to raise their own children may no longer apply. In family conflicts, the migrant parent, now the real authority because he or she pays the bills, can become a pawn in a power struggle (Dreby 2010; Yarris 2017). Visits home, at least occasionally, are then needed to reestablish discipline. The presence of a biological father for a child being raised by a female relative or friend can also be problematic, as the father either strengthens the resource environment by working with the women in charge or undermines childrearing by making competing claims on the child's loyalties and affections.

These dynamics challenge the very definition of parenthood, which is no longer the sole purview of moms (Hoang and Yeoh 2011). In Vietnam, Thailand, and the Philippines, for example, an increasing number of fathers are more actively engaged in parenting now that their wives are working abroad. When fathers do step up, children left behind are more likely to get the care they deserve (Parreñas 2005; Gamburd 2000; Yarris 2017). Yet throughout Mexico (Dreby 2010), the Andean region (Escrivá 2004; Leinaweaver 2010), and South and Southeast Asia (Lamet al. 2013), some households lack social networks extensive enough to provide adequate childcare and turn instead to paid caregivers. The support they purchase generally complements rather than replaces the care of family members and friends although, in some cases, paid caregivers are the sole providers.

The quality of care they receive strongly influences children's well-being and development. A study in Ghana found that children did less well with frequent changes in caregiving because they were constantly forced to "adapt to new environments, form new attachments, and accept new authority figures" (Cebotari et al. 2017, 1782). All caregivers have to balance that hard-to-find line between emotional attachment and remembering that these children are not their own. They struggle to maintain intimacy without usurping the biological parent's place. Sociologist Joanna Dreby (2010) calls these caregivers "middle-women" because of their in-between position.

Technology can help. The definition of good parenting, together with whoever is supposed to do it and what it entails, is renegotiated as new technologies make possible involvement without physical presence. The lower cost and greater accessibility of technological platforms such as WhatsApp and FaceTime mean that children and their parents can be in touch multiple times a day (Dreby 2010; Schmalzbauer 2005; Berckmoes and Mazzucato 2018). Parents can now watch their children take their first steps or say their first words. They can check homework, make sure their sons and daughters are appropriately dressed and eating properly, or even monitor their social lives by checking their profiles on social media (Madianou 2016; Peng and Wong 2013; Madianou and Miller 2011). But while technology creates the illusion of intimacy and connection, it cannot replace physical warmth and contact.

Support for Migrant Parents and Their Children

Even though transnational childrearing is increasingly common, migrant parents, children left behind, and their caregivers receive little institutional support. Counterexamples are discouragingly few.

A few sending states actively cultivate intergenerational intimacy across borders. The Philippine Overseas Employment Agency, for example, organizes mandatory pre-departure orientation seminars during which instructors remind migrants of their ongoing responsibilities to their families. They urge them to continue providing financial and moral support and to communicate with their families as often as possible (Guevarra 2010). The Tulay program[3]—a partnership between Microsoft and the Filipino Department of Labor and Employment, which has offices in Manila, Hong Kong, and Riyadh, Saudi Arabia—provides internet and webcam training to migrant women so they can stay in touch with their children (Madianou 2016). But this, of course, can be harder than it seems. In spite of the state's constant entreaties, some moms only manage to stay in touch minimally with their children. Their internet connections are unreliable, their long work hours leave them little time, or the psychological costs are just too high (Madianou and Miller 2011; Lam et al. 2013; Peng and Wong 2013).

Some sending states invest in programs to aid left-behind children. The Philippines is again an example, although it often promises more than it can deliver. The state allows left-behind children to apply for housing and small business loans, qualify for college scholarships, gain eligibility for low-cost life insurance policies, and access funds when a migrant-worker parent is deported or dies. While the Overseas Workers Welfare Administration (OWWA) administers these programs, it is notoriously underfunded (Parreñas 2005, 24).[4] In Romania, local authorities partner with schools to ensure that children growing up with one or both parents working abroad do not fall behind (Hatos 2010).

Other states invest in programs to discourage migrants from leaving instead of helping them when they do. In Poland, the government mounted campaigns stressing that working abroad is not the best way to provide for one's children (Wiśniewska et al. 2017). As budget cuts and austerity measures pushed many families to leave the country, the government strategically expanded the welfare system to persuade citizens, especially young parents and families, to stay put and have even more children. It launched the Family 500+ program in April 2016, designed to boost Polish birth rates and reduce child poverty by improving living conditions for large families (Sussman 2019). Parents receive a tax-free benefit of about 120 euros per month when they have a second child and any children born thereafter. The allowance lasts until the child turns 18 years old. As of 2018, the program covered about

55 percent of all children in Poland and helped many women to support their children without having to migrate (Magda et al. 2018).

Beyond the state, both nongovernmental organizations (NGOs) and the market also facilitate parent–child contact and communication. The Archdiocesan Commission for the Pastoral Care of Migrants and Itinerant People, the Embassy of the Republic of Indonesia, and the Humanitarian Organization for Migration Economics run short-term computer classes for migrant workers in Singapore and facilitate access to computers (Lam et al. 2013). Before social media and cell phones became so widespread, SingTel, one of the largest telecommunications companies in Singapore, offered migrant domestic workers discount rates to call and text the Philippines and Indonesia (Lam et al. 2013). Immigrant activists in Hong Kong fought to pass legislation protecting migrant workers' right to use these technologies because some employers and recruitment agencies actively restrict their cell phone use (Smales 2020). Yet, as Lam et al. (2013, 9) caution, these efforts are "uneven and disparate." In particular, migrants whose employers restrict their movements or who work for families in remote areas where there is limited access to the internet need more support (Boccagni 2013).

Noncitizen Children in the Receiving States

Across the world, large numbers of children are born abroad in countries where their parents are not citizens. The depth and breadth of the resource environments available to these children depends upon the extent to which they—and their parents—are recognized in countries of origin and destination.

Whose Child Is This: Responsibility Before Birth

The question of who is responsible for children who are born to immigrants begins before birth. Some governments try to deflect any responsibility by proactively trying to prevent pregnancy. Domestic workers in Singapore, for example, must take a pregnancy test before they are recruited and, then, each year thereafter. A woman found to be expecting a child is deported (Huang and Yeoh 2003). While Hong Kong allows domestic workers who get pregnant to stay in the territory, they often have a hard time getting access to public benefits after giving birth (Constable 2014). In Israel, female migrant workers and their newborn children have the right to remain but only with permission from their employers. In actuality, this means that most migrant mothers and their babies are deported (Kemp and Kfir 2016).

Once a child is born, questions of citizenship become paramount: the child's status not only affects what social protections the state is required to provide but also the kind of resource environment their parents can construct. Children born outside their parents' country of citizenship become citizens in two ways. In the many countries in which citizenship is determined by blood (*jus sanguis*), the children of temporary migrants—especially refugees, asylum seekers, domestic workers, and low-skilled migrants—are assumed to "belong elsewhere" (Constable 2014, 11). They are therefore not entitled to any protections from the receiving state. In countries that abide by the *jus soli* principle, or the right to citizenship on the basis of soil or birthplace, children born in a given territory have immediate access to rights based on settlement and to social benefits that sometimes extend to their parents. In such cases, both poor and well-endowed families are often accused of engaging in so-called birth tourism or purposefully moving to give birth in a place with generous benefits (Wang 2017). Critics claim that these "anchor babies" lead to "chain migration" because they pave the way for future migration by immediate and extended family members.

People's lives, of course, are much more complex than these heated debates suggest. Whether giving birth to a child abroad helps parents secure citizenship for themselves and their children depends on state polices and public attitudes. In 2017, the European Court of Justice confirmed that children with EU citizenship had a right to be raised in the European Union (EU) and their non-EU parents therefore had a right to remain within its borders (BBC 2017). Not surprisingly, critics greeted this decision with great dismay and some member states revisited their citizenship requirements for children with migrant parents. In contrast, undocumented immigrant parents in the United States regularly face deportation even if their children are native-born citizens. Because many of these deportees are men, women become de facto single mothers who struggle to provide and care for their children (Dreby 2015). At the same time, deported fathers—especially those who are detained and incarcerated for extended periods and have no possibility of returning legally to the United States—are likely to lose connections or even contact with their children (Andrews and Khayar-Cámara 2020). Traumatized by deportation-related family disruption, many children—even those who are legal residents and citizens—perceive the United States as a hostile, insecure place where they do not fully belong (Dreby 2015; Sullivan and Kanno-Youngs 2021).

Central to the controversies regarding birth tourism, of course, is who is defined as deserving or undeserving. In the larger, global context, birth tourism renders citizenship a resource. Families want to obtain another citizenship to strengthen and extend their resource environments. Parents who believe in the future of their homelands will be less likely to seek foreign passports for the next generation. Parents who are less hopeful about their homelands may turn to birth tourism as a form of transnational social protection.

Parents and children for whom citizenship is not an option face more limited resource environments. Domestic workers often work in countries where there is no pathway to citizenship. Taiwan, Hong Kong, Israel, and Singapore are just some of the places where naturalization is impossible unless the biological father is a citizen. In such cases, children born to migrant mothers are not legal residents and must eventually leave even though they are officially stateless (Constable 2014; Kemp and Kfir 2016; Friedman and Mahdavi 2015).

In the Gulf States, the resource environments for children born to temporary migrants are even thinner and the fate of these children is more precarious. In Kuwait, citizenship and related services are extended to children in three categories: children of unknown parents, children born to Kuwaiti mothers but with unknown fathers or unmarried parents, and children of destroyed families (where one or both parents have passed away, are incarcerated, or are otherwise incapable of raising them) (Mahdavi 2016, 121). If a temporary migrant gives birth but cannot identify the child's father, her child is ineligible for citizenship and becomes stateless if the mother's country of origin will not recognize her child as a citizen (Mahdavi 2016, 121).[5] Some of these children return to their mother's homeland. Some are allowed to stay in prison with mothers jailed for having sex outside marriage. Some are transferred to local orphanages, with or without their mothers' consent.

In the European Union, where member-state citizens have the right to live and work in other member states, time and location matter more than citizenship in determining benefits for migrants' children. The country of origin, not the country of destination, is responsible for EU citizens who have been working abroad for less than two years. In cases where it is not clear which agency is responsible for providing the benefits, the relevant national authorities step in and decide, normally based on a parent's country of employment. When children live in the same country as their working parents, benefits come from that country. If parents and children live in different countries, the country with the highest benefits pays. If the right to receive benefits is based on residence, the country where the children reside is responsible for benefits. If this sounds confusing, it becomes even more so when a child's parents are not EU citizens (CLEISS 2019).

Beyond the state, children assumed to "belong elsewhere" or children who are denied services often receive assistance from NGOs. These provide migrant workers and their "born-out-of-place" children with food, money, legal aid, temporary housing, and basic medical services. NGO staff in Israel have gone even farther, collaborating with other activists to create Israeli Children, an antideportation coalition. These advocates link "claims about 'cultural belonging' with demands for a 'just migration policy.'" They want to put an end to "the exploitative 'revolving door' of recruitment–deportation that creates illegality" (Kemp and Kfir 2016, 388).

Young people who are long-term residents without documentation make up another group of children whose legal and social belonging is contested. In the words of sociologist and education scholar Roberto Gonzales, these young people live their lives in a state of "legal limbo." (Gonzales 2015). The Deferred Action for Childhood Arrivals (DACA), an executive order issued by the Obama administration, allows certain eligible young immigrants who arrived in the United States as children without proper documents to access a renewable, two-year work permit and protection against deportation. Since its inception in 2012, more than 800,000 young immigrants have been able to stay with their families and communities. While the Trump administration made multiple attempts to dismantle these protections, the Supreme Court ultimately left it in place (Flores and Svajlenka 2021). DACA does not, however, provide a clear pathway to legalization or citizenship.

Many refugees and asylum seekers are also among the children who "belong elsewhere." They are protected by the United Nations and other international NGOs through agreements such as the Convention Relating to the Status of Refugees and the Convention on the Rights of Children (Nykanen 2001; Andersson and Nilsson 2011). Under these, children are entitled to protection because it is a human right. But, as we have already seen, multiple loopholes and caveats allow states to use their discretion in providing humanitarian relief (Fassin 2011). Indeed, over the past decade, France, Ireland, and the United States have restricted the rights of refugees and asylum seekers to work or receive public benefits such as cash, food stamps, and medical care (FitzGerald 2019).

These dynamics strongly affect the social, economic, and psychological well-being of refugee children and their families. Their liminal legal status, coupled with the restricted pathways to citizenship they face, makes long-term planning for work or education difficult, as we discuss in greater detail in Chapter 2. In places like Turkey, they are regularly forced to move between camps or temporary housing, making their lives unpredictable and strictly regulated (Strasser and Tibet 2019). In other countries, like the United States and the United Kingdom, refugees and asylum-seeking families are resettled in dangerous or unwelcoming neighborhoods where children have difficulties developing friendships and fear for their safety (Brown 2011; Spicer 2008).

Children Sent Ahead

Lily's experience stands in stark contrast to the lives of refugee children. She comes from a wealthy family in Hong Kong. She studied English at the international school she attended back home before moving to the United States to attend St. Paul's, an elite private school in New Hampshire. Her parents sent her there to boost her chances of getting accepted at a prestigious university—an investment in the family's future.[6] Her parents were not wrong. Most St. Paul's graduates go on to study at elite colleges and universities. But Lily's transnational upbringing came at a high cost. She was under tremendous pressure to succeed, she explained: "I have to do well. My parents remind me every day. They e-mail me and call me . . . I mean, I know why I'm here. My parents want something special for me" (Khan 2011, 189).

Lily's case sheds light on the resource environments of wealthy families. Even though they are the more likely to be able to transform capabilities into functionings, these families also worry about risks and uncertainty. From their perspective, social protection is a matter of personal responsibility and so they send their children ahead to better their life chances—a kind of insurance policy for the future. Such strategies go by many names—"parachute kids," "astronaut families," or "wild geese families" (Yeoh et al. 2005; Waters 2005; Ong 1999; Lee and Koo 2006).[7] They involve more than just paying tuition. Students need care and support, which requires even more money and strong social ties. In many cases, moms accompany their children on their educational quests while their spouses stay home and work to support them (Huang and Yeoh 2005; Chee 2005). In others, relatives or close friends step in to supervise and guide these children when their parents cannot (Zhou 1998; Sun 2014a). Or, as in Lily's case, care is part of the package her parents purchase from her private boarding school (Han 2012).

There are many more children sent ahead from the other end of the socioeconomic spectrum. They leave with their parents' blessings or sometimes on their own because it is the only way to protect themselves from the famine, poverty, or violence that plagues their homelands. Migration is not just a risk management strategy but a desperate act of last resort (Leinaweaver 2007; Øien 2006; Fonseca 2004; Leinaweaver 2014; Goody 1982). Indeed, in 2014, 70,000 unaccompanied children, mostly ages 12 to 17, arrived at the US border. In 2019, the numbers increased to 76,000 (Johnson 2019). The Trump administration tried to "deter" further migration by allowing deplorable conditions in migrant holding centers and instructing shelters to scale back activities "not directly necessary for the protection of life and safety" (Romo and Rose 2019). As we write, the Biden administration is struggling to cope with a recent surge of unaccompanied arrivals who are being held in facilities designed for adults (Sullivan and Kanno-Youngs 2021).

Europe faced its own migration crisis in 2015, when thousands fled war in Syria, Iraq, and beyond. Of the more than 1.3 million migrants seeking asylum, 96,000 were unaccompanied minors (Pew Research Center 2016). EU rules at that time mandated that asylum claims be filed and processed at the first point of entry, but many of these arrivals did not want to stay in Italy or Greece, nor did these countries have the capacity to handle the influx. Infighting between member states over who was responsible for these asylum seekers ensued. Unaccompanied minors, however, had special status: under EU regulations, they could be reunited with family in any member state regardless of their entry point.

A key underlying challenge in disputes over refugees in general, and unaccompanied children in particular, is agreeing on how decisions should be made. When the British and French governments wrangled over which state should be responsible for children stuck at an infamous border "chokepoint" in Calais, they used a logic tied to citizenship (Bochenek 2016). In contrast, the European Union's response to its crisis drew largely on the logic of human rights. According to the European Commission, "Protecting children is first and foremost about upholding European values of respect for human rights, dignity and solidarity. It is also about enforcing European Union law and respecting the Charter of Fundamental Rights of the European Union and international human rights law on the rights of the child" (European Commission 2017, 1). The European Union has encouraged member states to strengthen child protection systems along migratory routes and to cooperate around child protection and civil registration. It supports projects that foster regional migration reforms, help unaccompanied children stay put, decrease migration, and prevent smuggling and child trafficking.

Who, then, is responsible for unaccompanied minors? In the first half of 2019, a third of the refugee and migrant children who arrived in Europe came alone. While transnational institutions advocate on behalf of these children, who should their guardians be? The answer is largely decided by domestic law. Since 2017, for example, Italy has allowed regional governments to recruit volunteer guardians. Before this, the burden of guardianship normally fell to local lawyers and officials, who were sometimes caring for as many as fifty children at one time (Guerra and Brindle 2018). In most cases, children under the age of 12 are placed in foster care. Children between the ages of 12 and 18 are placed in group apartments, residential homes, or other supervised accommodations. France, Spain, Italy, and Portugal guarantee underage migrants the same protections afforded nationals (Guerra and Brindle 2018). The United Kingdom guarantees National Health Service coverage to unaccompanied child migrants. Still, even the most generous systems leave young people facing significant barriers to care. In France, the health care system is notoriously hard to navigate, and unaccompanied children regularly miss medical appointments. Having to move frequently and not speaking the local language prevents them from using available services.

The resource environments of unaccompanied children reflect the state's competing imperatives of caring, coercing, and keeping out (Galli 2020). In the United States, institutional actors, such as Customs and Border Protection officers and officials working in the Office of Refugee Resettlement or in the immigration courts are charged with caring for these vulnerable youth. At the same time, they must also decide who is "deserving" and "undeserving." As sociologist Chiara Galli (2020, 766) notes, "UACs [unaccompanied alien children] are not only subjected to state power through enforcement laws, but they also benefit from laws that protect them. The laws construe them as a deserving rather than a stigmatized social group, more similar to refugees than undocumented immigrants. Unlike refugees, however, whose protected status has already been recognized when they enter the United States, UACs find themselves in legal limbo and must engage with the humanitarian bureaucracy to seek rights and belonging." Because the few rights they are guaranteed constitutionally fall short, they must rely on the human rights apparatus for protection that, in many cases, also fails to adequately deliver.

In sum, across the socioeconomic spectrum, children are sent ahead as a form of social protection. This strategy comes with costs, benefits, and unintended consequences. Children entrusted to relatives or friends often feel abandoned or like "second-class citizens" in the homes where they live (Larmer 2017; Tribune News Service 2016; Titzmann and Lee 2018). Children raised and educated in contexts different from those of their parents often experience role strain. Their parents expect them to adhere to one set of rules, but they have been raised according to another. As their parents grow older, and the gap between parents and children increases, both generations can come to question the value of the sacrifices they made (Sun 2017).

Wealthy families who send their children to be educated abroad make it more difficult for students from less well-off families to compete. As more and more selective international schools open in places like China, Hong Kong, and Taiwan, these children get a major head start in competing in the global labor market—mastering English and a demanding curriculum that makes them competitive candidates for elite universities and graduate schools abroad. In contrast, for disadvantaged families, sending children ahead is often a matter of life or death. Unable to purchase the protections they need from the market, refugee and asylum-seeking children must rely instead on already stretched kinship networks or help from the state or international actors, which are neither sufficient nor guaranteed. They are pushed to leave in search of basic rights and protections.

"Satellite Babies" and Children Sent Home

Researchers estimate that, each year, parents working in Europe, Australia, and North America send thousands of infants home to be cared for by their grandparents (Bohr 2010; Da 2003; Orellana et al. 2001; Glasgow and Gouse-Sheese 1995; Smith et al. 2004).[8] These "satellite babies" circulate between their parents' home and host societies because the parents, having migrated, cannot care for them adequately while they work (Bohr and Tse 2009; Liu et al. 2017). Children also get sent home because their parents want them brought up according to homeland values so they will grow fluent in their ancestral tongue (Smith 2006; Bohr et al. 2018). Older children are sent home to "keep them out of trouble"—protecting them from what their parents perceive as dangerous schools and neighborhoods that encourage bad behaviors associated with the host society.

Javier Cárdenas, with whom our chapter began, is one such case. When he began failing high school, his mother sent him back to the Dominican Republic. By that time, though, he was too much for his grandmother to handle. When he returned to Boston, relations with his family became increasingly strained. Thus, he began years of moving back and forth between the United States and the island. Stories such as this ask us to redefine what we mean by a "good family" and "good parenting." In many cases, parents can care more effectively for their children by distributing the tasks of production and reproduction across borders rather than maintaining the nuclear family under one roof at all costs. Indeed, in some contexts, such household strategies build on long-standing traditions of grandparents becoming their grandchildren's primary caregivers or of fostering.

Sending children back to an ancestral home is not always a survival strategy. For some families, it is a strategy for gaining a competitive edge. Parents hope that the cultural resources their children will acquire by spending time in their ancestral homes will serve them in good stead in the global race to the top. Middle-class Chinese migrants around the world, for example, see China as a rising economic superpower whose star will only grow brighter as their children grow older. They believe that returning home to learn Mandarin and become familiar with Chinese customs will enhance their children's ability to compete in the global job market (Knowles 2017; Liu 2014).

Many studies reveal the emotional sacrifices that come from these economic gains. Sociologist Leslie Wang found deep psychological scars and intergenerational tensions resulting among the Chinese American former satellite babies that she studied (Wang 2018). On the one hand, these young people appreciated knowing about their parents' homelands and being able to strengthen their ties to relatives there. On the other hand, many never truly understood why they were separated from first their parents and later their grandparents. They vividly remembered the pain they felt leaving both settings. "Despite achieving impressive academic and professional successes that were bolstered through their parents' efforts," Wang (2018, 28) writes, "many former satellite babies retained an unsettling mixture of gratitude and emotional pain about being sent abroad long ago. Their ambivalence suggests that they are caught between different cultural expectations of family and parenting."

"Quiet Migration": International Adoption

Our last category of mobile children often flies under the radar when it comes to discussions of migration and social protection—international adoptions. Leslie Wang (2016) met 1-month-old Emma at Tomorrow's Children, a Western, faith-based organization that provides medical care to abandoned children and youth in mainland China.[9] Not only had she been abandoned by her biological parents, Emma had been diagnosed with a rare form of cancer. Tomorrow's Children sent Emma to Hong Kong where she received cutting-edge treatments. Eventually she recovered, and, at age 4, was adopted by a North American family, transforming her "from a forsaken girl to an American sweetheart" (Wang 2016, 50).

Unlike the other children we've described, international adoptees are technically "first-generation immigrants with citizen parents" (Leiter et al. 2006, 12). In most cases, they are adopted by affluent, white families in North America and Western Europe, which makes adoption a kind of transnational social safety net in its own right (Leinaweaver 2013; Dubinsky 2010; Wang 2016). "With recurrent crises in local economies following austerity programs or denationalization of industries," writes anthropologist Christine Gailey (2010, 89), "international adoption is a ready source of income for the poor in countries where the government is either indifferent to their welfare or unable to address their problems."

International adoption differs significantly from family migration because states recognize adoptees' right to citizenship. In fact, international adoptees in receiving countries like the United States, Canada, and the United Kingdom are often put on a citizenship fast track (Editor 2017; Gov.UK 2014). They have birthright citizenship through the principle of *jus sanguinis* because their parents are citizens, even though it is a fictive "by blood" relation to the state (Leiter et al. 2006). Similarly, *jus sanguinis* countries sometimes approve dual nationality for adoptees as a way of strengthening their ties to their biological birthplaces. For example, since 1995, the South Korean government has extended adult adoptees the legal status of "overseas Korean," which allows them to stay in Korea for up to two years to work, make financial investments, purchase properties, and access medical insurance (Kim 2007,

507). As of 2010, they can also become citizens. The government hopes these ethnic Koreans will act as "cultural ambassadors" and help build "economic bridges" between their two worlds (Kim 2007, 497). NGOs are also enlisted in this cause. The goal of Global Overseas Adoptees' Link, for example, is to ensure an instant social home for adoptees who arrive in Korea by offering them frequent weekend get-togethers, monthly meetings, seasonal retreats, and holiday parties (Kim 2007, 505). Yet, as is often the case with "return" migrants going back to a real or ancestral home, feeling truly comfortable and being truly accepted is much more complicated than it seems at first glance (Kim 2009; Kibria 2002, Christou and King 2015).

Transnational adoptions raise unique questions about transnational social protection. Are poor children, who would ordinarily only have access to an extremely limited resource environment, best served by adoptive families where social protections will be plentiful? To what extent should these children have a right to their ancestral culture? What should be done when the social context in a receiving country is hostile to interracial families or to a specific immigrant group (Leinaweaver 2012; Dubinsky 2010)? Adoptive parents try hard to respond to these challenges. They enroll their children in cultural activities such as dance or language classes or they schedule playdates with children from similar backgrounds (Louie 2015). Some go on family "cultural tours" to visit their children's birthplaces or, as children grow older, they go on tours of their own (Gailey 2010, 83). But these good-faith efforts at "culture-keeping" on the part of adoptive parents can also contribute to stereotypical views of culture and ethnicity—as something that can be statically commodified and consumed rather than something that is deeply felt, variable, and constantly changing (Louie 2015).

The world of transnational adoption extends beyond individuals and families. It is regulated by an ever-growing number of international conventions and supported by an ever-growing number of NGOs. Western NGOs, for example, donate significant resources to Chinese orphanages, transforming international adoption into a "means of individual family formation as well as an influential global institution central to the 'cultural economy of circulating relationships of power and exchange' between the PRC and Western countries" (Wang 2016, 15). Adoptive parents receive extensive pre- and post-procedure training to assure that children's best interests are protected (Frekko et al. 2015). The 1993 Hague Convention on the Protection of Children and Cooperation in Respect of Intercountry Adoption, which is based on the principle of "plenary adoption," ensures that birth parents and biological relatives can no longer claim rights to children who are internationally adopted (Beaumont and McEleavy 1999). As of 2018, more than seventy countries—including Brazil, China, Thailand, Ukraine, and Bulgaria—had signed the convention (US Citizenship and Immigration Services 2017).

But despite these many strict regulations and protections, violations still occur. In one case, state-run orphanages in Luoyang, Beijing, and Guangzhou allowed children over 14 to be adopted which was over the legal age limit. In some cases, they did so without official agreement from their birth parents (Wang 2016). Adoptive parents often have little information about what their children went through early on, including malnutrition and emotional deprivation, nor do they understand the possible long-term effects (Gailey 2010). Some parents learn that their adopted children are not "orphans" in the conventional sense because agents forged their stories and documents to make them more "adoptable" (Fenton 2019, 85).

The buck stops with the state. National policies profoundly affect the numbers of children who can be adopted and the resources available to them. Russia and Rwanda, for example, were once major adoptee-sending countries but both countries have since closed their doors (Jones 2015). China instituted stricter criteria for adoptions, raising the parental income requirement; imposing age limits for parents and children; and regulating marital status, health status, and sexual orientation (Wang 2016). As sociologist Estye Fenton (2019, 5) writes, "Since the year 2000, one sending country after another has shut down its international adoption program amid concerns over human rights abuses, corruption, and outright fraud; diplomatic disputes with the United States; or the political, social, and ethical implications of systematic migrations of children along traditional lines of global inequality." International adoptions, therefore, are increasingly out of reach. Providing social protection for an internationally-adopted child involves not only providing resources to improve their well-being but also taking an ideological stand on whether "exporting child[ren]" is a national disgrace, a global power struggle, or a fair distribution of resources (Selman 2012).

Conclusion

As this chapter makes clear, families can adopt a number of migration strategies when children are part of the equation. Bringing children across international borders to secure a better life, leaving them at home to receive remittances, or sending them ahead on their own may seem like disparate approaches. They are all, however, means of protecting children from violence, poverty, or uncertainty. They are also ways of expanding children's resource environments by appealing to humanitarian law; enhancing access to citizenship and, therefore, to public benefits; or generating additional funds to purchase protections from the market. Our analysis drives home, over and over again, the stark differences not only in the breadth and depth of the resource environments that transnational families construct but also in the vulnerability and risk that poor families experience compared to their well-off counterparts. While wealthy families who chose family separation may not anticipate its long-term emotional impact, poor families often have no choice. These dynamics affect both children who are protected and those who are not. Their fates are often linked because opportunities for some give rise to competition for resources for others.

Analyzing these different experiences under the same umbrella also makes clear the many widespread, fundamental changes in the nature of family life that are underway in our world on the move. For many families, the idea that a nuclear or even extended group will live under one roof in one place has long since disappeared. When cultural norms and state narratives continue to cling fast to a view of a "good" parent or a "model" family that is long out of date and out of reach for many of its citizens, they add insult to injury (Solari 2018). So is the idea that mothers alone raise their children. Clearly, transnational caring is gendered. At home and abroad, the people raising kids are more likely to be women, be they mothers, aunts, grandmothers, or older sisters. But fathers, uncles, and brothers are also increasingly involved.

Therefore, we need more supportive policies and narratives that take transnational family life squarely into account. Achieving this requires the cooperative efforts of multiple actors operating at multiple scales. Restrictive citizenship or migration policies have an especially negative impact on the life chances of children who are legally recognized as temporary and involuntary migrants, including undocumented youth, refugees, and asylum seekers. These are the children most in need of protection, most at risk of deportation, and most likely to be denied resources. State policies promoting inclusion, therefore, are essential to providing the protection and security that allow children and families to establish stable and productive lives.

We also see a role for direct services and campaigns aimed at shifting cultural expectations in response to changing family needs. Children left behind, for example, need help understanding why their parents are working abroad. If governments in countries where large numbers are affected address this issue publicly, it becomes a normalized collective experience, not just something an individual child and family has to deal with on their own. Parents who adopt internationally need guidance on issues their children might encounter—from hostility to discrimination to identity crises. Their children may also need support as they make sense of their relationships with their "homelands." Finally, children sent back to spend their formative years in their ancestral homes often have a hard time readapting when they return. In constructing and reconstructing community, these families need help negotiating intergenerational relationships and even basic communication when language barriers are high.

Finally, across groups of migrant children, legal status (e.g., citizenship, documentation, or refugee status) is often the most important resource, either allowing or denying access to state-provided benefits. Children who are citizens or who have proper documentation can depend on at least some measure of protection because of their constitutional rights or status, even though the welfare of their migrant parents may be outside the state's purview. They are theoretically protected under international conventions like the UN Convention on the Rights of the Child. But, as we have seen, whether children actually get what they need depends a lot on the discretion of state actors. The state can provide the protections children desperately need or it can overlook, reject, or challenge their requests (Galli 2020). It uses policy to care, coerce, or keep out. Care denied can deeply traumatize children and their loved ones (Dreby 2015; Andrews and Khayar-Cámara 2022). The continuous trade-offs and struggles that arise from choices benefiting some family members, at the expense of others, undoubtedly affect children long beyond childhood.

2
Education

Donato Soberano paid thousands of dollars to get his job teaching seventh-grade science in Arizona. It was 2016. School districts across the United States could not hire enough teachers already living in the country because the salaries they offered were too low. They looked to professionals from abroad to fill the gap and the Philippines, Soberano's home country, was ready and waiting (Goldstein 2018a). Teachers are just one kind of worker the Filipino government actively exports. As Mukul Bakhshi, director of the Alliance for Ethical International Recruitment Practices, says, recruitment companies and the Filipino government train teachers "in a way that it's easy for them to pass muster from licensing authorities here. They obviously speak English, and they are willing to work" (Goldstein 2018a).

Since 2015, the Pendergast Elementary School District in Phoenix, Arizona, has employed more than fifty teachers from the Philippines. Like au pairs and camp counselors, these workers hold J-1 visas that allow them in the country temporarily without a pathway to citizenship. According to the US State Department, in 2018, more than 2,800 foreign teachers arrived on American soil through the J-1 program, up from about 1,200 in 2010. School administrators welcome these recruits because they ease staffing shortages. They say foreign-born educators are efficient workers who diversify their classrooms and workplaces. Union leaders emphatically protest these efforts, claiming they are one more way that school districts can undermine their fight for decent pay for teachers (Goldstein 2018b).

Although Soberano's $40,000[1] salary is high by Manila standards, he makes major sacrifices to earn it. He gets up every morning at 4 a.m. to Skype with his wife and two daughters. He spent down all his savings and took out a bank loan to afford the $12,500 recruitment fee he had to pay to get his job.[2] When his J-1 visa runs out in three years, he will have to pay an additional $1,000 to extend it (Goldstein 2018a).

While J-1 teachers account for only a tiny share of Arizona's 60,000 public school teachers, international recruitment is on the rise in other parts of

Transnational Social Protection. Peggy Levitt, Erica Dobbs, Ken Chih-Yan Sun, and Ruxandra Paul,
Oxford University Press. © Oxford University Press 2023. DOI: 10.1093/oso/9780197666821.003.0003

the country. There are now clusters of recruits in Nevada, North Carolina, and several other states. In 2017, the Philippines became the top sender of J-1 teachers to the United States, followed by China and Jamaica. While the system generally works well, it has also resulted in cases of abuse. In 2009, the Louisiana Federation of Teachers sued the recruiting agency Universal Placement International (UPI). It charged the company with holding in servitude the Filipino teachers it hired as replacements after Hurricane Katrina. UPI allegedly retained large portions of teachers' wages and threatened them with deportation if they complained (NPR 2009). The union won a $4.5 million settlement in 2012 (Lansworth 2012).

Teachers are not the only ones under increasing pressure to cross borders. Students who want to maximize their chances of securing good, high-paying jobs after graduation know that getting an education at home is no longer enough. Employers around the world prefer candidates who have experience studying abroad (Trooboff et al. 2007). A 2014 European Commission study found that 64 percent of employers see study abroad as central to the university experience (European Commission 2014). In fact, the European Union (EU) has numerous programs supporting the mobility of students, trainees, teachers, and young people. From a young age, students are encouraged to envision a future of transnational education and professional training and to not assume that their homelands are the best place to train for the job market. The burden of responsibility increasingly shifts to the individual, who must piece together the most robust combination of domestic and international resources and knowledge. While a limited number of scholarships facilitate transnational studies, most students have to fund themselves out of pocket—another transfer of responsibility from public institutions to individuals and their families.

These stories are part of a broader reorganization of all levels of education across borders. They exemplify how risks and opportunities are redistributed transnationally in ways that empower some and create obstacles for others. Migrant teachers alleviate shortages in American schools and provide better education for American children. But this quick fix does little to alleviate the deep structural problems facing education in the United States, including the low salaries that give rise to teacher shortages to begin with. On the country-of-origin side, migrant teachers improve their families' lives but at tremendous cost and risk. Brain drain plagues the education sector as some of the most talented educators leave to teach elsewhere.

In some parts of the world, the transnationalization of education receives considerable support from international and regional institutions. The European Union supports partnerships between schools in different states (the Comenius program); university student exchanges lasting between three and twelve months (the Erasmus program); and training courses in school or adult education, including short work placements (internships) in other countries (the Comenius and Grundtvig programs). These efforts nudge teachers and students toward developing cross-border resource environments. They are based on the view of education as a commodity that individuals choose to purchase in the context of the global knowledge economy and the global market for talent. They are also an example of governance supersizing that the European Union puts in place to reduce the costs of competing effectively for its members.

Education, perhaps more than any other form of social protection, has been generally seen as the responsibility of the state. Schools play a central role in the socialization of children: They allow the state to exercise control of the nation's founding myths and ideologies, to set relatively uniform standards of learning, and to define the parameters of citizenship (Fabbe 2019). Schools train citizens but also workers: The future of a country's economy, in no small part, depends upon the strengths of its educational system. As such, states generally invest heavily in the formal education of their citizens and education is a constitutional right.

Yet, as we discussed in the introduction, the idea that education systems are solely state driven, territorially limited, and nationally bounded is out of date. In the United States, shrinking government resources prompt public schools to patch budget gaps by looking abroad, whether by hiring instructors like Donato Soberano at the primary level or by recruiting full-tuition-paying international students at the university level. For cases like Mexico and the United States that have deeply integrated migration corridors, both countries have an interest in preparing students to retain cultural—and hopefully economic—ties to their homeland. Well-educated, integrated, and healthy migrants are good for everyone, no matter where they live. This marks a turn away from educating children solely as nationals to transforming them into transnational or global citizens.

The developments we trace in this sector are enormous. Hybrid transnational social protection encompasses primary, secondary, and tertiary education, as well as teachers, learners, recruiters, evaluators, and regulators.

Our purview includes migrants who move with the intention of settling permanently and students who circulate in and out of different school systems because their families migrate seasonally or because they are forced to return home.

When the state downsizes its role in public education, individuals and families look to other sources to create resource environments. As a result, private institutions play an ever more prominent role in education provision, whether it be in the form of private universities, supplemental enrichment, or English-language programs families invest in to improve student performance. Nongovernmental organizations (NGOs) and religious institutions are also significant, especially in cases where children are not consistently connected to a single school system and are, therefore, at greater risk of falling behind. Families also rely on their social networks and communities to access information about educational opportunities and scholarship programs, to navigate application processes, or to care for children "sent ahead" to study far away from home.

We begin this chapter by briefly reviewing the history of education as a form of social protection. We then discuss broad trends in the globalization of higher education against which *migration-driven education*, *education-driven migration*, and *brain circulation* take shape. Migration-driven education includes education to meet the needs of migrants and their children. Education-driven migration refers to people who relocate in search of educational opportunities that are better than those in their countries of origin. Untangling the effects of a globalized education sector from changes produced by transnational migration is difficult because they are deeply entwined. While many of our examples focus on the higher education sector, as the story of Donato Soberano suggests, the developments we describe are also transforming primary and secondary education.

The History of Education: State Responsibilities, Human Rights, and Economic Globalization

Education is not always included in the bundle of rights associated with social welfare. How, then, does an education contribute to social protection? Conversely, under what conditions does social protection support education? Which actors assume primary responsibility for education? How abundant, versatile, and resilient are the resource environments they create?

The idea of education as a human or citizenship right and entitlement, or an integral part of social welfare, developed differently from the idea of elite travel for education. Although both involve education across borders, they operate on opposite sides of the socioeconomic spectrum.

The University of Paris (i.e., the Sorbonne) has educated some of the world's most brilliant minds and attracted some of its most distinguished intellectuals since its founding in 1150. During the eighteenth and nineteenth centuries, Eastern European elites sent their children not only to Paris but to Berlin and Vienna for better, more prestigious educations. These mobile intellectuals returned home with "disruptive" ideas about democracy, liberalism, nationalism, and socialism that inspired political movements like the Spring of Nations in 1848. Such opportunities, however, were largely limited to the rich. Being educated in the best institutions was a mark of status. Wealthy families from Eastern Europe regularly hired tutors from France and Germany to work with their children so they could make the grade. Famous universities also recruited foreign students on the basis of merit, providing scholarships because they believed that their presence enriched the educational experience for all.

The contemporary features of education across borders are in some ways a continuation of these trends. Education promotes social mobility. Sending a child to a good primary or secondary school or supporting a university education is a pathway to securing a better, higher paying job in the future. The hope for families and societies is that children who have these opportunities will live better lives and have more options with which to manage risk. Education is, therefore, an investment in social protection. It serves to expand resource environments, and—to the extent that it is widely available—mitigates inequality and poverty.

Education as a privilege, however, is distinct from education as a universal right—a tension with a long history. The right to education is inscribed in international law in Article 26 of the Universal Declaration of Human Rights and in Articles 13 and 14 of the International Covenant on Economic, Social and Cultural Rights (adopted by the United Nations in 1948 and 1966, respectively). These entitlements address public education provided by the state and, in many cases, prioritize perceived national interests. In the nineteenth century, socialist thinkers placed responsibility for ensuring the social and economic well-being of the national community squarely on the state. The individual right to basic social welfare thus included education.

This thinking stood in stark contrast to liberal arguments that deemed non-state, private, and/or local actors the primary providers of education and warned of the dangers of too much state involvement in schools (Friedman 1955). In the United States, the struggle over the role of the federal government versus individual states in education has a long history and continues to this day (Hornbeck 2017; Pelsue 2017). We see this mirrored around the world as increasingly popular neoliberal educational reforms drive forward decentralization and privatization (Turner and Yolcu 2014). States hybridize transnational social protection from above by encouraging citizens to exercise choice, assume responsibility for their students by being active consumers, and look beyond public education options by comparing the quality and outcomes afforded by other providers.

Religious and military institutions also played key roles in early public education. In Europe and the United States, some of the first schools were set up to train clergy. Many of the earliest European universities, founded in the Middle Ages, drew upon Christian principles. The Catholic Church instituted free education for the poor in 1179 and decreed that every cathedral appoint a master to teach basic reading, even to students too poor to pay. Parishes and monasteries also ran free schools with basic curricula (Orme 2006). With Latin as the lingua franca among educated Western Europeans, the affluent could travel for education while the poor received basic training at local schools. Even during the Middle Ages and the Renaissance, mobility was a sorting factor in access to education.

During the Renaissance, humanists emphasized the importance of education for men (but not women) as a pathway to excellence and to creating enlightened citizens who would actively participate in the civic life of their communities. The Reformation, which led to the spread of education in the vernacular as opposed to Latin, and the invention of the printing press, which made texts available to larger audiences, drove forward the rise of compulsory education for boys and girls throughout Europe and the United States (Boyd and King 1994; Soysal and Strang 1989). In the United States, the founders of the Plymouth Colony required parents to teach their children to read and write. Massachusetts mandated that every town with more than fifty families hire a teacher and every town of more than one hundred establish a school. In its quest to produce soldiers and obedient citizens, Prussia introduced compulsory education in the early nineteenth century and after the French Revolution, the Republican School in France, which was both free and secular, sought to break the hegemony of the monarchy and the Catholic Church (Chadwick 1997). In 1919, Vladimir Lenin launched a campaign to eradicate illiteracy in the Soviet Union by government decree (Brooks 1985).

In each of these cases, nation-states were the stars of the show. Today, national governments generally have the final say about curricula and public authorities monitor and regulate day-to-day school operations and performance. They also assume the lead in training, credentialing, and evaluating teachers. Yet tensions between the national and the transnational have always characterized public education. Mobile students and teachers promote the global circulation of knowledge even as national education systems stress the "national" to strengthen the bond between citizen and state.

At the same time, education is increasingly a global business and privatization is on the rise (Steer et al. 2015). Private schools increase students' range of learning opportunities—and enhance choice—but they can also deeply undermine efforts to provide universal access to high-quality education. Indeed, growing numbers of private institutions, both brick-and-mortar schools and virtual enterprises, have had their licenses revoked or diplomas invalidated because of the poor quality of the services they provide (Brownell 2013).

Today, it is not only students and teachers but institutions, administrative and governance structures, and curricula that cross borders. These developments are part and parcel of economic globalization. The global race for human capital fuels competition to educate the world's most talented students. Home countries hope their most promising students will return when they graduate and lend their talents and skills to the national cause. Recognizing that physical return is not always in the cards, governments create avenues and incentives to encourage these expatriates to continue to contribute via long distance. On the other hand, destination countries hope that some graduates will take their places among their own most talented and productive workers. In fact, in the United States, immigrants are responsible for more than half of the start-up companies valued at $1 billion or more. They are also key members of management or product development teams in more than 80 percent of these enterprises (Anderson 2018). What might Silicon Valley have become if these engineers, inventors, and entrepreneurs had studied in England or Germany instead?

Education-Driven Migration

For those who were lucky enough to attend, summer camp generally brings back fond memories. What could be better than making new friends, swimming in a lake, and sitting around a campfire? Today, though, summer camp is about more than just fun—it is also a site of transnational education. Children from well-to-do families swim and play baseball while also learning English and mastering American social norms. Like Lily in Chapter 1, who was sent ahead to study, students from China frequently go abroad to attend elite summer camps or private secondary schools thought to bolster their chances of economic success. In fact, journalist Evan Osnos (2014, 67) writes: "I stopped being surprised when Communist Party grandees told me their offspring were at Taft or Andover," two elite private high schools in the United States.

Families that migrate to access the "best" education for their children are engaged in one form of education-driven migration (Nyiri 2018; Lan 2018b). Another form involves international students who, with the help of education intermediaries, purchase access to a university education abroad. A third form consists of international students recruited by universities trying to attract talent, boost the quality of learning experiences on their campuses, and build diverse, cosmopolitan communities. They do so by offering financial aid to disadvantaged students who would not otherwise be able to attend, generally through channels operating outside the purview of the state. This freedom from government intervention is important. It allows students to escape corruption-ridden educational systems in their countries of origin, especially young people who do not have the money to pay bribes or who lack the necessary personal connections.

At least initially, migration for education is usually temporary—that is, most families move so their children can study and then plan to return home once the school year ends. What happens is often different. As the years go by, primary school abroad leads to secondary school and university abroad as well. Children who are primarily educated abroad are socialized into the laws, languages, and cultures of other countries at the same time that they lack basic knowledge about their own. Therefore, the goals of transnational education can undercut the emergence of strong national ties.

Migrants who work abroad so their children can access better schools and higher education back home are investing in an intergenerational social mobility strategy. They want to prevent their children from having to migrate to make a living. "I work abroad so they won't have to" was a frequent refrain among the Central and Eastern Europeans working throughout the European Union whom political scientist Ruxandra Paul interviewed. Not surprisingly, there are many unanticipated consequences (Paul 2020).

In villages in Northwest Romania, for example, Paul (2020) found mayors worried that migration undermined the value of education: "What is the point of going to school, to university," one asked, "if, in the end, you end up working on some construction site in France?" Halfway around the world, Dominican teenagers echoed this sentiment. Why go to high school in the Dominican Republic when what mattered was learning enough English to get a job in the United States (Levitt 2001)? In settings of high emigration, these ideas about the value of a home country education can subvert national workforce development.

Education-driven migration may depend as much on information as on funding. Prospective students need to know about international exchange programs and financial aid offered by foreign universities. Vast networks of schools, businesses, and civil society organizations are hard at work publicizing these opportunities. In cities like Sofia and Bucharest, certain high schools are known for preparing, counseling, and placing students in American or European institutions of higher learning. State-sponsored institutions with branches around the world, like the Alliance Française, the British Council, and the Fulbright Commission, disseminate information and even run courses that prepare students for standardized tests. International alumni provide input for admissions officers, sometimes conducting interviews with candidates who cannot travel for campus interviews. Admissions officers from foreign universities go on long tours to connect with potential applicants. Their mission is to identify talent and facilitate education-driven migration.[3]

Pursuing international education, however, comes with risks. Online applications may facilitate the process but the educational consultants whom many families hire to help navigate the admission process are not always trustworthy or competent. Many Western institutions dismiss them as money-making frauds because the more students they place, the higher their commission (Sklarow 2011; Thieme 2017). Most parents lack the wherewithal to assess the value of the services they purchase. Not surprisingly, many of these so-called parachute kids (who are supposed to parachute in and out for their studies) remain abroad, building careers and starting families, thereby precipitating a cycle of long-term intergenerational separation (Sun 2017).

Indeed, that is, in some sense, what universities and the international recruitment industry are hoping for.

Debt can also put international students at great risk. Student loans not only create grave financial and psychological burdens, but can also force students to accept exploitative work conditions after they graduate. In the United States, for example, some recruiting agencies are predatory, targeting high-skilled Indian graduates in the fields of science, technology, engineering, and math (Thomas 2017). Aware that these students are hard-strapped for cash and that they need employment immediately after graduation, recruiters place them in jobs for which they are overqualified and underpaid. The fees they deduct represent a big cut in salary. While taking such jobs is risky, "returning to India with debt and no money would have been equally embarrassing" (Thomas 2017, 1886).

Socialized into the ways of another country, where they now have strong social networks, students who study abroad can find it hard to return home, both personally and professionally. The social mobility plan families invest in so heavily unfolds but not in the place where it was planned. When students do return, they sometimes experience downward mobility because their training and credentials are not well regarded (Ho 2019). In mainland China, sociologist Elaine Ho (2019, 39) found that some returnees became "middling migrants (*zhongdeng yimin*)." They not only fell behind their nonmigrant counterparts, they were considered less competitive than their younger colleagues.

The European Union's solution to these challenges was to establish the free movement of people as a fundamental right. It was to educate a class of professionals who reap the benefits of European citizenship and are, therefore, productive and comfortable anywhere within its borders. The Erasmus Programme, or European Action Scheme for Mobility of University Students, promotes student exchanges among European universities. Since 1989, it has moved some 250,000 students per year. It officially recognizes studies completed in its member states as well as non-EU members such as Iceland, Norway, Turkey, Liechtenstein, and Switzerland (Recchi 2015).

To reduce vulnerability and brain drain, some countries help young citizens to access educational opportunities abroad. Governments provide scholarships in exchange for the promise that students will return and work at a government job for a certain number of years. The Romanian government offered scholarships covering the costs of a master's or PhD program in Western Europe or North America. In exchange, recipients signed contracts that committed them to work in the public sector for at least three years (InCont 2011). In 2020, national student organizations rejected an initiative that would have forgiven government loans to students who returned to Romania after graduation (HotNews 2021).

Migration-Driven Education

In cases of frequent, long-term circulation between sending and receiving countries, governments and NGOs may step in to help students whose needs cannot be met by a single education system. Cooperation between Mexico and the United States, involving a range of formal and informal programs, is a case in point that we discuss in depth here.

Mexico's federal government, along with the governments of various Mexican states, support these efforts as a form of statecraft. The government wants children of Mexican origin to stay connected to Mexican culture and to support the country economically and politically as their parents have done. The US government's involvement is also, in part, motivated by self-interest. Many children of Mexican parents are US citizens and may return to the country at their first opportunity. All parties, therefore, have an interest in educating fluent English speakers who are well integrated economically and politically regardless of their address.

Education programs at the US–Mexico border have a long history. In 1982, the Mexican and US governments created El Programa Binacional de Educación Migrante (The Bi-National Program for Migrant Education, or PROBEM) to meet the educational needs of child and young migrants. It targets children who circulate between the two countries on a regular basis, whether they are currently in the United States or have resettled in Mexico (Instituto de los Mexicanos en el Exterior 2016). The goals of PROBEM are to (1) facilitate access to schools by easing requirements for enrollment; (2) organize summer teacher exchanges; (3) provide educational and cultural supports by developing technological and pedagogical techniques to meet the needs of students on the move; and (4) ensure that families, teachers, and administrators know about the program and can access it easily (Secretaría de Educación Pública n.d. a, b).

The Mexican government created the *documento de transferencia* (transfer document) that is issued by Mexico's consular offices in the United States. It serves as proof of school attendance and provides a "report card" that enables students to be placed appropriately in any school in Mexico at any point during the school year. Mexican teachers also visit different US cities for three to eight weeks each summer to work with children of Mexican origin—either migrants or the children of migrants—to reinforce their Mexican identity, provide remedial academic support, bolster their Spanish language skills, and increase their self-esteem (Instituto de los Mexicanos en el Exterior 2016).

Back in Mexico, legislators passed reforms guaranteeing all minors in the country the right to education regardless of their migration status or citizenship. This provision refers not only to students of Mexican origin but to all migrant students living in Mexico, including those from Central America. The government also reduced the requirements for enrolling in a Mexican school. Rather than demanding the *documento de transferencia*, which was time-consuming and expensive, Mexican authorities now allow families to simply present their children's transcripts instead.

An active group of civil society organizations complements state efforts. Founded in 2013 with the goal of including migration policy in the next Mexican National Development Plan, the Colectivo Migraciones para Las Americas (The Migration Collective of the Americas) is a national and international network of organizations working together to protect the rights of migrants. Partner organizations communicate using WhatsApp so that when a family arrives in a new place, they receive the coordinated support they need (Colectivo Migración para Las Américas 2020). Deportados Unidos (Deportees United) is a transnational organization helping deportees in the United States and Mexico access information and services (Sánchez 2017). Dream in Mexico is a youth-led organization serving undocumented young people in the United States and those who have returned to Mexico. The organization assists in finding education and employment by identifying potential jobs, schools, courses, scholarships, and other resources (Dream in Mexico 2020).

Researchers find much variation across states in the impact and implementation of these programs. The right to education, their findings show, is not enough to ensure that students get what they need to succeed in school (Eunice Vargas Valle, personal communication, October 2018). Rather, successful integration depends on a host of factors, including language support. Second-language programs, like English as a Second Language programs in the United States, are not standard practice in Mexico and students who return knowing little Spanish have difficulty. Researchers also point to the distinction between mastering colloquial and academic Spanish. Even though students communicate easily on the playground, it does not mean they are able to do their homework (Eunice Vargas Valle, personal communication, October 2018).

Classroom culture—the norms for behavior of students and teachers—also shapes the learning experiences of return student migrants. In the United States, researchers find, students are trained to express opinions, participate in discussions, and challenge their teachers—a cultural expectation common among middle-class families and educational institutions (Lareau 2011; Calarco 2018). Back in Mexico, where schools demand more deference to authority, these students often experience a culture clash. Children considered gifted and talented in the United States have trouble fitting in. Students also need to catch up on basic knowledge about Mexican holidays, the national anthem, and addressing teachers using the polite form of "you."

Not all teachers in Mexico support these efforts. Some consider them a waste of time and energy because so many of these students are likely to return to the United States at the first opportunity. Some school districts balk at the cost. Others support small interventions, even if they only reach a fraction of those in need. Eunice Vargas Valle, a researcher at the Colegio de la Frontera Norte in Tijuana, established support groups for students and teachers, training them in education practices that are more "inclusive, intercultural, and sensitive to the needs of migrants" (personal communication, October 2018). But gaining support from administrators, she told us, brings challenges, as do teachers' unions that, in some states, oppose these efforts.

As we described in Chapter 1, in 2012, the Obama Administration's Deferred Action for Childhood Arrivals (DACA) program began allowing youngsters brought to the United States without documents to study or work without the threat of deportation. Aware that many of their citizens in the United States are undocumented, some Latin American countries are actively helping them apply for DACA. As international relations scholar Alexandra Délano Alonso (2018, 142–143) found,

> The Mexican government was able to mobilize and adapt a consular infrastructure developed over many years to provide resources and support to

help migrants access benefits available to them in the United States, in this case responding to a temporary change in the legal status of undocumented youth through the DACA program. The government offered assistance in obtaining the required documents and also organized workshops to help migrants complete their applications, in some cases even sponsoring some of the costs of application.

Why is the Mexican government willing to invest resources to help undocumented youth living in the United States? From their perspective, many DACA recipients—especially those who are activists—can help the Mexican government exercise greater political influence in the United States. They can contribute money and skills to their ancestral homeland. That is why Reyna Torres, the director general of Protection for Mexicans Abroad at the Foreign Ministry, told Délano Alonso (2018, 144), "the activism, leadership, and economic potential the Dreamers represent is clear: They are fighters. We know the profiles of other leaders, traditional leaders. But these leaders have a different profile. They will be senators, council members, doctors, investors."

These efforts on the part of the Mexican government receive mixed reviews. Critics claim they devote too many resources to help DACA-eligible youth in the United States and not enough to young people deported back to Mexico. A representative of the National Institute for Migration within the Ministry of the Interior, which is responsible for issues related to deportations and repatriations, told Délano Alonso (2018, 164) bluntly: "We deal with Mexicans abroad; when they return to Mexico it is no longer our responsibility."

The repeal of DACA, or a similar policy change leading to widespread deportations, would have a major impact on the Mexican university system. Large numbers of students who have never studied or worked in Spanish would be sent back to Mexico. They are not likely to return to their regions of origin but to move instead to urban centers like Mexico City or Guadalajara. While some of the courses they took outside Mexico might count toward a Mexican degree, other programs, like law and medicine, which require knowledge of the national system, would not. According to Rodrigo Aguilar Zepeda, an education researcher, students can transfer credit for courses in the humanities and some of the social sciences outside the country about 70 percent of the time, but not for majors unrecognized in Mexico, like Chicano studies (personal communication, November 2018). In addition, linguistic, social, and cultural barriers make it difficult for deported youth to adapt to school life in Mexico (Délano Alonso 2018).

Transnational Teacher Training

Migration-driven education poses unique challenges for teachers. How should they prepare students culturally and intellectually for lives in two settings? How can teachers become better informed about the different social and cultural challenges students face?

Informal, short-term efforts to address students' needs often last only as long as funding, interest, and the political climate allows. For example, during the 1990s, small numbers of New York City teachers traveled to the Dominican Republic each summer to receive "cultural training" so they could better understand the context where their students came from (Levitt 2001). German and Turkish officials have had high-level discussions about training teachers to work with the many students of Turkish origin in Germany. In 2008, Prime Minister Erdogan offered to send teachers to Germany to provide Turkish language instruction. The German government opted instead to emphasize German language instruction and to train teachers of Turkish origin to function better in the German school system (Ministerium für Bildung und Forschung n.d.).

Some teacher education programs that cross borders arise not in response to migration per se but to prepare nationals to compete more effectively in the global market. When the Malaysian government wanted to increase English language fluency among its citizens, it created a teacher-training program with the New Zealand government (Anderson 2014). Three hundred and fifty prospective teachers studied in New Zealand between 2010 and 2012 as part of a program connecting five Malaysian teacher education institutes with five Southern Hemisphere universities.

Education to Maintain Ties and Support Mobility

Nation-states use education to strengthen the ties that second and third generations maintain to their ancestral homes. These efforts are also designed to help return migrants to be better integrated and to encourage those who stay abroad to contribute from afar. Many consulates around the world host cultural events with an eye toward engaging their diasporas. The Moroccan Embassy in France offers language classes. The Dominican Embassy in the United States hosts events for Dominican migrants' children (Aguinas 2009). In the 1980s, the Turkish government established the Turkish-Islamic Union of Religious Affairs, which became the largest

Turkish diaspora organization in Europe. Its branch in Belgium, established in 1982, hosts teachers trained and funded by the Turkish government. The Yunus Emere Institute, established in 2009, also offers Turkish-language classes for young generations of Turkish migrants in Brussels (Gsir et al. 2017).

Some countries encourage diaspora members to consider studying in their ancestral homes. The Pakistani Embassy in the United States provides lists of internships, medical colleges, and universities in Pakistan (Aguinas 2009). Since 1999, there has been a dedicated department in the Romanian government (Departamentul pentru Românii de Pretutindeni or Ministerul pentru Românii de Pretutindeni or the Ministry for Romanians Everywhere) for Romanians abroad, which is charged with attending to the educational needs of Romanians outside the country. Its goals are to promote the Romanian language through education and mass media and to offer advanced training for children in neighboring countries where ethnic Romanians already receive basic language instruction at public school. It also supports churches, private and Sunday schools, and charitable organizations to preserve the "national cultural patrimony." Finally, the government offers scholarships and designates slots for students of Romanian origin who want to study back home. Some universities even offer a one-year remedial language course or summer language camp, with all costs covered except airfare, so that prospective students can become fluent enough to study in Romanian (Ministerul pentru Românii de Pretutindeni 2020).

A private version of this, aimed at enhancing student performance and, thus, future social mobility, is the supplemental education or enrichment programs common in many sending countries. In Korea, for example, even families with limited means scrape together their savings to send their children to *Hogwons*—after-school preparatory programs aimed at helping students excel on the entrance exams to the country's top universities. Children barely in preschool spend hours each week on an educational assembly line that extends through high school (PBS 2017). *Hogwons* (or *Buke/Buxiban*, as they are called in Greater China) are also opening up in Asian American communities across the United States. Indeed, sociologists Jennifer Lee and Min Zhou (2015) found these after-class programs were increasingly important tools for pursuing second-generation achievement and mobility.

Educating Refugees

Another form of migration-driven education involves involuntary migrants. The line between migrants who are forced to move and those who "choose" to move because of economic or political conditions is, of course, blurry. Those who qualify as "official" refugees or asylum seekers, however, are entitled to certain rights and protections. Although countries throughout the Global North adopt strategies to block forced migrants from entering their territories (Fitzgerald 2019), once these individuals are granted asylum, they are eligible for certain rights under the UN 1951 Convention Relating to the Status of Refugees and its 1967 Protocol (United Nations High Commission on Refugees [UNHCR] 2018). These include the right not to be forcibly repatriated to their home country but also the right to education, housing, and public relief and assistance. One hundred and forty-eight states have signed on to these agreements. How national law interprets this, and the ability of each state to fulfill its obligations, varies considerably.

Educating refugees presents unique challenges (Chopra and Dryden-Peterson 2020). They need "borderless" higher education because the skills and credentials they acquire must be valid wherever they resettle. As a result, while Canada used to fund individual Somalis to study abroad, it now supports training in camps in Kenya through a mix of online and blended learning. The goal, said Sarah Dryden-Peterson, an expert in refugee education, is to make their education and skills applicable in Somalia, Kenya, or Canada (personal communication, July 2018). Ideally, students will eventually return home and be well equipped to help rebuild their nation.

These programs are what Dryden-Peterson calls "stackable," as students can earn increasingly valuable credentials at multiple points along the way. A student who has time to complete only two years of study receives one kind of diploma. Someone completing three years receives a higher degree. Not surprisingly, refugees' options for accessing primary and secondary education vary considerably by country. In countries like Kenya, where movement is restricted, schooling takes place inside refugee camps. In countries like Uganda, where refugees are permitted to build homes, grow crops, and move about freely, they can enroll in public schools.

Religious institutions and NGOs are also important actors in refugee education. In Thailand and Kenya, Jesuit Refugee Services works with a network of Jesuit universities to place students, although national universities are sometimes reluctant to recognize their prior studies. JuSoor, a non-profit organization that supports Syria's (re)development and helps Syrian youth everywhere, began actively assisting refugees in Lebanon in June 2013 through educational programs and activities that offer psychosocial support. Between the program's inception and 2017, nearly 3,500 students attended JuSoor's schools in Lebanon, and twenty-two received scholarships to study at Lebanese universities (JuSoor 2018).

The United Nations High Commission on Refugees, in partnership with the United Nations Children's Fund, the United Nations Educational, Scientific and Cultural Organization (UNESCO), and national host governments, is responsible for refugee education policy worldwide. With displacement lasting an average of 10 to 15 years and most refugees now living in urban areas, the United Nations increasingly invests in national schools. As the third draft of the Global Compact on Refugees states, "States and relevant stakeholders will contribute resources and expertise to expand and enhance the quality and inclusiveness of national education systems to facilitate access by refugee and host community children (both boys and girls) and youth to primary, secondary and tertiary education" (UNHCR 2018). Newcomers should be enrolled in school three months after they arrive in a host country. When possible, support should be made available to train "refugees and members of host communities who are or could be engaged as teachers, in line with national laws and policies." Moreover, "support will be provided for the development and implementation of the national education sector plans that include refugees. Technical support will be provided where needed to facilitate recognition of equivalency of academic, professional and vocational accreditation" (UNHCR 2018, 13). Not surprisingly, what is guaranteed on paper is difficult to implement in practice. Even when educational opportunities are available, refugees and asylum seekers still face major bureaucratic obstacles, financial challenges, and discrimination that prevents them from taking full advantage of what is available to them (Gowayed 2018).

Beyond the Classroom: Promoting and Managing "Brain Circulation"

As we will discuss further in Chapter 4 ("Health"), governments use different strategies to stem the outflow of highly skilled workers—especially when the state foots the bill for their training. The challenges arising from the transnationalization of education and health care, and how governments respond, are often one and the same. Hungary, for example, introduced new rules in 2012 that require students to work in-country after graduation for a period equal to the length of their government-financed university educations. Those who leave earlier have to pay back their scholarships (Boros and Hegedűs 2016).

While these strategies are designed to keep an educated workforce in place, governments also institute policies to reap the benefits of the education and skills of migrants who remain abroad. In 2004, India created the Ministry of Overseas Indian Affairs, which became part of the Ministry of External Affairs in 2016. Its mandate is to monitor departure flows, protect expatriates, and harness the development power of the diaspora. The government also introduced the Overseas Citizenship of India scheme. In addition to the nonresident Indian (NRI), who lives abroad but retains Indian citizenship, a new category, person of Indian origin (PIO), was created for people of Indian origin who are naturalized citizens of other countries. Both statuses grant migrants a series of economic and educational rights, although not the right to vote from abroad, to encourage their enduring involvement in and commitment to India (Ministry of External Affairs 2020).

Other institutions also encourage the diaspora's long-term contributions. The Overseas Indian Facilitation Centre is a nonprofit group that works with the Confederation of Indian Industry to encourage investment and business development. The India Development Foundation of Overseas Indians facilitates philanthropic investments. The Global Indian Network of Knowledge is an electronic platform that encourages knowledge transfers so that India can benefit from the skills and knowledge of people of Indian origin living overseas. In 2003, the government celebrated the first Pravasi Bharatiya Divas, or Day of Non-Resident Indians, and, more recently, established a PIO/NRI university in Bangalore for children of Indian ancestry (Vezzoli and Lacroix 2010).

The Chinese government also actively promotes enduring ties to its educated citizens abroad. In 2013 alone, China sent an estimated 400,000 students overseas. At the same time, the rates of higher education in China have increased precipitously. While in 1978, only 1.55 percent of the Chinese population was enrolled in university, by 2013, that rate had increased to 34.5 percent (Mok and Han 2016). The country now has more graduates than its labor market can absorb. This mismatch not only increases pressure on the government to create more jobs but also heightens competition between graduates from national and international institutions, practically guaranteeing that at least some Chinese graduates will remain abroad. Either way, the government works actively to mitigate brain drain by offering generous incentives to return, either permanently or temporarily, to serve the country (Mok and Han 2016). These aim to "address the difficulties that returnees faced in obtaining residency visas [because China disallows dual citizenship], settling matters of housing and schooling for family members as well as the costs and technical difficulties of starting up research or companies in China" (Ho 2019, 30).

Local governments in Zhejiang and Jiangsu Province, for example, developed a "seagull plan" in an attempt to harness overseas expertise. "Seagulls" are talented professionals who commute between countries to promote transnational cooperation and boost national and local economic growth (Mok and Han 2016). In 2011, the government of Suzhou, in Jiangsu Province, introduced a program to encourage seagulls to take part-time jobs (no fewer than fifteen working days each year) or offer technical guidance online without physically returning. In Zhejiang Province, the government gets access to overseas talent by recruiting experts willing to work for two to nine months over a three-year period.

Educational Mismatch—Applying Knowledge and Skills from Abroad back Home

The extent to which brain circulation actually helps migrants' homelands varies considerably. Not all of the skills and knowledge they acquire abroad are suitable or applicable. In their study of returning health care professionals in India and China, Holdaway et al. (2015) found both positive and negative effects of studying and working abroad. International experience clearly contributed to personal growth. Practitioners adopted new practices that diminished the social hierarchy between doctors and patients. But returnees also learned things that reinforced institutional power dynamics and social inequalities. Ultimately, individuals tended to benefit more than the institutions they worked for.

Let's take the case of an Indian doctor who studied abroad to become a nephrologist. After completing his bachelor's degree back home, he settled in New York to do graduate work. He stayed there for many years, working for a successful group practice until a for-profit hospital chain convinced him to return to India by offering him the opportunity to open his own clinic. The wealthy patients who could afford his fees benefited from his services but those who could not had to wait in line for less-advanced care. Because the clinic earned money, the doctor received a disproportionate share of hospital resources. His colleagues held him in high esteem and were encouraged to follow his example (Holdaway et al. 2015).

Most of the Indian and Chinese clinicians studied by Holdaway and her colleagues received their training in Europe, Australia, and North America. While they learned new research, technical, and managerial skills, their courses focused primarily on health problems in developed countries and on protocols requiring sophisticated equipment and highly trained personnel. No one discussed whether what they learned would be relevant in poorer countries or whether this was an effective way to allocate resources. A more productive curriculum, many concluded, would be more holistic, public-health focused, and based on a rigorous socioeconomic analysis. They wondered why they had not been sent to Thailand or Sri Lanka instead—countries facing health challenges similar to those in India (Holdaway et al. 2015). These examples drive home an important point: Much of what practitioners learn while studying abroad may not fit the needs of the locales they return to. Although chronic "lifestyle diseases" like hypertension and diabetes are on the rise in China and India, the greatest burden of disease still requires prevention and primary care.

Geopolitics also affects brain circulation. Highly trained migrants can find their loyalties questioned when they seek to build bridges between their home and host societies. In 1999, Wen-ho Lee, a Taiwanese American nuclear scientist who worked at the Los Alamos National Laboratory in New Mexico, was arrested and indicted for the alleged theft of classified documents for the Chinese government. He spent nine months in solitary confinement before he was released when the charges against him were dropped (Purdy 2001).

Similarly, in 2019, Christopher Wray, director of the Federal Bureau of Investigation, expressed concern that international students and researchers, especially those from mainland China, were stealing important intellectual property. China, he stated, steals "innovation in any way it can . . . they're doing it through Chinese intelligence services, through state-owned enterprises, through ostensibly private companies, through graduate students and researchers through a variety of actors, all working on behalf of China" (Redden 2019). Indeed, the US Attorney's Office in Massachusetts arrested Massachusetts Institute of Technology Professor Gang Chen for failing to disclose contracts, appointments, and awards from various entities in the People's Republic of China to the US Department of Energy (US Department of Justice 2021). Federal prosecutors eventually dropped the case in January 2022 (Barry and Benner 2022). Whatever their merits, these claims arise from intense global competition and complex international politics that disrupt the free flow of highly skilled migrants and their knowledge and skills across borders.

Mobility, Skill, and Credentialing across Borders

Brain circulation begs the question of whether the credentials students earn in one country are actually recognized in another. Invalid professional credentials, be they university degrees or occupational licenses earned outside countries of reception, in health, education, or the law, block social mobility. Think of the many teachers from outside the United States who are working as teacher's aides within it. Think of the chemistry professors who must work as lab instructors. Until they get their licenses validated or complete additional coursework, they are overqualified and underpaid for the jobs for which they are eligible.

This is a worldwide problem and a variety of institutional solutions have been put in place to resolve it. The Bologna Process (BP) established a European Higher Education Area in 1999 that homogenized standards within its borders to foster student mobility and to make degrees earned in one part of the European Union valid in another. By creating a system that issued comparable degrees and approved credit transfers, it helped enable EU citizens to work in any place within its borders (Vögtle and Martens 2014).

The BP is the culmination of a long series of efforts (Hou et al. 2017). As early as the 1950s, the Council of Europe had conventions and information networks to encourage student mobility and ensure that credentials were recognized everywhere. The Lisbon Recognition Convention, or the Convention on the Recognition of Qualifications Concerning Higher Education in the European Region, created by UNESCO, the Council of Europe, and the European Union, was adopted in 1997. By 2013, fifty-three European countries had signed the convention. By 2012, forty-seven states had signed on to the BP, including all European and bordering states, except Belarus (Vögtle and Martens 2014).

Still, despite these advances, there is no automatic EU-wide recognition of academic diplomas. Students need to go through national procedures to get their degrees recognized in another EU country (Your Europe n.d.). The Bologna Declaration is not a treaty or a convention and does not have the status of EU legislation. Education is not among the policy areas in which EU member states have delegated decision-making authority to a supranational institution. Rather, it is an intergovernmental agreement that includes EU and non-EU signatories, but it is not legally binding (participation and cooperation remain voluntary). While participating governments have pledged to overcome obstacles to establish a European Higher Education Area, the terms are still quite vague. Signatories agreed to introduce a three-cycle higher education system consisting of bachelor's, master's and doctoral studies; ensure the mutual recognition of qualifications and learning periods abroad completed at other universities; and implement a system of quality assurance (European Commission n.d.). Member states committed to introducing automatic degree recognition by 2025 if these goals are accomplished.

Recognizing degrees earned outside the European Union, however, poses greater challenges. Reciprocal credentialing requires agreements between institutions that are not necessarily regulated by a national education system with a single set of rules and standards. In 1996, the Asia–Europe Meeting addressed this problem by establishing a regional network of information centers (Hou et al. 2017). National government bodies are responsible for co-recognizing qualifications earned in other parts of Europe and Asia. European networks of information centers and national academic recognition information centers then act as regional quality assurance agencies. These negotiations are often complicated by cultural differences, differing views of what constitutes quality education, and different state capacities to achieve it. Rather than attempting to achieve regional parity, some countries opt instead to sign bilateral or multilateral agreements, as China did with Germany in 2002, the United Kingdom in 2004, and France in 2015.

Asia is an interesting case. The Brisbane Communique, signed in 2006, attempts to coordinate educational approaches and frameworks for teacher and student evaluation across the Asia–Pacific region. Australia and New Zealand were especially keen to put in place these shared protocols, as they are the biggest providers of tertiary education in the region. Universities in China and India—their main competitors—were already aligned with the

European system and they risked losing students if they did not catch up (Olds 2008). The Brisbane Communique thus introduced a diploma supplement and made the Australian system for transferring credit more consistent with European metrics for course hours and workloads. To facilitate communication and demonstrate compatibility with Bologna policies, Australia and New Zealand also applied to join the European Register of Quality Assurance Agencies.

In 1983, Asian countries adopted the UNESCO Regional Convention on the Recognition of Studies, Diplomas and Degrees in Higher Education in Asia and the Pacific. The convention sought to ensure that degrees earned in one part of the region were recognized in another. In 2011, UNESCO member states updated this agreement in Tokyo. The new Asia–Pacific Regional Convention on the Recognition of Qualification in Higher Education promotes the widespread acceptance of studies, diplomas, and degrees in higher education across the region while also accounting for the diversity of education systems, histories, and socioeconomic contexts (Hou et al. 2017). As of 2019, twenty-one states were signatories.

Still, most quality assurance and credentialing in the region are the purview of national agencies, government bodies, or educational institutions themselves. In China, for example, the Chinese Service Centre for Scholarly Exchange, part of the Ministry of Education, is the only national body allowed to evaluate foreign qualifications for higher education. In Japan, the Ministry of Education, Culture, Sports, Science, and Technology regulates the recognition of foreign degrees by evaluating the degrees and credits acquired overseas. To be recognized, a foreign degree needs to match the number of years a student would study the same material in Japan (Vögtle and Martens 2014).

In contrast, in Latin America, where student mobility is much lower, efforts to harmonize degree requirements have met with greater resistance. Each country and institution has its own system of governance. Governments tend to be less directly involved in higher education. Furthermore, a burgeoning private sector for tertiary education, which operates outside the purview of the state, now accounts for approximately 47 percent of Latin America's enrollment (Vögtle and Martens 2014). The region has two networks—the Inter-American Organization for Higher Education and the Union of Universities of Latin America and the Caribbean—but it is universities that spearheaded efforts to harmonize policy. Universities that signed the Lima Declaration in 2009 are committed to making programs and institutions across the region more compatible—an effort aided by the fact that most South American countries share a common language and history. The Mercado Común del Sur (The Common Market of the South), which includes Argentina, Brazil, Paraguay, Uruguay, and Venezuela, is also active in educational regionalization, but the treaties and agreements it produces must be ratified by national legislatures (Azevedo 2014). So far, systematizing teacher training and validating medical credentials across the region are the focus of its efforts (Vitarelli Batista 2021).

In Africa, education reform has been driven by relations between European nation-states and their former colonies. Institutional change in the metropole puts pressure on institutions in the former colonies to act in concert. African universities that choose not to conform to the BP, therefore, run the risk of losing organizational legitimacy and the ability to operate (Vögtle and Martens 2014). In response, the African Union partnered directly with the European Union to develop a regional education space. Like the European Union, it has the institutional capacity and power to implement the policies it passes (Woldegiorgis et al. 2015). For example, between 2011 and 2013, the African Union launched the "Tuning Africa" pilot project, which brought together fifty-seven African universities and other higher education stakeholders (Hahn and Teferra 2013). They successfully developed conceptual and evaluation frameworks for degree programs such as medicine, agriculture, teacher education, and civil and mechanical engineering. Partners could not further institutionalize these efforts, however, because they relied too heavily on international funding. Subregional fragmentation and the shifting political commitments of member states also blocked the way (Woldegiorgis et al. 2015).

A last barrier to greater integration within and between regions is national governments' views of international decision-makers such as the World Trade Organization, the Organisation for Economic Co-operation and Development, and the International Monetary Fund. Countries like Singapore and Malaysia that want to become "education hubs" need to cooperate with potential partners, so their national governments tend to acquiesce to the supranational system of "network governance" with partner foreign universities (Mok 2008). In China, where most transnational education programs involve partnerships between foreign and Chinese institutions, the national government still has the last word in regulating content and structure (Huang 2003).

Conclusion

More than any other form of social protection, education is of utmost importance to the state. As a result, although we cite numerous examples of resource environments constructed from the private sector, NGOs, and social and familial networks, the state still looms large as an education provider, funder, credentialer, and regulator. This is because whether in a liberal democracy or a tightly held autocracy, primary and secondary education systems are the means by which states cultivate citizens—and, as such, legitimize their rule. As children get older, the education system also becomes the pipeline for training the workers needed for the nation's economic future.

Strategies to mitigate risk and enhance opportunities by assembling educational resources across borders throw into sharp relief the competing logics that determine access to schooling. Education is alternatively justified through a combination of citizens' constitutional rights, universal human rights, as a commodity, or as a community responsibility. In each configuration, the state is often asked to extend or voluntarily extends its reach across borders. In many cases, it does so in partnership with other states and with assistance from the nonprofit sector.

The wider range of choices generated by extending the educational resource environment across borders is liberating for some and creates additional challenges for others. They allow well-off families more opportunities to translate capabilities into functionings by sidestepping poorly run and underfunded state systems or admission systems that only allow in students with friends in high places. These families can send their children to school in what they see as the best places to prepare them to find work wherever the greatest opportunities are. These young people acquire broader cultural competencies, credentials unavailable in their home countries, and degrees from prestigious institutions, together with the elite social networks that these provide.

Families with less financial and social capital are doubly disadvantaged. As we will see in the case of health, the quality of state education declines as the market woos away more and more paying customers. NGOs step in, but the efficacy of their efforts ebbs and flows with their funding cycles. It is especially difficult for these families when the onus is on them to navigate between different providers in different settings.

For both groups, insufficient information makes decision-making onerous. Education brokers may serve the interests of institutions rather than prospective students. Geopolitical shifts may change visa policies. The credentials that students earn in one country are not always recognized by another. Private actors with little, if any, accountability leave even elites vulnerable to exploitation in an unregulated market.

As private-sector providers become increasingly central to the business of education, the more we shift from a logic of education as a constitutional or human right to a logic of commodification. It also becomes clearer how these logics are in tension. The logic of commodification gives priority to those who can afford to pay, threatening the universal access guaranteed by the logic of education as a human right. Institutions of transnational governance are the key guarantors of education as a human right, but they rest on the compliance of states that may be vulnerable to shifting political winds. Universalism is particularly important to refugees and asylum seekers and for migrants without legal documents who are the most at risk of educational neglect. These groups, however, cannot rely on the constitutional logic of social protection because they are not citizens in a context in which states are still the primary providers of education. While NGOs can pave the way to access for these groups, they too may be vulnerable to the whims of the state. Finally, the logic of citizenship suits the ends of states who see schools as nation-building tools over which transnational and private education weaken their control. Rather, private education proceeds with fewer safeguards and regulations and has little interest in or ability to guarantee education as a basic social protection. Therefore, hybrid transnational social protection may not just run parallel to existing systems but, in some cases, may undermine them.

3
Labor

In the year 2000, Gama, a construction company based in Turkey, won a contract with the Irish government to develop and build infrastructure for power and transportation. Under the agreement, Gama would hire more than 1,000 Turkish workers to do most of the labor. Despite trade unions' concerns, the Irish National Roads Authority promised that Gama knew it "would have to comply with Irish labour law and construction industry wage rates" (Yeates 2001). In 2005, however, the Gama contract became a national issue when Joe Higgins, an Irish politician in the Dáil,[1] charged the company with not only significantly underpaying its workers but also taking some workers' passports to stop them from leaving their jobs. Higgins argued that companies like Gama "undermine wages and conditions for all workers, and underbid, through crooked means, other companies who pay the full rate" (O'Halloran 2005). But as the case made its way to the courts, the first order of business was to establish jurisdiction. Who was responsible for the plight of the Turkish workers? Gama in Turkey? Gama in Ireland? The Irish government? The Turkish government? The European Union?

The answers to these questions depended upon who was asked. According to Gama, the case involved a Turkish company employing Turkish workers and therefore should be under the jurisdiction of Turkish labor and employment law. But according to a representative from the Service Industrial and Professional and Technical Union, Ireland's largest trade union, the Irish state was at fault for its lack of labor inspections. The head of the Irish Congress of Trade Unions, the country's main umbrella organization for organized labor, cited a "culture of impunity" related to labor violations among Irish businesses (*Irish Times* 2005). Legal representatives for the workers even claimed that Ireland had a moral responsibility to the Gama workers, given its long history of sending emigrants out to work (D'Arcy 2015).

The core issues raised by the Gama case reach far beyond the borders of Ireland. They remain relevant more than a decade later: How and where are labor protections ensured when migration and mobility become an integral part of everyday life? Given the pressures of global capital, is labor

Transnational Social Protection. Peggy Levitt, Erica Dobbs, Ken Chih-Yan Sun, and Ruxandra Paul,
Oxford University Press. © Oxford University Press 2023. DOI: 10.1093/oso/9780197666821.003.0004

protection—backed by the state, unions, or global civil society—available to anyone? What role can states, markets, nongovernmental organizations (NGOs), and social ties play in protecting labor rights? In particular, what is the role of unions organized at the local and national levels when workers and employers operate transnationally? Can unions scale up or, if not, can other actors such as NGOs and international regulatory bodies act as substitutes? Answering these questions requires rethinking the variety of resource environments workers can create from sources available at various scales, as well as the complex relationships they have with potential providers.

In this chapter, we find that when it comes to labor protection, the old system of state-driven, territorially and nationally bounded labor protections is clearly breaking down and has been unevenly hybridized for some time. Both capital flows and labor markets have become increasingly globalized, but transnational resource environments that can potentially protect workers have yet to catch up. The breakdown of traditional labor protections is driven by changes in both domestic and global political economy; namely, shifting ideas about the role of the state in regulating commerce and business activity. These changes are interrelated: neoliberalism is a driving force behind both. That said, to quote Gramsci, "the old is dying, but the new cannot be born" (Hoare and Smith 1971, 276); emergent forms of transnational labor protection have been juxtaposed with the old, creating hybrid transnational social protection. The logics of human rights, citizen entitlements, market forces, and community provision often clash in the contexts of economic globalization, thereby exacerbating precarious conditions for laborers.

Previous chapters have covered how the labor of social protection often falls heavily on the less well-off and is heavily gendered. As these individuals facilitate the social protection of their patients, students, and wards (not to mention their own families), we ask: How are they, in turn, protected as *workers*? This chapter uses different cases to analyze the hybridization of labor protection in transnational settings. Our goal is not to summarize the field of global labor studies, which several excellent reviews have already done (Ford 2019; Tsogas 2018; Brookes and McCallum 2017). We discuss, only in passing, the experiences of highly trained, professional migrants who work for companies or come from countries where their social protection needs are more than adequately covered (these workers will be covered extensively in the following chapter on health). Instead, we offer an in-depth examination of how poor and middle-income individuals turn to the state, the market, NGOs, and their personal ties to create resource environments in the context of these shifting sands. As we will see, these workers are overrepresented in so-called 3-D jobs: dirty, dangerous, and demanding. Therefore, the scope of how we define "labor protection" for the purposes of this chapter is limited to policies governing workplace conditions, rather than the direct provision of material benefits such as unemployment. Our focus on workplace conditions also means that we are particularly interested in the role that unions and other workplace associations play in labor protection.

Because this chapter centers on "workers" as a very broad group, rather than a specific mobile population like "children," "elderly," or "providers," it is structured somewhat differently than our other chapters. Rather than being centered on the key actors who are piecing together resource environments, we focus instead on breaking down different types of resource environments. We also discuss how the different logics of social protection as constitutional rights, human rights, commodities, or community manifest—or are limited—via the state, the market, and NGOs. Our analysis is organized into sections. First, we highlight key tensions within the shifting context of global enterprise and the global labor supply, and the challenges of legal frameworks when global workers fall under the purview of national governments. We then unpack how states, NGOs, and civil society can enforce labor protections in a world of transnational labor and capital. Finally, we consider the specific predicament of migrant domestic workers, a group that is often rendered invisible, whether for the nature of their work, their legal status, or their gender. It is with domestic workers that the greatest tensions in the hybrid transnational social protection regime become most starkly visible: protection for some means precarity for others.

Setting the Context: Global Enterprise, Global Workers

Over the last forty years, cross-border flows of global capital have increased exponentially, from $500 billion to a peak of nearly $12 trillion prior to the 2008 global financial crisis (Lund et al. 2013). The salaries of the CEOs who run the world's most profitable companies have also increased astronomically, rising to an average of $4.8 million in 2019 (AFL-CIO 2021). Whether these individuals construct their resource environments nationally or transnationally, global executives, and the high-level managers who work for them, do not lack for social protection. Their jobs still come with generous benefits, including health insurance, stock options, and pensions.

But the increase in capital flows we have witnessed is driven, in no small part, by the rise of outsourcing and offshoring, practices that are, in turn, facilitated by international migration. This movement of money, goods, and people has increased profits but also raised concerns about social precarity, in general, and precarity for workers, in particular.

Footloose Capital: Outsourcing and Offshoring

Named by the *Financial Times* as one of the "fifty ideas that have shaped business today," outsourcing involves the transfer of a specific business function to an outside firm (Plimmer 2013). For example, a hospital may opt to outsource its security, housekeeping, and food service functions to another company, thereby allowing it to focus on clinical care and lower costs. A growing number of multinational corporations have emerged to fill this heightened demand, among them Sodexo and Aramark in food services, Securitas and G4S in security, and Aon and Compass in human resources. Outsourcing is by no means limited to private firms. Since the 1980s, as neoliberal reforms have swept postindustrial economies, local and national governments have opted into outsourcing strategies as well. States even outsource some of their key functions to private corporations, including schools and prisons.

Proponents argue that outsourcing allows organizations to focus on their core competencies or on more high-value endeavors (Craumer 2002). It also enables them to reduce their employment liabilities. By off-loading key functions, a firm or arm of government is no longer responsible for those doing the work (Weil 2014; Bernhardt et al. 2016). Critics say this allows firms and states to renege on their basic commitments to workers. Indeed, with contracted firms themselves often passing off basic functions to other subcontractors, working conditions can continuously deteriorate. There is no single entity that is responsible for workers' safety and security.

Offshoring, the practice of moving the production of goods and/or services abroad, is also a popular business strategy. Firms save on production costs by moving labor-intensive production or, increasingly, services overseas where labor is cheaper. Offshoring also adds value because companies can offer a more comprehensive customer experience, such as a twenty-four-hour help line, without increasing costs (McKinsey Global Institute 2003). But offshoring almost always leads to lower wages for low- and medium-skilled workers in a given industry (Wolszczak-Derlacz and Parteka 2018). This is in no small part because it undermines labor unions, limiting their bargaining power when firms threaten to move operations abroad (Bronfenbrenner 2000).

While it is private firms evaluating market conditions that ultimately choose to outsource their operations or to move offshore, their decisions are heavily influenced by the state. Favorable trade and tariff arrangements and local regulatory environments strongly influence where companies opt to locate or source production (Mudambi and Venzin 2010). The passage of the North Atlantic Free Trade Agreement, for example, accelerated the distribution of US automobile company supply chains across the region. In electronics manufacturing, both technical support as well as some key engineering functions are contracted out to smaller firms or individuals. More than half of the world's iPhones are now produced in Zhengzhou, China (Pun and Koo 2015; Jacobs and Zheng 2018). Nonetheless, not all jobs can be offshored; landscaping, delivery services, security personnel, food preparation, and janitorial and housekeeping services require physical presence. Therefore, as more and more businesses turn to outsourcing services as a way to lower costs, they end up competing over labor costs. A key cost-savings strategy is to hire migrants.

Global Workers

According to the International Organization of Labour, in 2017, the numbers of migrant workers worldwide reached 164 million (ILO 2015). Because they are overrepresented in the 3-D jobs, they are recognized as "among the most vulnerable members of society" (Moyce and Schenker 2018, 352). The industries where migrant workers concentrate are notorious for their lack of adequate training characterized by high numbers of on-the-job injuries; undue exposure to high temperatures, noise, pesticides, and chemicals; accelerated production demands and worker abuse; and, in the most extreme cases, human trafficking (Flynn 2014; Chan et al. 2016; Pérez et al. 2012; Quandt et al. 2006). While some industries, such as construction, are unsafe for all workers, migrant workers face disproportionately high risks. As such, the decision to work abroad, often made to ensure social protection for family left behind, leads to greater physical and economic precarity for individual workers.

Because migrant workers are recruited to take 3-D jobs, outsourcing and migration are deeply intertwined (Li 2017). Many outsourced jobs not only pay poorly but are also low status. But what is considered a menial job in one's host country is not necessarily a low-status job in one's homeland. Even when they work in low-level positions, many migrants experience a rise in social status because they earn more money and savings according to homeland metrics (Levitt 2001). Given wage and economic disparities between countries, therefore, what looks poorly paid to natives often looks like a step up to immigrant workers (Anderson 2010). Migrants may also be willing to accept low pay and poor working conditions in the hopes of quickly meeting their earning goals and then returning home (Piore 1979; A. Paul 2015). For employers seeking to minimize costs and commitments, immigrants are ideal candidates, because they are willing to do undesirable jobs and accept relatively low pay.

Low-wage workers, who lack licensed expertise or recognized credentials, are typically forced to migrate to places where they will receive only minimal protections. Indonesian labor migrants tend to view Japan and South Korea as ideal destinations because they offer comparatively higher salaries and better safety standards. Both countries, however, require migrant workers to have a high school diploma and a certificate of language competency to enter, thereby leaving many potential migrants out (Chang 2021, 6). In contrast, Taiwan, with its lower wages, can still attract a stable flow of labor migrants from Indonesia, in large part because it has "no formal educational or language requirements, sets few limits on the intake of guest workers, and permits contractual extension for 12 years" (Chang 2021, 6). Blue-collar migrant workers in Taiwan, though, receive little labor protection and their high rates of on-the-job injuries and accidents are constantly in the news.

Taken together, these conditions ensure that workers in industries organized around outsourcing are particularly vulnerable. The construction and janitorial sectors in Los Angeles, California, are a case in point: the intersection of subcontracting, undocumented immigration, and unions in decline led to a decrease in real wages beginning in the 1980s (Waldinger et al. 1996; Kitroeff 2017). This is typical of what economist David Weil (2014, 12) describes as the "fissured workplace"— a particularly hard organizational model for unions to crack because firms are so fractured and spread out across the world and workers are so vulnerable (Barenberg 2015).

Migration is increasingly entwined with offshoring as well. Just as firms relocate to comparatively low-wage countries to take advantage of low-wage labor, workers in low-wage countries seek to migrate to comparatively high-wage countries. Sometimes these firms and workers move at the same time.

Western European companies that relocated production to new Eastern European accession states to save money on labor costs ended up facing labor shortages. They had to raise wages because so many local workers had already moved West in the hopes of better pay (Fairless 2018).

Governments respond by looking for replacement workers elsewhere. The Romanian government explored entering into an agreement with Pakistan that allowed migrant workers to access the country's labor market more easily. Romanian ambassador to Pakistan Nicolae Goia said that Romania could absorb about a million skilled and unskilled workers from around the world to meet its need for drivers, doctors, engineers, construction workers, and IT specialists (Obucina 2019). This effort followed a 2018 accord with Vietnam to bring in workers to address shortfalls in construction (Botea 2018). When less-industrialized countries develop export-processing zones—internal regions dedicated to production for export that generally operate outside the purview of prevailing trade and employment laws—they encourage offshoring, which may, in turn, trigger internal and international migration (Arends-Kuenning et al. 2019; Kopinak 2017).

Yet while the reorganization of production into global supply chains and the fissuring of the workforce are relatively new phenomena, the clustering of immigrant workers into key employment niches is not. A number of conditions—the undesirability of certain kinds of jobs, the skill sets of immigrant workers, and the familial or social networks that channel immigrant workers into particular sectors—contribute to immigrant clusters in particular parts of the labor market, regardless of fissuring. They also make immigrant workers vulnerable to exploitation by family members who demand that they work longer hours or accept lower pay in the name of family loyalty (Li 2017). In the United States, more than half of all seamstresses, housekeepers, agricultural workers, and construction workers are immigrants (Eckstein and Peri 2018). Clustering and fissuring, therefore, complement each other.

Global Workers, National Governments

In this context, what are the foundations of social protections for workers? What do workers use to construct resource environments and on which understanding of rights are these based? States play a central role in establishing labor protections, not just through labor law, but also through immigration law. International law may also play a role in setting labor standards, although not always their enforcement. The parameters that state and supranational actors set out affect how they then "see" individuals who are eligible for rights and, in turn, extend protections to them.

Labor Law

Labor laws are at the heart of labor protections. They establish a baseline set of workplace standards that employers are expected to follow. They mandate who is actually an "employer," an "employee," or a "contractor" and recognize certain activities as "work." As such, they also define who gets access to state assistance programs like disability or unemployment. Finally, labor laws determine the extent to which unions play a role in the workplace.

Perhaps the most contentious issue in labor law today is the question of who is an employee. While outsourcing made this distinction contentious, the "gig" economy brought it to the forefront of debates over labor protection and accountability. The formality of the labor market also matters for social protection because it affects the ability of the state to see workers. Informal employment is defined by the ILO as (1) work that is self-employment in informal sector enterprises, such as unlicensed street vending; (2) workers engaged in production solely for household use, such as subsistence farming; or (3) employees who are generally not subject to social security agreements, taxation, or labor laws because they work under the radar of the state (Hussmanns 2004). While more than 60 percent of the world's workers labor in the informal economy, levels of informal employment vary significantly by region. In sub-Saharan Africa, more than 85 percent of employment is informal; in Europe, the rate is 25 percent (International Labour Office 2018). Informal work is not, however, the same as contract and temporary work, which may be unstable but remain part of the formal economy. The informal labor market remains outside the purview of the state and the protections that the government offers. Not surprisingly, the informal economy is a key entry point into the labor market for migrant workers, especially those without formal work permits.

Finally, labor laws affect the extent to which organized labor can act as an agent of workers and the strategies that unions can use (Gordon 2005).

In the United States, federal labor law is considered so hostile to organized labor that some unions actively avoid conducting organizing campaigns and elections under the auspices of the National Labor Relations Board. In contrast, across much of continental Europe, unions not only negotiate labor contracts but participate in the creation of labor policies through institutionalized tripartite bargaining cycles between business, labor, and the national government. They often have strong ties to political parties.

Immigration Law

Immigration law also plays an important role in protecting workers. States set the terms of entry, and by doing so, not only regulate access to the labor market but also strongly influence whether those with the right to work do so with protections or not. Immigration law affects labor rights in a few key ways, including whether individuals are considered guests or permanent, tethered to their employer or free agents, or legally present or undocumented.

A wide range of countries have relied on guest worker programs at different points in their histories. Northern European countries used them to help rebuild after World War II. Today, many Persian Gulf countries depend upon guest worker programs, so much so that foreign workers outnumber citizens by as many as three to one. In Qatar, for example, there are more than two million foreign workers in a country of 2.6 million people (Cousins 2020). A key difference between European and Gulf states, however, is the extent to which the temporary can become permanent. Guest workers in Europe often come to stay (Rogers 1985). As one European official quipped, "we wanted a labour force, but human beings came" (Muchowiecka 2013). Like other liberal democracies, Germany found restricting immigration difficult once it had begun because of international law, international economic demands, and pressure from immigrant rights groups and domestic business interests (Sassen 1996; Joppke 1997; Freeman 1995). In contrast, non-democracies, such as the labor-importing states of the Gulf, have far more leeway to make sure that guest workers remain guests rather than future residents or citizens.

Another key distinction is whether or not immigrants granted entry to work are tethered to a specific employer or free to seek out work from anyone. For example, in the United States, the H1-B visa program for highly skilled immigrant workers is an employer-sponsored program: A specific employer petitions for the visa to be granted. The individual's right to work depends completely on his or her affiliation with the employer. In Singapore, migrant workers are also expected to work for the employer who initially contracts them and to remain in the occupation stated on their work permit; foreign workers thus "remain under the control of an employer and the state in relation to both their employment and migration status" (Kneebone 2012, 373). In contrast, individually driven systems, such as those in Canada or Australia, admit migrants on the basis of a desirable set of skills. They operate according to "point systems," which assign candidates scores based on a combination of age, skills, language, and education. Under individually driven systems, migrants may change jobs but are guaranteed only entry, not employment (Papademetriou and Sumption 2011).

Critics argue that employer-driven systems are rife for worker exploitation. Because the worker's ability to stay in a host country depends upon the employer's goodwill, that worker is extremely vulnerable. In the Gulf, the *kafala* system, under which an individual's immigration status is tied to an individual employer or sponsor (*kafeel*), is widespread. Migrant workers cannot enter a country, leave a country, or change jobs without permission from their *kafeel*. Here, too, sponsors control their workers by taking their passports, withholding wages, or in the worst-case scenario, abusing them. Because neither migrant workers nor citizens enjoy full civil liberties in these countries, major reforms are unlikely. Rather, national governments continue to perpetrate labor exploitation. "The more vulnerable workers are," observed development scholar Lan Anh Hoang (2016, 9), "the more productive and disciplined they become . . . The state, through its instrumental rules, is complicit in the rise of infirmity, irregularity, and illegality in cross-border flows and labor markets"—a point we return to later in this chapter.

Finally, the most important distinction that a state can bestow upon an individual is permission to enter (and permission to work once he or she has entered the country). Without legal residence papers or work permits, migrant workers are extremely vulnerable to exploitation, wage theft, and worse. Certain sectors of the economy are somewhat open to the undocumented—domestic work, for example—but these sectors are rife with labor violations. Even when migrant workers have permission to enter and work in a given country, the process to *stay* in compliance with immigration and labor law can throw individuals into a state of illegality. This may not be a bug, but a feature: what the sociologist Kitty Calavita (1998, 11) calls "the legal construction of illegality" generating a "flexible" labor force for employers and creating an entire class of workers who are intentionally rendered precarious.

International Law

An important question that remains is who regulates the state? Governments play central roles as gatekeepers, recruiters, and exporters of labor. They are also party to worker protection and worker exploitation. Rarely do governments volunteer to stand up for migrant workers on their own; rather, they are pressured by national and international civil society actors. Organizations like the ILO and the World Bank propose social policy guidelines in the hope of shaping national policies, but as we have seen, they do not have the power to force governments to abide by them. The Migrant Workers Recommendation of 1979 (No. 151), for example, stipulates that migrant workers and their family members who are legally present in the territory of a country should enjoy equality of opportunity and treatment with nationals in their life conditions and social services, including education and health (R. Paul 2017). In 1998, the ILO Declaration on Fundamental Principles and Rights at Work stated that universal principles and rights apply to all migrants, whether they are temporary or permanent, legal or undocumented.

But the stark truth is that all ILO conventions concerning nondiscrimination and equal opportunity for migrants in host countries have abysmal ratification rates, even though they are "soft law" and therefore not binding. Only twenty-three states ratified the ILO's Migrant Workers (Supplementary Provisions) Convention of 1975. Only four states ratified ILO Convention 157, the Maintenance of Social Security Rights Convention of 1982, which was created to establish a global regime of portable benefits (Olivier and Govindjee 2013; R. Paul 2017). Therefore, in many cases, despite their ideological grounding in universal human rights, transnational conventions and the institutions they put in place offer little to migrant workers on the ground.

Some migrants turn to regional institutions created by regionally integrated labor markets such as the European Union, the Association of Southeast Asian Nations (ASEAN), or the Caribbean Community. These trading blocks, which lower barriers to the circulation of capital and goods, rely on the circulation of laborers who need protection. As in the European Union, this reliance means making benefits such as pensions and health insurance portable. The 2018 ASEAN Consensus on the Protection of the Rights of Migrant Workers is one such effort. It calls upon the Universal Declaration of Human Rights, Convention on the Elimination of All Forms of Discrimination Against Women, Convention on the Rights of the Child, and other appropriate international instruments to which ASEAN member states are party, "to safeguard the human rights and fundamental freedom of individuals" (ASEAN 2018).

The ASEAN consensus promises to recognize the rights and dignity of migrant workers as stipulated in these international and regional conventions, in accordance with the national laws of member states, and to "uphold fair treatment with respect to gender and nationality, and protect and promote the rights of migrant workers, particularly women" (ASEAN 2018). These rights include freedom of movement, visits from family members, the ability to retain passports and other personal documents, and permission to file grievances and seek assistance from embassies and consulates. Migrants are also assured the same rights as citizens in matters of criminal justice, in accordance with national laws (ASEAN 2018).

Similarly, the Commission of the Economic Community of West African States (ECOWAS) met in Abuja in 2019 to draft the Directive on the Harmonisation of the Labour Laws in the ECOWAS region. Its goal is to "achieve the much needed harmonization framework while respecting the diversity of legal cultures, systems of working relations, areas of regulation and practices existing within ECOWAS" (ECOWAS 2019). The European Union supports these efforts. While regional attempts to provide worker protections face the same barriers to implementation as their transnational counterparts, they do represent another institutional layer to which migrant workers can turn.

Since regional economic growth and integration is linked to the circulation of healthy, decently paid laborers working under decent conditions, we may see more regional efforts at labor protections in the future. What is clear, though, is that national laws on the books, and the power behind them, matter. They determine who is eligible to work and to have their work regulated by the state, and the likelihood that unions play a central role in that monitoring process. They determine who has the right to be present, to work formally or informally, or to work for whom they see fit. As such, both labor and immigration law affect whom the state sees. But, as political scientist James Scott (1998) notes, states really see only what they are interested in. And even when the state sees workers, its record of enforcing labor laws has grown worse over the last few decades, even in countries well equipped to implement them.

States and Enforcement

In this world on the move, then, who actually enforces these national, bilateral, and international statutes, and from where? This is an especially complicated question. States' commitments to protect their citizens often bump up against international labor laws based on human rights principles.

Traditionally, enforcement came from a combination of bureaucratic execution, private lawsuits, and oversight from labor unions (Glynn 2011). These regulatory sources generally worked in tandem: for example, health and safety inspections took place more frequently in workplaces with unions. In union shops, inspections were more thorough and penalties for infractions higher than in workplaces without them (Weil 1991). But these traditional mechanisms of enforcement are failing (Fine and Gordon 2010), in no small part due to political and economic changes that have undercut unions in many advanced industrial economies. Although some unions have tried to adapt by actively recruiting migrant workers and transnationalizing labor disputes, steep declines in formerly unionized sectors have left organized labor without the political heft it needs to protect even the statutory right to organize. State bureaucracies are trying to adapt as well, particularly since systems of labor monitoring designed for large factories are ill-suited for regulating today's working conditions (Weil 2008).

Countries of Destination

Receiving states play a central role not just in the creation but in the enforcement of labor protections. However, their willingness and ability to enforce existing statutes and agreements depends on their relationship to other states and their own internal dynamics. Receiving states grapple with a series of competing logics that affect enforcement: the struggle between the logic of the market versus the regulatory state, the logic of state–society relations, and the logic of bureaucratic action. All of these are mediated by regime type: democracies behave in a fundamentally different way than autocracies or "hybrid" quasi-authoritarian regimes.

The extent to which states enforce their own statutes is, at its most basic, about their willingness to confront and regulate capital on behalf of labor. Enforcement outcomes reflect how much political weight capital and labor command. In some systems, this weight is carefully calibrated through tripartite or corporatist arrangements: Labor, business, and government all have an institutional role in setting social policy—including labor policy—at regular intervals (Lijphart 2012). Countries with corporatist systems may grant labor a seat at the table within firms. Thus, institutionally, unions are much better positioned to ensure some degree of enforcement of the law in corporatist systems than in countries where interest-group competition is more of a free-for-all.

We do not mean to suggest, though, that corporatist arrangements are universally good for all workers. In fact, countries with corporatist systems may have strongly bifurcated labor markets. "Insiders" covered by national bargaining agreements are protected while "outsiders" are subject to temporary labor contracts and poor wages and working conditions (Häusermann and Schwander 2012; Rueda 2014). Unfortunately, in a world on the move, these outsiders are quite often immigrant workers (Gorodzeisky and Richards 2013).

States not only have different models of political economy and interest group politics, but different logics of bureaucratic action. These logics have implications for enforcement as well. As Piore and Schrank note, the US system can be characterized as "diffuse and punitive" (2008, 5). Multiple agencies have jurisdiction over labor protection, and violations are assumed to be the product of strategy, rather than sheer ignorance or incompetence. Subsequently, violations are penalized with fines that are then paid, which leaves the underlying problem intact. On the other hand, the "Latin model," which is prevalent throughout the Mediterranean Basin, Latin America, and various Francophone countries, is "conciliatory and tutelary" (Piore and Schrank 2008, 5). Regulatory responsibilities are more centralized, so inspectors have a more holistic view of their work. Violations are assumed to result from poor management. Violators are not just made aware of the problem, but regulators work with them to bring them into compliance.

Finally, the last key factor affecting enforcement is whether a government is democratic or nondemocratic. Rule of law, property rights, the right to protest, protection of a free press, and responsiveness to citizen demands are all components of a liberal democratic society (Dahl 1973; Schmitter and Karl 1991). These conditions guarantee some degree of labor protection—whether through the freedom to form a union, exposés of labor abuses in the media, or lawsuits against unscrupulous employers for wage theft or other workplace violations. In contrast, quasi-democratic and authoritarian regimes frequently lack some or all of these safeguards (Levitsky and

Way 2010). The heavy hand of the state generally constrains workers, and poor people seeking to mobilize are on their own (Silver 2005, Piven and Cloward 2012). The less democratic a given society, therefore, the weaker the regulatory framework tends to be, and the more citizen and noncitizen workers alike are prone to experience labor abuses. It is no accident that most global supply chains have shifted some production sites to "labor repressive regimes" in autocracies or quasi-authoritarian states (Anner 2017, 56–57). In a globalized world where countries compete economically, democracies can withstand the pressure to weaken labor rights better because workers have the right to vote and unionize (Wang 2020). While authoritarian states may offer labor repression as an asset to multinational firms, democracies can offer strong property rights—something that many autocracies lack (Wang 2020).

That said, certain kinds of enforcement mechanisms can work at cross-purposes. The Taiwanese government, for example, holds employers accountable for their workers' mobility. Employers must deposit a bond equivalent to two months' salary and pay a monthly fee. If a migrant worker "runs away" or "disappears," the employer is still responsible for paying the fee until the worker is caught or the contract expires. If employers fail to do so, their quotas for hiring labor migrants may be temporarily frozen (Lan 2006, 56). In response, many Taiwanese employers withhold wages or confiscate travel documents to make sure their employees stay put (Hoang 2016, 7). In some cases, the fact that the state holds employers responsible for their workers' whereabouts ends up increasing migrants' precarity. When these workers run away from their abusive employers without money or legal documents, they are forced to enter the black market labor pool.

Countries of Origin

Faced with the possibility of worker exploitation, some states actively try to protect the labor rights of their citizens abroad. The Romanian government is one example. The Ministry of Romanians from Abroad mounted an ongoing national campaign called "Information at home! Safety in the world!" to inform citizens who want to work abroad about things like legal versus illegal work contracts, the risks of undocumented status, and human trafficking. The first phase of the campaign primarily targeted students and young people, but it also reached teachers, school directors, and representatives of student leagues and organizations.

As we have noted throughout, the Philippines stands out for its heightened involvement in all aspects of the training, placement, and support of migrants while abroad. This state-generated safety net explains why Vietnamese workers in Taiwan are much more vulnerable than their Filipina counterparts (Hoang 2016). Having "strong backing from the Philippine government and civil society groups within and beyond the home country" (Hoang 2016, 9), Filipino migrants are in a somewhat better position to negotiate for better working conditions.

Nonetheless, even "activist" sending states have trouble protecting their citizens abroad. Critics claim that government programs pay insufficient attention to sexual harassment, which many migrant women encounter (Parreñas 2015). As sociologist Anna Guevarra (2010, 83) writes, rarely can Filipina migrants or their advocates find "mention of any official procedures for reporting cases of sexual abuse or identifying any organizations that can help workers." Fighting back against abuse threatens the security of dependents back home who need the money that migrants earn. If repatriated, migrants still have to repay brokers' fees. Their conditions can also result in diplomatic ruptures. In February 2018, when the body of a Filipina maid was found in the freezer of a family in Kuwait, President Rodrigo Duterte banned new employment contracts for Filipinos in Kuwait and pushed for suspending the right to work in Saudi Arabia because it also failed to commit to basic labor protections.

As these examples illustrate, the sending state's role as a labor broker is often at odds with its role as a protector of its citizens. The competing imperatives of defending workers overseas and catering to the demands of profitable labor markets are not always reconcilable (Rodriguez 2010; Guevarra 2010). In another example from the Philippines, a major labor dispute erupted in Brunei's export-processing zones in 2001 when Filipino workers realized that the contracts they had signed before departure were not the same as the contracts they were asked to sign when they arrived. Rather than insisting that Brunei respect the original, the government tried to convince workers to accept the new contract (Rodriguez 2010). Employers in Brunei thus avoided a prolonged labor dispute and were absolved of all legal responsibilities. The Filipino government not only supplied workers to employers but also "brokered" a settlement that benefited all parties—except the workers themselves (Rodriguez 2010).

States that rely on the market to monitor and regulate labor rights can also exacerbate migrant precarity. Labor brokers, contracted by sending states to prepare migrants for life abroad, are part of the problem. In the predeparture training sections for workers from Vietnam, Indonesia, the Philippines, and Cambodia, they are told to expect harsh working conditions (Constable 2014; Guevarra 2010; Lan 2006; Hoang 2016; Yea 2019). By presenting exploitation as something to be tolerated and handled by each individual, brokers create a docile, divided labor force unlikely to demand its rights. In addition, market actors tend to stereotype certain groups of migrant workers in ways that increase risk. Muslim men, for example, are frequently deemed "backward" and "unsuitable" for "modern" factory work. They are more likely, therefore, to be placed in countries with lower wages and higher safety violations (Chang 2021, 15).

Civil Society and Enforcement

Another set of actors in enforcement who bring with them their own set of complications and tensions are civil society organizations. Let's take the example of a labor dispute at the University of Miami (UM) in 2006. Like many universities, UM outsourced its cleaning services, in this case to Unicco, a company that specialized in janitorial services for colleges and universities. As is the case with many cleaning subcontractors, Unicco employed a workforce disproportionately composed of migrants, primarily from Cuba, Haiti, and other Caribbean countries. Even in South Florida, where wages are generally low, UM stood out for its poor wages and benefits. An article in the *Chronicle of Higher Education* placed the university near the bottom of a list of poorly paying institutions (Werf 2001).

In response, Unicco janitors worked with the Service Employees International Union (SEIU) to demand better wages and affordable health insurance. When Unicco blamed the low wages on UM, university administrators responded that the janitors did not work directly for the institution and that, therefore, it had no role in the dispute. After months of negotiation, the janitors walked off the job, launching what would become a two-month strike, made possible by staff and financial support from other SEIU locals and the union's international headquarters.

In the middle of the strike, University President Donna Shalala flew to Haiti to participate in a panel on the nation's health care challenges. She cared deeply about this issue, having worked hard to revamp the US health care system during her time as secretary of Health and Human Services. Her trip must also have served as something of a respite from the escalating tensions on the UM campus. During her speech, however, members of the Haitian union Batay Ouvriye presented her with a list of demands from the striking workers back home (Batay Ouvriye 2006)—a surprise confrontation made possible by transnational activist networks uniting workers in Miami and Haiti.

Unions as a Bulwark

Unions matter not only for crafting labor policies but also for enforcing labor rights. The presence of unions increases health and safety workplace protections and can decrease fatalities and serious injury (Morantz 2013). Blue-collar workers, laid off from union jobs, are more likely to get unemployment benefits than similarly employed nonunion workers (Budd and McCall 1997). Overall, the presence of a union makes individuals more likely to know and exercise their labor rights and to file the complaints that trigger workplace inspections (Weil and Pyles 2005). This is key because not all workers are willing to complain on their own: immigrants, the less educated, and those working in informal sectors of the economy tend to be less likely to demand their rights, in part because they may not know they have any.

Despite their importance to the well-being of both native and foreign-born workers, unions' strength has declined considerably over the past several decades. Within the Organisation for Economic Co-operation and Development, membership has fallen from 30 percent of workers in 1985 to 17 percent of workers in 2015 (McCarthy 2017). The relative power of unions is, in part, a function of politics and, in part, a function of the market. Unions are politically stronger when they not only play an institutional role in politics but also align clearly with a political party that enjoys national power (Anzia and Moe 2015). Not surprisingly, public-sector unions across much of the industrialized world are extremely strong, relative to their private-sector counterparts. This is because their members also tend to be stalwart supporters of left-wing political parties that influence public-sector budgets and policies (Anzia and Moe 2015). Unions are also stronger when their members work in economically important industries; if an industry is shedding jobs, workers enjoy far less leverage during contract negotiations. Finally, as traditional unionized industries shrink, so does membership, which leaves unions with far less political clout.

As such, unions may need immigrant workers as much as immigrant workers need unions. The United States and the United Kingdom are prime examples. The terrible irony, however, is that in continental Europe, unions that are strongly connected politically are less likely to reach out to migrant workers. This is because their organizational health depends upon their institutional position rather than on how effectively they mobilize their membership (Gorodzeisky and Richards 2013). In Asia, unions' efforts to extend membership to migrant workers have met with varying degrees of success. In Hong Kong and Malaysia, unions willingly took up the cause of labor rights for migrant workers although their efforts generally extended only to those employed in certain sectors, such as domestic work (Ford 2019; Piper and Ford 2006). In Japan and Taiwan, transnational labor activists have made minimal inroads. Outreach in Singapore and South Korea prompted symbolic rather than substantive change. The narratives and rhetoric about workers' rights became more inclusive without actual changes in union actions and policies. Unions worry that extending social protections to labor migrants will come at the expense of local workers. They see the creation of resource environments as a zero-sum game (Ford 2019).

Transnational Unions

As more and more corporations operate transnationally, local campaigns are reorganized across space as well. Some union leaders, such as Stephen Lerner, an architect of the SEIU's Justice for Janitors campaigns that began in the late 1980s, have long argued for a geographic logic when organizing workers who supply on-site services. While manufacturing has fragmented and extended across borders, Lerner reasons, the finance industry has consolidated in a few key cities (Sassen 2001). These sites are thus good targets for worker mobilization. Janitors are concentrated in one place and their work cannot be offshored (Lerner 2007). Many firms that own commercial buildings in New York also own buildings in London and other global cities with large immigrant populations. They are familiar foes for the SEIU. The union's time and experience spent mobilizing immigrant workers could help unions in other countries facing similar economic and demographic challenges.

Lerner tested his logic in London, one of the world's preeminent financial hubs, by mounting a campaign aimed at cleaners working in buildings in and around the city. Primed by earlier efforts to raise wages, community organizations in East London stepped in as coalition partners with local unions. Taking inspiration from the SEIU's success with Justice for Janitors in the United States, the Transport and General Workers' Union also partnered with its American counterpart to map out strategies for recruiting new members. Other tactics included bargaining by city zone rather than by individual building or employer, shaming building owners for failing to abide by their own corporate social responsibility agreements, and partnering with faith communities that had strong contacts with workers (Wills 2008).

Often, the role that transnational labor unions play is to raise local unions' awareness of migrant workers' rights to protection. They redefine migrants as workers as well as newcomers. As Michele Ford (2019, 65) notes, "the impetus for the development of the global unions' migration programs ultimately came not from Asia but from Europe, where developments in the lead-up to the expansion of the European Union brought the issue into focus within the United Nations system and shaped the agendas of the global unions and the SSOs [Solidarity Support Organizations] that fund much of their project work."

Workers Organizing outside of Unions

Traditional trade unions are not the only groups coming to the aid of migrant workers. Worker centers and local NGOs are also involved in collective action on their behalf, although coordination between traditional unions and worker centers is not always easy (Fine and Gordon 2010). In fact, partly because of local unions' ambivalence about labor migration, NGOs, particularly those in Asia, have stepped into the breach.

Again, the Catholic church is an important example. As Mexico became a more important transit country and the border a site of even greater migrant vulnerability, the so-called Tex-Mex Bishops supported a range of local and international NGOs, including Catholic Charities, Catholic Legal Immigration Network, and Catholic Relief Services, that provide humanitarian, hospitality, social, and legal services (Hagan 2006). Their efforts got a boost in 2009, when six US and Mexican church groups established the Kino Border Initiative to provide shelter and food services, education, research, and advocacy (Kino Border Initiative n.d.). In their first joint pastoral letter, "Strangers No Longer" (2003), Mexican and US bishops declared, "We speak as two episcopal conferences but as one Church, united in the view that migration between our two nations is necessary and beneficial." This letter called for systematic reforms to US immigration policy, a path to citizenship, family reunification rights, and protections for migrant workers (Scribner 2013). Moreover, the Mexican Church has been an outspoken critic of the state's failure to promote jobs in emigrant regions and of its unjust treatment of Central Americans transiting through Mexico (FitzGerald 2009).

The success of these efforts depends upon the sociopolitical context (Ford 2019). In Hong Kong, Singapore, and Malaysia, where the plight of migrant domestic workers has attracted the attention of politicians and lay people alike, NGOs have actively publicized their exploitation. They have pressured governments to help women before they migrate and while they are working abroad (Ford 2019). In contrast, NGOs in Japan, Taiwan, Thailand, and South Korea have focused their attention on migrant workers employed in formal and semiformal sectors such as construction, manufacturing, and hospitality. In each case, NGOs step in where unions do not because those unions see migrant workers as a threat to their membership.

One interesting example is the Worker Rights Consortium (WRC), "a global team of field investigators" with an "extensive network of relationships with unions, human rights groups, women's organizations, and other civil society groups around the world." While corporate brands inspect their suppliers by interviewing workers on-site, the WRC talks with them outside their workplaces, thereby enabling the organization to "uncover labor rights abuses the brands and their auditing organizations routinely ignore." Their publicly available reports and policy briefs have "compelled brands and their suppliers around the world to implement vital remedies: tens of millions of dollars in back pay, reinstatement for nearly two thousand unjustly fired workers, and far-reaching safety improvements." (WRC n.d).

Despite small successes, transnational labor organizing clearly faces challenges. One issue is how receptive the surrounding community is to unions and corporations. Volkswagen in North America offers a case in point. Volkswagen is headquartered in Germany where standard practice includes plant-based work councils, or groups of nonmanagement employees who negotiate strategies and working conditions with managers. When Volkswagen proposed building a new plant in Tennessee, a "right to work" state in the American South that is not particularly union friendly, the United Auto Workers, which represents most workers in car manufacturing, announced its intention to organize prospective employees into a bargaining unit. In Germany, Volkswagen's high-level managers responded with equanimity, but in Tennessee, local politicians were outraged. Both the governor and a senator publicly opposed the union, and the company's Tennessee workers rejected unionization in 2014 and again in 2019 (Greenhouse 2014; Scheiber 2019). This example illustrates the damage that a hostile political environment can do. The likelihood of loss is even greater outside liberal democracies where unions are often tightly controlled by the government, if not banned outright.

Faced with the challenges of global supply chains, the practice of outsourcing and offshoring, and governments unwilling or unable to make or enforce labor law, organizers of campaigns for international worker justice generally deploy three tactics. The first is to actively target the lead firm. As the case of the UM strike makes clear, focusing on the more high-profile company in a labor dispute allows activists to build coalitions that are well covered in the media. A second tactic mobilizes civil society to use private regulation through certifications and codes of conduct, such as food or clothing labels, that assure customers they are buying something produced ethically (Locke et al. 2013). A third tactic relies on informal hybrids of state and private systems of governance (Amengual 2010).

How effective are these tactics? As one might expect, the results are mixed and vary around the world. Because targeting lead firms is illegal in many places, unions must use this strategy with care. Even nonunion groups, such as student organizations, must proceed with caution. Private regulation has shown its limits time and again. We know, for example, that private monitoring alone did little to improve working conditions in textile plants (Locke et al. 2007; Clack 2020). We also know it can exacerbate the divide between the haves and have-nots in already divided labor markets in developing countries. In Costa Rica, workers employed in plants that process food for export to the European Union receive better pay and enjoy better conditions than their counterparts in factories exporting food to other parts of the world. This is because companies that export products to the European Union are held accountable to stringent labor standards (Lee 2010). Finally, a recent study of textile worker campaigns in Bangladesh suggests that transnational labor governance comes up short when best practices don't get institutionalized among local actors (Kang, forthcoming).

In sum, as economist David Weil reflects, "the greatest hope comes from leveraging private sector pressures from these supply chain systems to strengthen national public policies. Without the laws—and the enforcement systems that make them real—the attention of companies is transient, but their participation can be used as a regulatory fulcrum. Examples where this has happened are promising. But there are no single silver bullets to the transnational labor regulation problem" (personal communication, March 2021).

Public Tactics, Private Workers

Domestic workers and the undocumented, who are often one and the same, are particularly vulnerable populations. The undocumented are generally overrepresented in industries that rely heavily on cheap, temporary labor or in settings where under-the-table payments in cash are standard practice—for men, day labor and low-skilled construction jobs, and for women, domestic work. Undocumented workers are particularly vulnerable to violations of labor rights for several reasons. For one thing, they are reluctant to complain to the government. Since so many work without contracts and are paid through informal channels, they do not have adequate documentation to verify their claims. For another, because they lack the legal right to be working, they fear that the state will choose enforcing immigration law over protecting unauthorized workers (Weil and Pyles 2005). Employers who knowingly hire undocumented workers often take advantage of their vulnerability by ignoring regulations, underpaying, withholding wages, or engaging in other workplace abuses. If undocumented workers threaten to complain, their employers threaten to report them.

Migrant domestic workers typically have a destination hierarchy in mind (A. Paul 2017); most want to move to a place where they will be better protected and able to become naturalized citizens. Who, then, ends up working in the countries with the poorest standards but women migrating with the least resources. Indonesian and Filipino domestic workers in the United Arab Emirates and Dubai, for example, typically come from poor, rural areas where they received limited education. Because they do not have the social or cultural capital to compete in the global domestic labor market, they end up in the Middle East rather than in more desirable positions in Hong Kong or Canada (Parreñas et al. 2019). Some deploy a "stepwise migration" strategy, hoping to move once they gain more experience and savings, although most are unable to achieve this goal (A. Paul 2017).

Working conditions for migrant domestic workers also vary by political regime (A. Paul 2017). In authoritarian states where even citizens lack basic rights and civil liberties, noncitizens receive few, if any, government protections. But in liberal democracies, immigration policies, welfare arrangements, and cultural attitudes come together to shape the experience of domestic work. Within Europe, for example, workers who migrate to Spain and Italy benefit from a perfect confluence of supply and demand. Their services are desperately needed because so many native-born women have entered the workforce. The informal economies in Italy and Spain are much larger than in the rest of Europe. Employing people under the table is quite common, which increases opportunities for migrants without documents. At the same time, despite the fact that both countries are now major transit countries for people trying to reach other parts of Europe, neither has a comprehensive immigrant management policy. A steady supply of migrants, therefore, arrives to meet the growing demand for care work, but they work outside the purview of regulatory institutions that would ensure their basic rights.

Gendered assumptions about domesticity, including the blurred boundary between work and home, also deeply compromise the rights of migrant care workers (A. Paul 2017). While most male migrants are theoretically protected by industrial codes, female domestic workers live behind closed doors under someone else's roof (Chang 2018). Because abuses in private settings are difficult to detect and regulators rarely enter these spaces, migrant women are left to fend for themselves and resolve their own problems.

These women have few places to turn. Worker centers and unions, such as the International Domestic Workers Federation, with its national and regional affiliates, try to help. The ILO's programs and conventions are in place but, as we have seen, these conventions often result in few protections on the ground. To have more of an impact, these efforts must involve alliances with the broader civil society. In Hong Kong, for example, representatives from Southeast and South Asian migrant NGOs worked with local organizations such as the Hong Kong Domestic Workers General Union to address issues like abuse and underpayment (Lim 2016). Even then, liberal and conservative politicians alike were reluctant to grant the right of abode[2] to migrant domestic workers (Lim 2016). Discussions about who is worthy of what level of protection take place against the backdrop of larger debates about who can become "one of us." Once again, the logic of citizenship rights contradicts the logic of social protection based on human rights.

Countries of origin can also step in on behalf of their domestic workers abroad. Knowing that the need for elder care workers will only increase, Indonesia now requires domestic workers to get at least 400 to 600 hours of training and to be licensed before they emigrate. Doing so not only gives migrant workers an edge up in the international market, it also allows the government to pressure employers and public sector actors in countries of destination to provide better protection. Because Hong Kong, Taiwan, and Singapore compete to hire migrant domestic workers from Indonesia rather than Sri Lanka or Cambodia, those workers can demand better labor conditions. In July 2020, during the height of the COVID-19 pandemic, "Indonesia unilaterally declared that, starting in January 2021, foreign employers would be responsible for shouldering emigrants' pre-departure expenses" (Chang 2021, 11). These examples point to the enhanced role countries of origin could play in advocating for their workers abroad.

Conclusion

This chapter examines hybrid transnational social protection in the realm of labor rights. The increasing globalization of capital, labor, and production have given rise to fundamental transformations in where people work, how they perform their jobs, and what kinds of entities operating where are responsible for their protection. We focus here on how migrant workers and their families create resource environments from a mix of protections in countries of origin and destination, which increase choice and opportunity for well-educated professionals and precarity for their low-skilled, less educated counterparts. These two groups need each other. The transnational professional class can do what they do because the transnational class of low-skilled workers cares for their elderly parents and children and attends to their daily needs. This tension—between support and vulnerability—is a defining feature of the ever-changing global economy and the context within which its workers negotiate their labor rights.

As with education and family care, nation-states are central to the direct and indirect protection of migrant workers. Despite appearances that the state is downsizing and stepping back from its involvement in welfare provision and in migrant workers' affairs, our overview suggests otherwise. Receiving states still actively shape conditions affecting protection for workers, often in ways that protect labor and exploit it at the same time (Faist 2018). They do so by regulating markets and occupational safety and health. Their policies influence the power and resources wielded by NGOs and unions working with migrants. They also determine who is recognized as a migrant and as a worker and, therefore, who has the right to work and reside legally within their borders. Sending states that extend labor protections to their citizens working abroad also protect and render them vulnerable (Délano Alonso 2018; Guevarra 2010; Rodriguez 2010; Chang 2021; Yea 2019). Ultimately, collaboration between countries of origin and destination is necessary for effective labor protections on a global scale. How effective these efforts are depends on promulgating and implementing transnational agreements that can be strongly and effectively enforced.

The global reach of business drives forward labor mobility. Outsourcing moves business functions to satellite firms. Offshoring moves entire plants beyond national borders. Global supply chains make it more difficult to agree on who is responsible for upholding labor standards and how they will be held accountable (Plimmer 2013; Pun and Koo 2015; Wolszczak-Derlacz and Parteka 2018). These developments allow firms to seek lower-cost labor and avoid regulations, thereby diminishing the power of the state to establish and enforce labor regulations. They can pit migrant workers against local workers who worry they will be replaced by migrants willing to accept lower wages and harder working conditions.

To be sure, a range of third-sector actors, such as investigative journalists, NGOs, and unions working nationally and internationally, pressure states and employers to address abuses (Ford 2019). They have achieved some notable successes. These, however, are limited and often short-lived. They are of little comfort to the most vulnerable workers. To have a broader and more durable impact, a transnational workers' rights regime would need to encompass multiple interlocking mechanisms for redress and enforcement, including policies corresponding to capital's global reach, worker, and other advocacy organizations, and a variety of methods that would bring private companies to the negotiating table.

What is clear is that the market will not regulate itself nor protect the well-being of migrant workers on its own. Private regulation and a civil society that works across borders can advance the cause of protecting workers, but the former depends upon the latter (Hoang 2016; Locke et al. 2013). With the exception of firms that are extremely conscious of their global reputations, companies rarely do enough to regulate and safeguard, with some even failing to meet basic labor standards. Basic human rights, labor rights, and citizenship rights rely on different legal and ethical commitments. Therefore, greater gains will only be achieved if there is greater cooperation and alignment across social protection sectors and across actors operating at different scales rooted in these different logics.

4
Health

In 2004, Howard Staab, of North Carolina, faced a terrible decision. During a routine physical, his doctor discovered a life-threatening heart valve disorder. With no insurance, the estimated out-of-pocket cost for the surgery he needed added up to a stunning US$200,000. Purchasing additional coverage after his diagnosis would drive his premiums up to US$1,600 a month. He would have to wait more than a year for the operation.

Staab felt as if he were between a rock and a hard place—choosing between financial ruin or possible irreparable health damage. Instead, he chose a third option: traveling abroad. In India, the total cost of surgery, including preliminary testing, hospitalization, and doctors' fees, came to $6,700. In testimony before the US Congress, his partner, Maggi Ann Grace, reported that he received state-of-the-art care from a surgeon trained abroad. Even with private insurance, Grace said, she would consider traveling to India for elective medical procedures. Services there are excellent, she testified, and paying cash in India is cheaper than her deductibles, copayments, and supplemental private insurance in the United States (Grace 2006).

Howard Staab's story is just one example of the myriad ways in which families procure health care across borders. When the care options available to them in the countries where they live fall short, families turn to hybrid transnational social protection, creating cross-border resource environments from the public, private, and nonprofit sectors and their social networks. In Staab's case, the principal logic of social protection at work was that of health as a commodity. In fact, individual patients benefit from competition between providers and between countries where medical care businesses are located. In contrast to social protections founded upon constitutional rights, both citizens and noncitizens can purchase these services. The only requirement—which, of course, is no small feat—is that they can pay.

Care seekers have long ventured abroad for medical treatments. Their ability to do so grows with each more advanced mode of travel (Jenkins 2021).[1] Doctors, too, have long gone abroad to work. Again, India is a case in point. In 2007, one out of every twenty doctors in the United States hailed

Transnational Social Protection. Peggy Levitt, Erica Dobbs, Ken Chih-Yan Sun, and Ruxandra Paul,
Oxford University Press. © Oxford University Press 2023. DOI: 10.1093/oso/9780197666821.003.0005

from India, recruited largely through a visa program aimed at attracting physicians willing to work in underserved rural areas (NPR 2007). India's ties to Britain's National Health Service (NHS) run even deeper: 8 percent of doctors in the NHS are from India or Pakistan and more than a quarter of all NHS doctors are foreign-born (Kentish 2018). Yet, while the crown jewel of the British postwar welfare state relies heavily on immigrant providers, anti-immigration voices clamor to restrict the numbers of foreign-born doctors in the United Kingdom (Bulman 2018).

The globalization of the health care sector complicates the configuration of transnational resource environments in several ways. Emigrating health care professionals and the societies to which they move need one another. Doctors from countries like India or Romania who work in highly specialized fields might not be able to practice their skills or train on the most up-to-date equipment if they remain at home. From this perspective, migration turns a potential case of "brain waste" into a case of "brain gain." But what generates helpful resources in one country often results in losses to another. India is not only one of the world's leaders in the emigration of health care professionals, it is also one of its leaders in the emigration of citizens with higher education (World Bank 2016). Internal brain drain is an issue as well: The Indian government subsidizes medical education at public universities, but most graduates go on to work in the private sector. Like Howard Staab, they are seduced by the allure of gleaming clinics stocked with state-of-the-art equipment (Block 2018).

At the same time, the rise of Western-style clinics can also drive forward return migration. Young doctors may go abroad for advanced medical training, but at least some return home to practice (Levitt and Rajaram 2013b). One of the world's best-known examples is cardiac surgeon Devi Shetty. Born in India and trained in London, Shetty returned to India and went on to establish Narayana Health, a hospital chain that provides world-class care at rock-bottom prices while still making a profit. In fact, his chain became so successful, Shetty opened a satellite clinic in the Cayman Islands to attract well-heeled patients like Staab from the lucrative North American market (Altstedter 2019).

The increasingly complex relationship between migration and health care globalization also affects people who stay behind. When large numbers of physicians emigrate, it produces care deficits but also means that more families can purchase the care they need with the remittances they receive. In fact, several studies show that households receiving remittances spend more money on health care than households without them—a disparity that is particularly stark in India (Mahapatro et al. 2017), Europe (Kalaj 2014), and Latin America (Amuedo-Dorantes and Pozo 2011; Howard and Stanley 2017; Chezum et al. 2018).

For example, nearly 31 percent of the gross domestic product in the southwestern Indian state of Kerala comes from remittances. In one out of five households, there is at least one member working abroad (Rajan and Zachariah 2010). These funds allow people to bypass the much-maligned public health system and turn to private medical care. By doing so, they ensure the growing importance of private hospital systems like Narayana, both as care providers and as magnets to attract return medical staff. They also increase the gap between the privileged and the disadvantaged. People who receive remittances can choose between a broader range of available options while the poor only have recourse to declining and overextended state institutions, nongovernmental organizations (NGOs), or their social networks. This is social protection as a commodity that individuals are responsible for securing themselves, par excellence.

Of all the sectors we describe in these pages, health care is, perhaps, the most transnational and hybridized. We focus on six sets of institutions, caregivers, or care seekers where this occurs: (1) health care professionals on the move; (2) medical institutions that operate transnationally; (3) individuals accessing medical care through remittances; (4) the provision of health care for undocumented migrants; (5) medical tourism and travel; and (6) the global governance of health care in the context of transnational migration. While several scholars have written about aspects of what we describe in isolation, we bring their analyses into conversation with one another to offer readers a more comprehensive picture (Cohen 2011; Connell 2016; Villa-Torres et al. 2017; Mathijsen and Mathijsen 2020; Raudenbush 2020).

Medical Professionals on the Move

After World War II, many high-income countries began offering more generous health care to their citizens. To sustain this level of care, they needed more medical labor power. Thus began what became a steady stream of medical recruitment. Across wealthy Western countries struggling with aging populations and the costs of care, foreign medical workers—doctors, nurses, and technicians—have become indispensable. More than a quarter of the medical workforce in Australia, Canada, Ireland, and the United States is foreign-born (Kingma 2018). These providers come disproportionately from a small set of countries. Not surprisingly, India and the Philippines top the list.

As foreign medical staff become "essential workers" in the health care systems of the Global North, their impact on the countries they leave grows ever stronger. While India leads the world in the emigration of college-educated workers, the Philippines, whose nurses are ubiquitous in high-income hospitals and clinics, follows close behind. These workers' departure strongly affects the Filipino labor market: 35 percent of overseas Filipino workers have college degrees but only 14 percent of the domestic workforce is university educated (Ducanes 2015). The loss of these highly skilled health workers in poor and middle-income countries affects not only private but public health care.

Sub-Saharan African countries and the Caribbean also suffer from brain drain. These countries are home to only 3 percent of the world's medical staff but they shoulder 25 percent of the world's disease burden (Rubagumya et al. 2016). Fifty-five percent of medical staff in Tanzania emigrate, while in Mozambique and Guyana the numbers rise to 65 and 72 percent respectively (Kollar and Buyx 2013). Although medical training is heavily subsidized by home governments, when these graduates migrate, it is wealthy countries that benefit most from their expertise. We have already noted this problem in India, where a 2008 study tracking the careers of top medical school graduates found that between 1989 and 2000, 54 percent were living and working outside the country (Kaushik et al. 2008). The numbers for the Caribbean are even more striking: from 1965 to 2000, 78 percent of Jamaicans, 79 percent of Haitians, and 80 percent of Guyanese with university degrees emigrated to the United States (Mishra 2006).

These outflows profoundly affect health care access. Romania is a case in point. In 2014, official estimates claimed that more than 21,000 Romanian doctors had emigrated since 1990; 14,100 left the country between 2007 and 2014. In 2014, officials at the Colegiul Medicilor, a Romanian professional organization representing physicians, estimated that these doctors had gone to France (4,500), the United Kingdom (4,000), Germany (3,000), and Belgium (2,600). As a result, staffing shortages plague the health care system and the country's health indicators rank among the poorest in Europe. In 2013, for example, life expectancy for men was 70 years while in France it was 79 years.

The infant mortality rate in Romania was 9 per 1,000 live births compared to an average of 4 per 1,000 live births in the European Union as a whole (Pison 2013; Séchet and Vasilcu 2015).

Push factors prompt medical professionals to migrate. These include low pay, poor working conditions, and social problems such as crime, corruption, and weak physical and institutional infrastructures. If unemployment is high or health services are underfunded, surplus workers may be forced to migrate. Work culture also sows the seeds of emigration dreams. South Korea is a prime example. While the country boasts a stable, prosperous democracy, it is also known for its rigid, hierarchical workplaces where people are expected to work long hours and, essentially, be "married" to their jobs. Younger workers, in particular, are attracted to jobs in Europe or Australia because they believe they will be able to achieve a better work–life balance (Forney 2017). Gender discrimination also operates as a push factor, as evidenced by the increasing proportion of migrant doctors who are women. In fact, 70 percent of the Romanian doctors practicing in France are female (Séchet and Vasilcu 2015).

Policies in countries of origin drive medical migration as well. As we have seen, some governments actively export health care workers. For more than a century, nurses have been one of Kerala's biggest exports. During the colonial period, the British government recruited Indian women to work in the British Military Nursing Service. The Hindu community viewed nursing as impure, but Malayali Christians were more than willing to answer the call. Missionaries encouraged them by describing nursing as "God's work" (Asianet Newsable n.d.). Today, nurses from Kerala are so widely respected that international hospital chains use them as a selling point to attract medical tourists.

The Philippines is also a global go-to place for nurses. As we discussed in Chapters 2 and 3, because the economy is not able to absorb enough workers, the government trains students to work abroad. By framing their work as a source of remittances and social protection rather than as a loss of care, the state sidesteps hard questions about what it owes its citizens working outside its borders (Masselink and Lee 2013). This transnational commodification of labor is even greater in Cuba, where exporting doctors (often in exchange for energy or investment) is a cornerstone of the government's foreign policy (Groll 2013). In both cases, these exchanges result in improved social protection for citizens in other countries while limiting health care services for national citizens.

Pull factors also inspire people to move. Some governments actively recruit doctors and nurses for their public health systems. They institute preferential visa programs to attract professionals to serve in high-need rural areas or in understaffed specialties like geriatric health. International wage competition even drives migration between countries in the Global North. Comparatively high salaries in the United States are often enough to lure away English-speaking doctors working in Ireland and the United Kingdom. The Irish case, in particular, highlights the strong push-and-pull dynamics driving the international market for skilled practitioners: Ireland graduates more medical professionals per capita than any other country in the Organisation for Economic Co-operation and Development (OECD n.d.) but more than 35 percent of its practicing physicians received their training outside the country (Nolan 2018).

Just as governments compete for health workers from abroad, or actively export their excess workers overseas, they also put in place policies to keep them home. By far the most common response to brain drain is to try to convert it into brain gain or, at least, brain circulation. Whether this is the best way to respond to large-scale skill flight remains to be seen. Some researchers find the dangers of brain drain exaggerated. They say that migration only leads to "brain strain," which gives rise to both positive and negative outcomes. Expatriate doctors practice at a high level, using advanced equipment unavailable at home, thereby avoiding brain waste (Raghuram 2009). Some of these doctors stay in touch with their colleagues while they are away and start joint projects that lead to skill, knowledge, and technology transfers.

Other researchers find the effects of brain drain more serious. The solution, they say, is to actively intervene by addressing the poor socioeconomic conditions that push educated citizens to migrate to begin with (Benedict and Ukpere 2012). Others argue that redesigning medical education so that it focuses on local problems and trains more students from underrepresented areas would stem the outflow of medical staff (Eyal and Hurst 2008). Still others propose punitive policies that would require students receiving tuition assistance to repay some of the cost of their schooling (Record and Mohiddin 2006). Proposals that rely on state intervention in the labor market evoke especially loud dissent. When asked about regulating the migration of health workers, South African doctors objected strongly, arguing that freedom of movement is their right. The state does not interfere in the movement of accountants and lawyers, so why should it do so for them? (Mahlathi and Dlamini 2017).

While most policies addressing brain drain put the onus on countries of origin, others look to countries of destination. One example is the Medical Education Partnership Initiative (Kasper and Bajunirwe 2012). The US Department of Health and Human Services and several US medical schools partnered with twelve sub-Saharan African countries to develop new medical schools and health care training programs (National Institutes of Health 2019). Increasing the supply of medical professionals within developing countries, however, does not guarantee that they will stay put. For that to happen, the Global North would need to cure itself of its reliance on immigrant providers. States would have to commit voluntarily to limiting the numbers of doctors they recruit overseas—an unlikely scenario as populations age and the demand for medical care increases.

Recognizing these challenges, some governments direct their efforts toward getting migrants to return after stints abroad. They do so by improving socioeconomic conditions and by creating hospitals and clinics where doctors want to work. They offer tax incentives and support training, research, and development (Gaillard et al. 2015; Arah et al. 2008). Policy interventions, such as immigration laws, strongly shape how effective such efforts can be. Most countries granting work visas to noncitizens have strict rules about residency status and limit the time spent abroad to qualify for visa renewal or permanent residency. These make it difficult for noncitizens to return home for long periods because they risk losing their work visas. Visa policies that take personal and private transnational lives into consideration could enhance social protection in countries of origin and destination.

What might also help are regulations that address the needs of sending and receiving countries. In 1999, for example, Britain's NHS issued an internal Code of Practice that set ethical limits on the numbers of medical staff recruited from abroad. In 2003, the United Kingdom signed a bilateral memorandum of understanding with South Africa to limit the latter's brain drain and enhance cooperation between the two health care systems. This cooperative arrangement resulted in hospital "twinning," more residency exchanges, and a decline in the numbers of South African nurses registered to work in the United Kingdom (Robinson and Clark 2008). Labor market regulation, therefore, can support countries with fewer resources to provide more effectively for their own citizens using the resources they have at hand.

Many governments, however, recognize that most skilled emigrants will not come home. They focus instead on encouraging expatriates to contribute skills, money, and technological know-how to national development from afar (Levitt and Rajaram 2013a). They also encourage short-term visits to facilitate these exchanges. A study of Malawian emigrants, for instance, found that two-thirds would be willing to return for short-term skill transfer programs, although they expected the government to fund their travel and expenses (Masanjala 2018). The Singaporean and Chinese governments entice leading scholars and practitioners to spend time back home by offering incentive programs and generous financial benefits, including research funds (Zhou and Liu 2016). In these ways, countries of origin make it easier and advantageous for health professionals to retain membership in professional, scientific, and other communities at home.

For countries with a large-scale exodus of doctors, investing in education is a losing game. To meet their own pressing health needs, poor countries have to devise proactive, holistic, and progressive policies "to train, retain, and sustain" the medical professionals upon whom their health care systems so desperately rely (Doyle 2014). Restrictive or hostile attitudes toward migration, however, are unlikely to solve the medical brain drain anytime soon. Emigration of health care professionals is an outcome, not a cause, of deeply rooted structural problems. Curtailing it requires treating the disease rather than the symptoms that make migration a necessity to begin with.

A final set of actors that affect brain drain is international lenders. One of the biggest challenges to training and maintaining an adequate health care workforce in very poor countries is overcoming the restrictions that institutions like the World Bank and the International Monetary Fund place on government spending (Benedict and Ukpere 2012; Kasper and Bajunirwe 2012). These governments cannot afford to improve infrastructure or create the health care institutions they need even when they want to. Offering manageable financial terms to poor countries is to recognize health care as a human right that, to be achievable, requires international and national support.

Health Care Institutions that Go Transnational

Taking their cues from patients and providers, institutions are also restructuring themselves transnationally to provide care. We offer examples of two different approaches. In the early 2000s, Narayana Health launched a full-fledged campaign to attract clients from the US market. The hospital chain went to the government of the Cayman Islands with a set of demands. It wanted the government to recognize Indian medical qualifications; approve work permits for Indian staff; and support a "health city" complex with hospital centers, research facilities, and a medical school. To develop the "city," Narayana partnered with Ascension Health, a US-based Catholic health care network looking for a place to perform expensive procedures offshore (Doyle 2014). By 2017, however, Ascension backed out of the deal, claiming that Narayana had failed to deliver on its promised target of 17,000 US patients per year (IMTJ 2017). The facility ended up catering instead to wealthy Caribbean residents seeking tertiary care[2] unavailable back home.

The Johns Hopkins Medicine International system, a spinoff of the Johns Hopkins University's hospital system in Baltimore, Maryland, is another case in point. While Johns Hopkins long provided services to international patients who came to them, it now goes to its patients. For instance, after caring for Emirati patients who traveled to Baltimore for decades, the university began working in the United Arab Emirates directly. In 2006, it signed a management contract with Tawam Hospital in Abu Dhabi that included a two-way residency program with its international network. In 2018, the government in Abu Dhabi upped the stakes by donating $50 million to a new stroke institute that operates in Abu Dhabi and Baltimore.

Johns Hopkins Medicine International has entered into similar agreements with hospitals around the world. Its administrators help with operations, raising the bar to meet US standards of care. Medical students can do residencies in many countries. Staff in Maryland offer second opinions on more difficult cases. Their partners enjoy enhanced legitimacy because they are now part of the Hopkins brand. The improved quality of care also forces competing regional hospitals to improve (McDaniels 2017). Hopkins is not alone in extending its brand beyond US borders. The Cleveland and Mayo clinics have also established international partnerships in high- and middle-income countries throughout Asia, the Gulf, Eastern Europe, and Latin America.

Of course, these efforts don't always work smoothly. Critics chastise Western hospitals for partnering with institutions in countries with serious human rights abuses (McDaniels 2017). International clinics catering to international patients exacerbate internal brain drain by luring away doctors and nurses working in public-sector institutions. This compromises public health and diminishes state capacity. In Thailand, while international facilities like Bumrungrad Hospital attract patients from around the world and medical personnel from around the country, Thais in rural areas are increasingly underserved (Wibulpolprasert and Pachanee 2008). The expansion of international hospital chains provokes heated debates about whether hospitals, particularly publicly funded institutions, should be profit-making entities (Connell 2016). What happens to the quality of care, critics ask, when management decisions are market driven? Treating health care as a commodity sets a dangerous precedent that people who can pay are more entitled to care than those who cannot.

Market-based binational health insurance schemes are also on the rise. Private insurance programs—most notably Blue Cross, Blue Shield Access, and Baja HMO—now operate along the US–Mexico border. Under these plans, subscribers get their primary care in Mexico and their emergency care in California. Access to these programs is market-bound rather than country-dependent. In the United States, states rather than the federal government regulate the insurance industry. While private insurance plans operate transnationally in states like California, allowing combinations of services across the US–Mexico border, the Texas state legislature successfully blocked a similar scheme.

Partnerships between European and African countries also gave rise to cross-border insurance arrangements. France and Belgium worked with NGOs and government agencies in Mali and Congo. Migrants contribute funds to health insurance accounts in Europe that their relatives back home can then access to pay for health expenses. European governments also supported the construction of clinics initially intended to serve migrants' families but which later opened up to serve local populations as well (Lafleur and Lizin 2015).

Even states are getting into the business of providing health care across borders. The Mexican government's Ventanillas de Salud exemplifies the diasporic institutional growth we discussed in our introduction (Gomez et al. 2017). Established in 2003, the Ventanillas de Salud is a network of mini-clinics in consular offices across the United States. They provide screenings; health education; vaccinations; and diagnostic tests for HIV, high blood pressure, and diabetes to Mexican citizens who are often uninsured and unable to afford care. These individuals are considered "at risk" given their "limited access to health insurance, low income, lack of information about health services, and fear of accessing health services due to individual or family migration status" (Délano Alonso 2018, 84).

Some migrants return to get care in their homelands, in part, because new institutional arrangements enable them to do so (Mathijsen and Mathijsen 2020; Sun 2021). Authorized Mexican migrants living close to the border can seek care through the Mexican Social Security Institute. They were previously also covered under Seguro Popular, a public health insurance scheme that was even available to expatriates before it shut down in 2020. The Instituto de Salud para el Bienestar, which provides health care to people not covered under any other public health insurance scheme, replaced it (Agren 2020; Block et al. 2012). These efforts, at least in theory, extend social protection as a constitutional right to citizens not physically present inside the national territory. They work through a network of institutions that supersize the welfare state by extending its reach to émigrés, vulnerable citizens, and their descendants abroad.

Interestingly, immigrants in the United States are not always big fans of these transnational health care projects. Many of the New York–based immigrants whom sociologist Robert Smith and his colleagues studied did not know about Seguro Popular or were confused about how the program operated. They greeted these government efforts with skepticism and worried about falling through the bureaucratic cracks. They did not want to return to Mexico to get services (Smith et al. 2020). At the same time, due to their limited social networks, concentration in informal occupations, and absence during major enrollment periods, many returning or deported migrants were not enrolled in the program and, thus, remained uninsured (Wassink 2016). By and large, Seguro Popular also failed to curb outmigration. For families who view emigration as a social protection strategy, it did not go far enough in guaranteeing "free, effective, and timely access to healthcare to the uninsured" (García and Orraca-Romano 2019, 183).

Accessing Health Care with Remittances

While remittances generally allow families to manage risk and secure protection across borders, this is especially true with health care. Studies show that households receiving remittances spend more on health care than those that do not (Amuedo-Dorantes and Pozo 2011; Kalaj 2014). Women are more likely than men to use remittances to pay for health and education. Since the numbers of women migrants are on the rise, this contributes to better health outcomes for their children (Cortes 2015; Piper and Yamanaka 2005). Children in remittance-receiving households do better with respect to height and weight and are more likely to be vaccinated and dewormed (Ponce et al. 2011). These gains are not sustainable without enough medical providers. Whereas remittances tend to reduce child mortality, medical brain drain increases overall mortality (Chauvet et al. 2013). Countries receiving the most remittances are generally those with the highest levels of brain drain and health care labor shortages.

It is not just money, however, that is being sent home. Migrants often send their families medications that are unavailable in their countries of origin or they bring medicines to relatives who need to replenish supplies (Sun 2021). As we explained in Chapter 1, though, these exchanges often come at a high price. The Vietnamese migrants whom sociologist Hung Thai (2014) studied, for example, scrimped and saved so much to send money home that they sacrificed their own health. Sudanese refugees and asylum seekers in the Netherlands also skipped meals or spent less on food so they could send more remittances (Mingot and Mazzucato 2018a).

Social remittances also circulate continuously between countries of origin and destination—exchanges of skills, knowledge, ideas, practices, and social capital between migrant and nonmigrant family and community members (Levitt 2001; Levitt and Lamba-Nieves 2011). These constant, iterative transfers lead to changes in thinking about what it means to be healthy, the need for exercise and a proper diet, and who is responsible for providing health care. Because social remittances also challenge conventional wisdom about what states and individuals should do and expectations of the state and personal responsibility, they shift understandings about social protection as a constitutional right, a human right, a commodity, or community or personal responsibility.

Questions about harnessing remittances remain. Should the state regulate flows or let households use their money as they wish? Left to decide on their own, individuals and families can contribute to what Drabo and Ebeke (2010) call "sectoral glide." Spending more money on private health care, they weaken the public sector. Evidence about the effects of social and economic remittances is contradictory. Economic remittances can decrease support for taxation and redistribution policies that fund public social services and thus lead to their decline (Doyle 2015). Social remittances, in contrast, can increase support for a more proactive government. One study found families that remained in close contact with migrant members abroad were more likely to favor a more interventionist state (Meseguer et al. 2016). Social and economic remittances thus push people to re-evaluate state–society relations in countries of origin, but not in predictable ways.

Supporters believe that remittances mediated by the state offer two key advantages. First, when funds are channeled through organized programs, senders tend to feel more confident that their money is well spent. Second, by pooling funds through hometown associations, groups of migrants can magnify the impact of remittances, distributing them more widely and equitably. A well-known partnership scheme is the Three-for-One program in Mexico. The program matches funds raised by hometown associations in migrant-receiving communities to pay for social services and infrastructure upgrades in sending communities at a 3 to 1 ratio (i.e., the federal government matches contributions from the state and locality). Because the program leads to improved sanitation and water provision, it also improves health outcomes (Duquette-Rury 2014). The program also generates democratic dividends: Mexican communities with high emigration and active hometown associations are more likely to be politically active (Duquette-Rury and Chen 2019).

Critics believe that states are only guided by their self-interest. The Mexican government's regulation of the Three-for-One program raises eyebrows about corruption and nepotism (García 2020). Recent research also finds that the millions of dollars sent back to Mexico inadvertently drive up violence and homicide rates across remittance-receiving municipalities. Organized criminal groups target these municipalities due to the financial resources concentrated there (García 2020).

Caring for the Undocumented

The extent to which nation-states provide health care to noncitizens, both those residing legally and those without documents within their borders, varies considerably and is the subject of much debate. Canada provides universal health care for its citizens but unauthorized migrants are ineligible (Siddiqi et al. 2009). Twenty of twenty-seven EU countries offer unauthorized migrants access to emergency care (Cuadra and Cattacin 2010). In contrast, EU citizens who fall ill during a temporary stay in another EU member state are entitled to care for any condition that requires immediate attention.

The migrant has the same right to health care as any citizen of that country through the European Health Insurance Card, which is available for free in the individual's country of origin (European Commission 2021).

In the United States, the federal government's policies regarding access to medical care for undocumented migrants are increasingly restrictive (Portes et al. 2012; Marrow 2012a; Marrow 2012b). Even though the Affordable Care Act, passed in 2010, enabled approximately 20 million previously uninsured people to access care, unauthorized immigrants were excluded. This was because, as sociologists Helen Marrow and Tiffany Joseph observe, "in the controversial context of health care reform, any attempt to include them [unauthorized immigrants] may have been accurately perceived as a danger to its [the act's] supporters' legitimacy and ultimate chances for success" (2015, 2258). As a result, without paying out of pocket, unauthorized immigrants have two choices. They can seek care in hospitals specifically funded to treat emergencies regardless of a patient's ability to pay or they can go to safety-net hospitals, such as federally qualified health care centers.

Advocates who believe that state and local governments should provide more actively for this population make three key arguments: (1) utilitarian prevention, or keeping medical problems from becoming so severe that patients need care in higher cost emergency rooms; (2) human rights, or the view that all disadvantaged and underserved groups should have access to a "safety net"; and (3) the worthiness of unauthorized immigrants because they contribute positively to American society (Marrow 2012a; Marrow and Joseph 2015).

In response, some locales have become "sanctuaries" that provide limited access to basic health services. In 2002, San Francisco allocated substantial public funds to programs such as San Francisco Healthy Kids. Since 2007, it has supported Healthy San Francisco, which assists uninsured residents regardless of their legal status (Marrow 2012a; Marrow 2012b). Vermont's health care reform expanded Medicaid coverage, established a state health exchange, and used state funds to insure the small numbers of undocumented immigrants living there (Joseph 2016). Massachusetts established the Health Safety Net program, which allowed all uninsured residents with incomes below 400 percent of the federal poverty line to access care from designated providers (Marrow and Joseph 2015).

Advocates for the undocumented in Spain made similar arguments. In 2012, a proposal by the conservative national government to limit care for undocumented migrants met with major pushback. Many of Spain's autonomous communities flatly refused to comply with the policy, deploying human rights and "positive contributions" arguments. Most were provinces where liberal opposition parties were in power, but in Galicia, the lone conservative region that rejected the government's proposal, supporters argued that public health concerns should take priority over party politics or immigration status (Huete 2015). This is an example of a "gray zone" created by a lack of alignment between federal, state, and local policies that created a window of opportunity for provincial governments to act when the federal government declined to do so (Dobbs and Levitt 2017).

The case of US health care reform, however, shows the difficulties of extending basic care to unauthorized migrants. Bureaucracy is a big hurdle. People without documents cannot prove the local residency or income eligibility needed to access care. Language barriers and lack of knowledge about available services further complicate accessibility (Light 2012). Long-term access to services depends upon the changing political and economic climate. Care for the undocumented is often the first thing to go during economic downturns (Joseph 2016). Many unauthorized migrants are also too scared to use services even when they are available (Sexsmith 2015). As a chief administrator at a nondenominational, nonprofit hospital in San Diego pointed out, undocumented migrants are often so worried about getting arrested they do not seek "proper medical care on a regular basis" (Portes et al. 2012, 15). An immigrant rights activist in Boston recalled similar stories about immigrants on their way to the hospital who turned around when they saw police cars on the road ahead (Marrow and Joseph 2015, 2265).[3]

Medical Travel/Medical Tourism

Although migrating to get health care has a long history, there are now many new ways to access care abroad (Raudenbush 2020). What used to be individual ad hoc transactions are increasingly mediated by institutional actors, including hospitals, insurance companies, and governments in both departure and destination societies. What's more, what used to be a mostly one-way movement from the Global South to the Global North has become a multidirectional flow of people seeking care in a much wider range of destinations. Some patients travel to access rich country standards of care at developing country prices. Others travel long distances for cutting-edge services not widely available closer to home.

Two images of medical tourists who travel abroad for medical care dominate the media. One is wealthy elites from the Global South who can afford private services at world-renowned hospitals and clinics in the Global North. The other is a select group of travelers from the Global North who seek out elective procedures, such as cosmetic surgery, that are not covered by their insurance back home. But assumptions about medical travel are misleading. Most travel takes place within regions (e.g., intra-Asia, intra–European Union, and between the United States and Mexico), and most medical travelers cross "the nearest, sometimes familiar, borders, amid people with broadly similar cultures" (Connell 2016, 539).

Some of these individuals seek specialized care like cancer treatment, reconstructive surgery, and organ transplants or complex tertiary procedures like pediatric cardiovascular surgery. Most, however, cross borders for routine health examinations and treatment (e.g., dental care) regardless of whether a binational health insurance scheme is in place or not (Connell 2016). These travelers are not tourists. They move to access care because the cost can make or break their monthly budgets. Sociologist Héctor Carrillo (2017) found that disparities in HIV-related health care between the United States and Mexico led Mexican gay men to cross the border regularly or even settle in the United States to use HIV/AIDS care in San Diego. Inequalities are thus key drivers in people's search for transnational health care (see also Villa-Torres et al. 2017).

Cultures of medicine also motivate people to cross borders to seek health care. Sensing that providers in the United States are driven more by profit than by patients, some Mexican immigrants feel frustrated with the lack of personal attention they receive. They believe US providers are " 'milking' patients for as many appointments as possible" (Horton and Cole 2011, 1851). They also find American providers to be too cautious because they worry about potential lawsuits. Doctors in the United States, in their opinion, prescribe too much acetaminophen (also known by the brand name Tylenol) instead of the stronger medications and alternative treatments that are readily available in Mexico (Horton and Cole 2011, 1850). South Korean immigrants in New Zealand similarly sought medical care during their visits home, not only to bypass the country's cumbersome referral system but also to avoid racism and linguistic and cultural barriers to care (Lee et al. 2010).

Medical travel and tourism has profound effects on countries of both origin and destination (Johnston et al. 2010). Proponents argue they help struggling patients access care and benefit the local population by stemming brain drain and encouraging return migration. Given the global reputation of its doctors, for example, India figures high on the list of destinations for medical tourism. But this position is not just a function of the market. The Indian government has instituted a special medical visa for patients, issuing more than 170,000 in 2016 alone (Block 2018). The thinking behind such policies is that rising demand will promote more high-quality clinics and hospitals to open. These will then entice expatriate providers to return, which will improve services for locals and medical tourists alike. But "shopping" for doctors internationally can also raise expectations about "appropriate" care back home. The exposure "to nurse-to-patient ratios that far exceed norms in most systems, hotel-like care spaces, and the ability to choose one's physician from a website may result in patients demanding similar 'consumer as king' treatment at home" (Johnston et al. 2010, 8).

Detractors worry that seeking health care transnationally can complicate patients' medical conditions (Chen and Wilson 2013). What happens when complications arise after they return home and proper post-op care is not available (Johnston et al. 2010)? Medical experts worry about the risks of "reusing syringes or equipment without adequate sterilization, exposure to falsified or substandard medications, and inadequately screened blood donations" in other countries (Chen and Wilson 2013, 1757). Such risks and uncertainties, exacerbated by uneven regulation across national settings, might come as a surprise to poorly informed medical tourists.

But the most important questions arising from the growth of medical tourism concern equity, equality, and allocation of public resources. In many cases, states actively promote medical tourism and travel. They directly and indirectly support the expansion of private health care provision. They build new public hospitals that offer care to foreign visitors. Some even establish "medical tourism coordination offices" to market their services to interested "clients" (Yılmaz and Aktas 2020). While the government argues that the benefits of these efforts will trickle down to average citizens, others accuse states of putting economic gains before public welfare.

In India, the private medical tourism industry has grown, in part, because of "the provision of public land, corporate tax breaks and reduced tariffs on imported medical equipment for use in private hospitals serving medical tourists" (Johnston et al. 2010, 5). Malaysia and Korea have similarly supported medical tourism industries "through advertising, tax reduction, or infrastructure support" (Connell 2016, 539). Throughout the African continent, medical tourism creates a two-tier health care system: one for those with financial means and the other for local people. Foreign patients are cared for using cutting-edge medical technologies, techniques, and services, while "a large local population endures rudimentary health, insufficient clean water and inadequate sanitation" (Mogaka et al. 2017, 6). As more and more countries join the race to become the next medical destination of choice, a key question remains: Wouldn't citizens be better served through direct investments in health care infrastructure? If governments choose not to make these investments, they may be forced to "outsource" care for their own people, creating a kind of second-class medical tourist. Conflating "patients" with "clients" not only reinforces the neoliberal idea that the market is the solution but gives states permission to abdicate responsibility for the health of their citizens.

We close this section with a brief discussion of "reproductive tourism." We include this in these pages because we see it as a type of medical tourism where patients travel to other countries for infertility treatments. While, as we noted in Chapter 1, the second decade of the twenty-first century witnessed a decline in international adoptions, families seeking fertility services are on the rise. Cross-border reproductive care includes activities "surrounding patients who travel outside their country of domicile to seek assisted reproductive services and treatment" (Ethics Committee of the American Society for Reproductive Medicine 2013, 645). Families leverage global resources in two ways: seeking sperm or egg donors, and securing surrogate mothers from abroad (Hertz and Nelson 2016). Cross-border reproductive care thus complicates our understanding of transnational resource environments even more because it makes people in less-developed societies into "resources" used by wealthier ones.

Prospective parents hoping to have a baby might seek suitable sperm or egg donors across national borders to protect themselves from a range of risks. They may not be comfortable with the options available to them in the countries where they live (Hertz and Nelson 2016). They might be trying to get around restrictive legal regulations back home (e.g., being a single or LGBTQ parent). Some live in countries that ban particular types of assistive reproductive treatment or gamete use (e.g., donated eggs and/or embryos) (Glennon 2016). Some find the price of pregnancy more affordable or the waiting period shorter in other countries (Paraskou and George 2017). Some seek surrogates who look more like them. Still others seek privacy. In Spain and the Czech Republic, donor anonymity is protected for life (Kroløkke 2014).

The ability to turn to the market to create a family is strongly influenced by geopolitics. India and Thailand used to be popular sources of surrogacy because of their accessibility and affordability (Scherman et al. 2016; Crawshaw et al. 2012). These markets shrank, however, when critics raised concerns about the human rights of surrogate mothers. They believed that poor women were being forced to sell their reproductive resources because they had no other economic choice (Huber et al. 2018). Transnational reproduction may also drive up the costs of medical care in destination countries (Storrow 2010).

Legal scholars also warn against the possibility of producing "stateless children":

> If the state where the child is born operates under an absolute *jus soli* principle, the child will be a national of that state once born, and so will not be stateless. However, if the state where the child is born operates a *jus sanguinis* approach, then the child's nationality is precarious, and will be dependent on who is recognized as a "parent." Problems arise if the state of the intended parents, state B, operates under *jus sanguinis* but differs in its rules in terms of how parentage is decided by state A. . . . As neither state's law can be imposed on the other, the result is that a child born through surrogacy in state A could be left stranded in state A with uncertain legal parentage, and without nationality of either jurisdiction; that is, stateless. (Ní Ghráinne and McMahon 2017, 329)

For these reasons, countries like India, Thailand, and Nepal have closed their doors to international surrogacy (Ní Ghráinne and McMahon, 2017). Former surrogate mothers are forced into further financial precarity, giving rise to an underground economy in which no stakeholder is legally protected (Huber et al. 2018). Prohibiting international surrogacy in one country often causes the practice to migrate elsewhere. Cambodia, for instance, replaced Thailand and India as a destination of choice (Cook 2015).

Global Health and Transnational Governance

The recent outbreaks of severe acute respiratory syndrome (SARS), the Ebola virus, and COVID-19 make it abundantly clear that illnesses do not need a passport. Migration and mobility make such diseases more difficult to manage. Although "state sovereignty is an alien concept in the microbial world" (Aginam 2002, 946), most governments respond to communicable diseases and transnational public health crises by closing their borders (Paul 2015). These incidents fuel xenophobia, bringing the boundary between "us" and "them"[4] into sharper focus. Strategies such as the "militarized rollout of containment measures, the ratcheting up of data surveillance systems, [and] point-of-transit screening protocols" are the typical national toolkit for maintaining national sovereignty and minimizing disruptions to international travel and business (Kelly 2018, 137).

The world's response to the COVID-19 pandemic and other global outbreaks drives home that any state's unilateral measures to restrict movement are bound to fail. They are out of sync with the everyday lives of ordinary individuals. During the Ebola outbreak, for example, countries such as Cameroon, Gambia, Ivory Coast, Kenya, Nigeria, and Senegal halted or limited air travel from Ebola-hit Guinea, Liberia, and Sierra Leone. Some airlines suspended flights to and from West Africa. South Africa refused entry to all noncitizens and permanent residents coming from Ebola-affected countries (Chishti et al. 2014). But these protocols assumed that all migrants travel legally, directly, along a clear set of routes, and that checks at borders and airports would catch them. They overresponded to the small numbers of legal migrants and under-responded to or even exacerbated the needs of displaced migrants and asylum seekers (Paul 2015).

Earlier episodes of infectious diseases, dating back to cholera epidemics in Europe during the nineteenth century, led to the creation of multilateral institutions to govern health. These homogenized national responses to disease, standardized screening, facilitated the exchange of epidemiological information and established international health organizations (Aginam 2002). Between 1851 and 1938, a series of conferences known as the International Sanitary Conferences worked to combat cholera, yellow fever, and bubonic plague. Today, the most prominent global health organization is the World Health Organization, created in 1948, which includes 194 member states. Other international actors include the United Nations Children's Fund and the United Nations World Food Programme, as well as the United Nations Millennium Development Goals and Sustainable Development Goals, with their systems for addressing global health.

Global epidemics do not drive greater public health coordination alone. The lack of a comprehensive nursing system and a systematic way to treat those wounded in war also contributed to greater coordination. In June 1859, the Swiss businessman Henry Dunant, on his way to Italy to meet Emperor Napoleon III to discuss business interests in Algeria, witnessed the Battle of Solferino, one of the bloodiest in the Second Italian War of Independence. More than 40,000 soldiers died or were left wounded in the field. An appalled Dunant abandoned his travel plans and set to work treating the wounded. Dunant's book, *A Memory of Solferino*, which he self-published in 1862, inspired leading European political and military figures to follow his lead and coordinate efforts to improve medical care in the battlefield.

These efforts laid the foundation for the International Red Cross and Red Crescent Movement and for the International Federation of Red Cross and Red Crescent Societies. The International Committee of the Red Cross, a humanitarian institution that works in states that signed the 1949 Geneva Conventions, protects victims of armed conflicts, including prisoners, refugees, civilians, soldiers wounded during war, and other noncombatants. Today's global responses to health crises build upon this legacy of human rights and on early efforts at transnational governance (Dromi 2020).

NGOs like Médecins Sans Frontières (Doctors Without Borders)—founded in 1971 by a small group of French doctors and journalists to expand accessibility to medical care across borders irrespective of race, religion, or political affiliation—are part of the current set of organizations working in conflict zones and areas affected by endemic disease. In 2015, with support from private donors, more than 30,000 doctors, nurses, administrators, and water and sanitation engineers volunteered to provide care in over 70 countries. The organization, however, eschews systems of transnational governance and deliberately limits the money it accepts from governments or intergovernmental organizations so that it can maintain its independence and impartiality. Another group, Médecins du Monde, established in 1980, provides emergency and long-term medical care to the world's most vulnerable through a global network in fifteen countries. Its slogan is "to go where others will not, to testify to the intolerable, and to volunteer."

Conclusion

We are no longer solely eligible for health care on the basis of our constitutional rights. Resource environments extend beyond the state—as both a place and an actor—to encompass numerous institutional arrangements for providing care. These draw on multiple logics simultaneously—of the market, the community, human rights, and social and political rights. The changing landscape we describe has emerged in response to the lived realities of the millions of people who move or are affected by movement around the world.

The nation-state, however, still matters in health care provision. It is deeply implicated in training medical staff. It is a—if not *the*—main source of care for millions of people and it facilitates the movement of transnational staff, patients, and institutions. As their citizens' needs extend beyond national territories, states are rethinking their role in health care provision and collaborating with new sets of actors to meet needs within and beyond their borders. Because disease knows no borders, health care must cross them as well.

The migration of health care workers clearly pits the concerns of actors against one another: states versus individuals, wealthy countries versus poor countries, and states versus the market. Emigrating health care professionals and receiving societies need one another, but this happens all too often at the sending country's expense. The global market for talent means that poor states generally cannot compete salary-wise for health care workers. Even when they try to attract personnel by upgrading their facilities, a new set of problems emerges, including internal brain drain and skyrocketing costs that make care out of reach for their own citizens. In more critical situations, such as war or global health emergencies, some NGOs and international NGOs coordinate research and care. However, this rarely translates into a systematic, institutionalized effort once the crisis subsides. They are not a reliable part of the resource environment that families can depend upon.

Just as medical professionals spend parts of their working lives practicing across borders, so too more and more health care institutions are restructuring themselves transnationally. Targeting the global market, local hospitals try to attract clients from abroad, partner with international providers, or establish branches overseas. While health care institutions shift their focus toward international clients, they are still responsible for local patients. How the competing logics underlying understandings of eligibility for care are resolved determines who benefits and who loses from this redistribution of attention and resources.

The extent to which states provide health care to noncitizen residents, both legal and unauthorized, varies considerably and is the subject of much debate. Advocates argue that offering all residents preventive care makes good public health sense. They say that health is a human right, well deserved by people who make valuable contributions to the society, regardless of their documentation status. Again, despite these overtures, nonresident citizens still face significant barriers to care, including bureaucratic hurdles, language barriers, political and economic opposition, and fear of arrest and deportation (Marrow and Joseph 2015).

These changing dynamics also affect those who stay put. Receiving remittances, especially on a regular, predictable basis, goes a long way toward helping nonmigrants access care and toward improving health outcomes. Efforts to attract medical tourists exemplify the trade-offs involved in transnational approaches to managing risk very well. As we have seen, they generally give rise to a two-tier system that exacerbates rather than diminishes economic and social disparities (Mogaka et al. 2017). People with the financial means can purchase the highest quality health care services but many local residents cannot. Likewise, wealthy prospective parents choose to travel across borders to realize their dreams while poor women may feel they have no choice but to become a surrogate. Hybridized transnational social protection produces clear winners and losers and the losers come disproportionately from the world's poor.

Infectious diseases like COVID-19, which readily cross borders, bring into stark relief just how inadequate national responses, alone, are to global health problems. International cooperation is the only way to respond effectively to global health challenges. This is a tall order, as evidenced by the high vaccination rates in countries in the Global North compared to the abysmal vaccination and high mortality rates in countries throughout the Global South. Yet as populations age in some parts of the world and swell in others, and both patients and providers remain willing to cross borders in search of better care or working conditions, the urgent need for national governments to recognize the transnational dimensions of care will remain.

5
Aging and Elder Care

John Leung moved to the United States in the late 1970s with a dream.[1] He imagined he would work hard, save money, and then move back to Taiwan where he would live out his golden years in full middle-class comfort. But as John Lennon famously said, "Life is what happens to you while you're busy making other plans." Even though John Leung conscientiously put away money toward his retirement, he lost almost all his savings. His fiancée, whom he met through a matchmaking agency when he was aged nearly 60, took most of his money and eloped with another man. Feeling heartbroken and discouraged, John gambled away what remained.

Single, childless, and almost bankrupt, John returned to Taiwan when he was in his mid-sixties. He found work as a janitor and gradually lost touch with his friends in the United States. His failures filled him with shame. Even so, life in Taiwan felt better than life abroad. It cost less to make ends meet and, as a dual citizen, John qualified for public benefits such as housing subsidies for seniors and public health insurance. He could now consult doctors at will, without having to worry about costs or language barriers. When he finally took care of a root canal that troubled him for years, the entire treatment cost less than US$25. A social worker helped him apply for a grant to offset seniors' dental costs.

While John concluded that life in Taiwan was not as bad as he had expected, he recognized that many Taiwanese did not welcome back return migrants like him with open arms. Indeed, many criticized returnees, labeling them opportunists who spend their productive years abroad and come back to use scarce resources when they retire. Had he stayed in the United States, John might also have been the target of criticism. Older migrants are often perceived as burdens to countries of destination, which can complicate their efforts to achieve permanent residency and citizenship, especially in places with generous social welfare (Ho 2019; Brandhorst et al. 2019). Even when they succeed in becoming official members of the societies where they move, the extent to which nation-states should be responsible for older immigrants is the subject of much debate.

Transnational Social Protection. Peggy Levitt, Erica Dobbs, Ken Chih-Yan Sun, and Ruxandra Paul,
Oxford University Press. © Oxford University Press 2023. DOI: 10.1093/oso/9780197666821.003.0006

These controversies are not unique to Taiwan. Like John, many older individuals devise strategies that enable them to take advantage of resources available in several countries at the same time. They are a heterogeneous group, differently equipped to manage the challenges they face. Some acquire the legal, social, and financial resources they need by moving to another country. Some stay behind and combine various resources—paid help, public benefits, local kin support, and economic remittances—to construct a resource environment for themselves and their loved ones. And, as we saw in Chapter 1, younger family members from poor countries are often forced to leave their aging parents behind so they can earn abroad the money needed for their care. Those who leave often hire migrant workers to look after elderly relatives in their absence.

The 2011 movie *The Best Exotic Marigold Hotel* depicts one of many new facilities throughout the Global South that cater to older migrants from the Global North. In the film, the British retirees who relocate to Jaipur, India, for its cheaper cost of living and easier, more interesting lifestyle all live happily ever after. Similar facilities are opening in Europe, where some retirees move from wealthier to less-expensive countries. Senior citizens' homes in Poland, for example, are designed to attract well-heeled Germans whose euros stretch farther across the border (Pytel and Rahmonov 2019). Locals, for whom the cost of care is out of reach, must then turn to less-expensive facilities, hire migrant care workers, rely on their families or communities, or seek help in a country with even lower costs. In Japan, because there are so many elderly citizens without enough young people to care for them, the government has relaxed visa and citizenship regulations to make it easier for migrant care workers to enter (Lan 2018a). In late-developing societies, like Korea and Taiwan, the expansion of public benefits inspires some older migrants to move between countries of origin and destination so they can take advantage of benefits in both (Sun 2018, 2021).

The resource environments in which older migrants and their caregivers are situated are increasingly hybridized and stratified. The different sets of resources they have access to sharply reveal the myriad risks and opportunities that stem from the intersection of aging, migration, and social inequality. We focus here on the experiences of four groups negotiating later-life transitions: (1) international retirement migrants, (2) parents whose children emigrate abroad, (3) older immigrants who return to their countries of origin, and (4) migrant elder care workers.[2]

One of the state's primary roles during this life cycle stage is to mandate what kinds of resources can and should be provided across borders and who is eligible for them. In some national and regional contexts, such as the European Union (EU), various social protections for seniors can be transferred across borders.[3] Nation-states, however, can limit public benefits to residents, tying eligibility to being present for a certain amount of time (Hunter 2018). In addition, even within the EU, the right to export means-tested benefits is not guaranteed (Gehring 2017). The role of the state is both downsized and supersized. It is not just a provider but a gatekeeper that actively regulates the allocation and availability of resources.

Finally, the cases of transnational aging and elder care make clear that legal citizenship does not always guarantee social rights. It is true that citizenship allows older migrants to access important care resources and improve their well-being (Newendorp 2020). But, as we spell out in these pages, the social rights of older migrants are not only regulated but also challenged, even when they are naturalized citizens of destination states. The general public often criticizes them for receiving public benefits without having spent enough time working to earn them (Ho 2019; Sun 2021). While some elders are able to create plentiful resource environments, the resulting exchange of people, money, services, and information between societies creates new dilemmas and controversies. These dilemmas can be resolved, we argue, by clearly defining the basic legal and social rights that citizens and noncitizens are entitled to and by specifying which entities are responsible for fulfilling them.

Rebooting the Golden Years: International Retirement Migration

Julia and her husband are American citizens. They lived most of their lives in the United States but relocated to Lake Chapala, in Mexico, when he was diagnosed with Parkinson's disease (Sunil et al. 2007). For them, the border between Mexico and the United States clearly divides two different resource environments. In the United States, the costs of living and health care were beyond their reach. In Mexico, with permanent residency permits, they became eligible to purchase coverage from the national insurance program for a small monthly premium.[4] Not only was their health plan affordable, it was also comprehensive, covering treatments for all major illnesses. The money they saved allowed Julia to hire round-the-clock care for her husband. "We came to Mexico because we could find affordable care," she said. "It has been a perfect solution" (Sunil et al. 2007, 500).

Julia and her husband are what researchers call international retirement migrants (IRMs) (Toyota 2006; Zechner 2017). Older people from countries across the world, be it Asia (e.g., Japan and Korea), Northern Europe (e.g., Britain, Norway, and Sweden), or North America (e.g., the United States) move to less-developed but more affordable societies such as Spain, Thailand, Mexico, Indonesia, Malaysia, and the Philippines for the last stage of their lives (Vega and Hirschman 2019; Božić 2006; Casado-Díaz and Casado-Díaz 2014; Ono 2015; Wong and Musa 2015). They seek better weather, a more manageable and affordable lifestyle, and less-expensive medical care. They meet their needs by creating transnational resource environments.

Why and How Do Seniors Migrate?

Retirees circulate in a variety of ways (Horn and Schweppe 2015; Walsh and Näre 2016; Pickering et al. 2019). Some migrate seasonally, dividing their time between two or more locales. Some settle in the host society permanently and rarely go back home. Still others settle in a new place for an extended period before eventually relocating to their country of origin. In today's world, seniors with enough financial resources enjoy a range of choices about where to live, how long to stay, and, perhaps most importantly, what strategies to use to meet their social protection needs (King et al. 2017). Less well-off retirees enjoy far fewer choices. Some even "retire" in name only, as they must continue to work in some form to support themselves and their families (Gavanas and Calzada 2016).

What motivates these seniors? They may be "amenity seekers" who move for cultural and recreational opportunities. They may be, like Julia and her husband, "care seekers" who want good medical and long-term care (Sunil et al. 2007). Sociologist Maria Casado-Díaz (2006) found that the Northern European retirees living in Spain whom she spoke with sought sunshine, affordable health care, and a lower cost of living. Well-off Japanese retirees are more likely to move to a highly developed country like Korea, while those with fewer savings generally move to more affordable Southeast Asian destinations, where their pensions last longer. As social science scholars Thang, Sone, and Toyota (2012, 243) note, "Since 2006, Western countries or locations such as Australia, New Zealand, Hawaii and Canada are gradually giving way to Southeast Asian destinations such as Malaysia, Thailand, the Philippines and Indonesia because of the lower cost of living, tropical climate and their relatively close distance from Japan."

Where one moves depends largely on one's social networks. The risks and costs of movement drop considerably if friends or relatives are already nearby, allowing migrants to easily construct community. While many international retirement migrants (IRMs) consider themselves cosmopolitan citizens, they still need social support. These retirees typically create or integrate into communities with co-ethnics who come from similar national and linguistic backgrounds. They interact in only limited ways with the local population (Sampaio et al. 2018; Wong and Musa 2015). They also try to maintain connections with families and friends back home (King et al. 2019). These ties are not only a source of emotional support but generate valuable resources such as advice, company, information, and hands-on care (Oliver 2013).

Seniors' choices are gendered (King et al. 2017). Western male retirees may look to the Global South as a place to form a romantic relationship with a local partner. Thailand is a prime example. Not only do their savings stretch far, but social norms allow these men to date or marry Thai women who are significantly younger than themselves (Howard 2008). Similarly, widowed or recently divorced Japanese women migrate to Southeast Asia to escape oppressive kinship networks back home. They feel liberated in Thailand and Australia because they are no longer beholden to the strict gender norms in place in Japan (Toyota and Thang 2012).[5] As a Japanese retiree in Perth put it, "In Japan, you can't be different from the others, as others will start to say behind your back and ostracize you" (Thang et al. 2012, 250). These studies speak to the intricate connection between what IRMs desire and the social protections they need. Both can be satisfied by migrating to a new country where it is possible to make a fresh start.

Shaping (and Reshaping) the Resource Environment

The resource environments that IRMs create pose new opportunities and challenges for the state and the market. Many places have "underground markets" for transnational elder care (Geest et al. 2004). The city of Genoa, Italy, for example, became a major destination for retirement migrants.

Because the city's port and manufacturing sectors are in steep decline, numerous young people are ready and waiting to provide hands-on care for older migrants in exchange for money and accommodations. These transactions frequently happen outside the formal labor market (Geest et al. 2004, 445). Changes in the destination country's medical industry also have unintended consequences for local residents. Many Western retirees, for instance, move to Thailand because medical tourism is booming there. The country offers excellent private hospitals staffed by professionals trained in the West (Howard 2008). While these institutions do not cater exclusively to older foreigners, the fact that these elders can pay transforms them into the primary target population rather than locals.

State policies regarding immigration, settlement, and the protections that "settled" retirees are entitled to also strongly affect their resource environments (Gustafson 2008). Some countries purposefully put in place policies to attract migrant retirees because governments see them as potentially profitable. The Thai Longstay Management Company Limited, in which the Tourism Authority of Thailand is a major shareholder, was created in 2001 to promote retirement to Thailand. The government created new visa categories for foreign-born older migrants, but they were only open to people who could prove they could pay for their own care (Toyota 2006). An applicant, writes sociologist Mika Toyota (2006, 523), had "to be over 50 years old and was required to pay a deposit of 800,000 baht (about US$20,000) into a [local] bank." Malaysia offers a "multiple-entry social visit pass under the MM2H [Malaysia My Second Home Program]." The "'Special Resident Retiree's Visa (SRRV)' in the Philippines, and '*lansia or lanjut usia (retirement)*' visas in Indonesia" also signal to retirees that they are welcome but only if they have enough money in their bank accounts (Ono 2008, 154).

Here again, regional institutions work alongside national policies to shape the lives of older migrants. The classic example is the European Union. As EU citizens, retirement migrants have the option to export their social security from one member country to another.[6] In Norway, a member of the European Economic Area and, thus, equal partner in the EU internal market, the state actually developed a business for transnational elder care: Norwegian municipalities create and manage nursing homes in Spain that are designed not only for patients who come directly from Norway but also for members of the Norwegian diaspora. The Alicante region recently became home to a number of new geriatric and rehabilitation centers run by Norwegian municipalities and staffed almost exclusively by Norwegians. While these state-sponsored efforts are rare, they may signal important future trends (Gustafson 2008; Fuchs 2007).

In the European Union, however, what one is eligible for on paper is not always easy to access in real life. Despite the transferability of social security, EU citizens typically cannot access means-tested benefits in countries of settlement. The right to export pension entitlements across member states is protected but social assistance for the disadvantaged "do[es] not fall under the scope of the regulation" (Gehring 2017, 5; D'Addio and Cavalleri 2015). As political scientists Ackers and Dwyer (2004, 457) note, "a migrant's social status in the host state and the welfare claims they can make there vary considerably and depend upon their present or past relationship with the paid labour market." This also explains why retirees who live on social welfare are less able to move within the European Union than those who are better off. "Those who are financially better off have more freedom to choose their preferred migratory pattern and have more options to maintain a dual lifestyle," writes legal scholar Anoeshka Gehring (2017, 6). "These migrants are also less affected by legal gates that may limit, channel, and regulate their mobility because states do not have the capacity to impose rules on the export of their pension payments."

In fact, well-off retirement migrants rarely depend on just the state for protection. Instead, they purchase what they need from the market. Many Dutch migrants who retire to Spain purchase private health insurance, even though they are eligible for public medical insurance programs (Gehring 2017). They want to make sure they get high-quality care and can avoid long lines and language barriers. Elder care in Spain is largely privatized or provided by family members. In Sweden, the government generously supports seniors. Still, Swedish retiree couples generally hire caregivers, especially when one spouse is no longer self-sufficient (Gavanas and Calzada 2016).

But, again, what is the state's responsibility to its elderly citizens? What support should the state be expected to provide to older persons who live outside its borders for extended periods? When countries market themselves as retiree destinations, what should they be expected to provide? While destination states see retirement migrants as potential paying customers, they are hesitant or politically unable to treat them as their own citizens. They tend to see only young people or highly skilled migrants as capable of social integration and of contributing positively to national development (Brandhorst et al. 2019).

What happens to immobile populations, both the locals among whom retirees come to live and those in countries of origin whom migrants leave behind?

For one thing, when retirees with savings come to stay, a second stream of qualified service providers generally follows, ready to meet their demands. The result is a sharp rise in demand for supplies and in the cost of care, which local elders are least equipped to deal with (Dossa and Coe 2017). Even some retired migrants from Northern Europe feel that traditional retirement destinations are now unaffordable and are searching for new areas that are less expensive and touristic (King et al. 2019).

Germany and surrounding countries illustrate this concern. Because of its rapid demographic transition, together with the high cost and shortage of labor, Germany has become a leader in outsourcing elder care. Even though long-term care insurance has been mandatory in Germany since 1995, it is still too expensive for many families. Therefore, less expensive care for the elderly in long-term care facilities of neighboring countries like Poland, Slovakia, or the Czech Republic is a more attractive option. In 2012, about 7,000 German pensioners were living in facilities abroad (Connolly 2012; Deutsche Wirtschaftsnachrichten 2014; Schölgens 2013).

Private companies are quickly jumping on this bandwagon, developing transnational models for long-term care, most commonly in Eastern Europe and Southeast Asia. In Eastern Europe, a group of German and local private investors received support from the European Union to upgrade elder-care facilities. While they created high-end institutions that provided excellent care to elderly Germans who could afford them, these facilities were beyond the reach of many local Eastern Europeans. Germany's inability to deal effectively with its aging population and to reform its long-term care sector, therefore, disproportionately burdened Eastern Europe by importing net-payers (i.e., young immigrants who come to Germany to provide elder care) into the social security system and by exporting net-users (i.e., German retirees who move to Poland, Slovakia, or the Czech Republic for more affordable long-term care). Public debates about these issues can become emotional. The Sozialverband Deutschland (Social Association of Germany), a German organization that advocates for social rights, called the export of the elderly a "deportation" (Cohen 2015; Connolly 2012).

When migrants access services in ways seen as displacing local populations, a rise of anti-immigrant sentiments typically follows. Tensions are often characterized as "cultural conflicts." For example, in Bocas del Toro,

Panama, the presence of lifestyle migrants, about a third of whom are retirees, has increased "pressure on social services and infrastructure, while imported values and expectations ten[d] to clash with traditional ways of life and influence behavior, particularly in younger generations" (Spalding 2013, 80). Similarly, in a survey of local people's attitudes toward migrants retiring in Turkey, 63 percent of respondents disapproved of foreigners buying property and 62 percent preferred not to live in foreigner-populated neighborhoods (Balkır and Kırkulak 2009, 136–137). The decisions of retired migrants, therefore, have profound consequences for people who stay put.

Parents Whose Children Emigrate Abroad: Staying behind, Moving Abroad, and Migrating Transnationally

Gurazie and Fari live in Albania but their children are all working abroad (Vullnetari and King 2008). While they miss them dearly, they recognize the limited economic opportunities postcommunist Albania offers. They also depend upon the remittances their children send home. This money is a sign of their children's love and appreciation. Even if they are physically separated, Gurazie and Fari know they are not forgotten or abandoned.

Parents like Gurazie and Fari are what scholars call "left-behind" or "stay-behind" parents (Sun 2017). They have much in common with the left-behind children described in Chapter 1. Some of these individuals cannot afford to join their children or are unable to reunite with them because of visa restrictions. Others live transnationally, spending part of the year with their children and grandchildren and then returning home. Some relocate permanently. Each strategy strongly affects the resource environment they have access to.

After living apart for some time, and despite concerns for their aging parents, the migrant generation is frequently reluctant to return home. They grow accustomed to life in the countries where they settle and they want to continue to work toward their professional and educational goals (Kim 2012; Lee and Zhou 2015; Sun 2012). Indeed, the so-called sandwich generation, the cohort of people raising children and caring for elderly parents at the same time, often left for better educational or job opportunities to begin with.

Migrant adult children must figure out ways to support their at-home parents (Baldassar et al. 2007; Kim 2012; King 2012; Sun 2017). One is to provide material and symbolic resources. They visit, send money, and pay for short-term care (Amin and Ingman 2014; Kim 2012; King et al. 2014; Sun 2012; Zechner 2008). They supplement the support parents receive from other kin and from public benefits (Lee et al. 2010; Sun 2012, 2017). Migration studies scholar Valentina Mazzucato (2007) found that the money Ghanaian migrants sent back from the Netherlands allowed their parents to afford better housing and personal and medical care. Jeehum Kim (2012) found that male Korean migrants who could not return to take care of their relatives themselves "remitted" other family members—usually wives and children—to do so. The unequal gendered division of caregiving is, in this way, reinforced rather than undermined, even in this transnational environment.

Children also support their parents emotionally and socially. Just as migrant mothers stay actively involved in the daily lives of their children through the internet, communication technologies allow migrant children to be present and involved in the everyday lives of their parents (Baldassar 2016; Millard et al. 2018). In some cases, children continue to coordinate their parents' care, even over long distances (Ciobanu et al. 2017). Some of the Italian women that Loretta Baldassar (2014) studied in Perth, Australia, for example, still supervised the daily care routines of their parents back home.

To organize and sustain care via long distance, migrants need strong, on-the-ground networks they can turn to in an emergency. Being able to do so depends not only on what supports migrants provide from afar (i.e., sending remittances or not) but also on how family caregivers back home value migrants' efforts to "protect" and provide for them (i.e., whether they experience empowerment or disempowerment). In their study of adult children caring for parents left behind in China, sociologists Ken Sun and Nazli Kibria (2022) identified four types of dynamics between family members abroad and at home: (1) collaboration, (2) intrusion and interference, (3) voluntary takeover, and (4) feeling left behind. While some nonmigrant caregivers view the financial and material assistance provided by migrants as generous contributions, others perceive it as inappropriate meddling. Still others appoint themselves as the "moral head of the family" who is forced to step in because their siblings abroad do so little. Finally, some migrants just feel left behind. They experience their brothers' and sisters' lack of involvement in elder care as a sign of the power imbalance between them. They see these "selfish" and "apathetic" family members as letting the family down.

Not surprisingly, the state plays a central role in these decisions. It not only strongly influences which countries migrants move to but whether or not it is possible for the family to reunite. In Australia, the price of a family reunification visa is exorbitant, costing as much as AUD$50,000 (around US$32,000), with processing times of up to "30 years" (Brandhorst et al. 2019, 6). The points-based system in Canada, which favors working-age applicants with language proficiency and higher education, significantly reduces the chances of elderly parents moving to live with their children (Ho 2019). Sociologist Yanqiu Rachel Zhou found that many Chinese seniors who traveled to Canada late in life returned home because they were unable to get a residency visa. The visa application, they felt, was unnecessarily "complicated, restrictive, discriminatory and expensive":

> To get a visitor visa they had to pass the physical check-up when requested to do so, and present various kinds of evidence, such as a notarized bank statement and proof of home ownership, to prove they had no intention of staying in Canada illegally. Some had to travel from their home towns to cities with Canadian Embassies or Consulates, and some were rejected for a visa the first time, and had to go back, and wait for months, and re-apply. (Zhou 2012, 236)

As a result, many parents turn to temporary visitor visas to be able to spend extended periods with their children (Karl and Torres 2015). Here again, family relations can get complicated. Because they have few social ties and little cultural understanding of the destination-country context, intergenerational conflicts arise. This happens because one generation depends too much on the other (Dossa and Coe 2017; Horn and Schweppe 2015; Walsh and Näre 2016; Sampaio et al. 2018; Sun 2017; Vullnetari and King 2008, Solari 2018). In one study, Indian grandparents who came to help raise their grandchildren, for example, called the United States the "land of no time" (Lamb 2009, 218–219). They resented that their grandchildren's art classes or soccer games took precedence over their visits with relatives or to the local temple (Levitt 2009). Similarly, Chinese seniors in another study described the United States as a "lonely paradise" (a place where life was peaceful but monotonous) and their homeland as a "happy hell" (where the quality of life was less than ideal but more dynamic) (Sun 2012, 1248).

Reunited seniors also struggle to get adequate care (Purkayastha et al. 2012). The struggles are especially dramatic in countries like the United States that lack universal healthcare coverage. A survey of Chinese seniors living with their children in Los Angeles found they were at higher risk of poor parent–child relations and declines in psychological well-being (Guo, Xu et al. 2016, 1473). Even when recently arrived senior migrants looked to their children for support, the younger generation could not live up to their expectations (Guo et al. 2020). Because the unpaid domestic labor they perform is not formally recognized as productive work, these seniors rarely qualify for public benefits. They stop visiting or come less frequently because they are afraid that they will experience a health emergency and be ineligible for care (Zhou 2012). This becomes even more of an issue when these individuals become the "frail elderly" (Sun and Cao 2022). It is much more difficult to manage care for the enfeebled and infirm who can no longer care for themselves and who require a unique set of policies and programs of their own (King et al. 2017; Guo, Liu et al. 2016).

Because destination states frequently restrict access to basic services based on legal status, nongovernmental organizations (NGOs) figure much more prominently in seniors' resource environments. Religious institutions are particularly important. They offer seniors company, information, and social support, allowing them to create new social networks that help them adjust to their new homes (Zhang and Zhan 2009). In Australia, community organizations help seniors develop digital literacy and set up home computers so they can keep in touch with their friends and family (Millard et al. 2018, 145). Health organizations advocate for culturally and linguistically sensitive services for aging immigrants (Mui and Shibusawa 2008; Victor et al. 2012). Many hospitals or clinics in major immigrant-receiving cities in the United States, Canada, and Australia try to meet the needs of aging Chinese immigrants by offering care in Mandarin or Cantonese (Ho 2019, 46).

These services vary significantly by place and are often few and far between in new immigrant destinations (see Marrow 2011; Schmalzbauer 2014). They depend upon the cultures surrounding social welfare provision. In Australia, migrant organizations have stepped in to provide care in a context characterized by a widespread acceptance of the rights of racial and ethnic minorities coupled with the privatization of social services (Brandhorst et al. 2019). Germany, in contrast, offers fewer services to older immigrant newcomers because the expectation is that most people migrated and assimilated long ago. Fewer NGOs, hospitals, and long-term care facilities are prepared to provide culturally sensitive services, such as translation, to senior newcomers (Brandhorst et al. 2019).

The Warmth of Familiar Suns: Aging and Return Migration

When Saleem left Morocco to work in France, he never imagined he would remain there until he reached his sixties. While he still misses his family and friends and makes regular visits to see them, he believes resettling in Morocco would be difficult, if not impossible, at this late date. His need for health care is his primary concern. In fact, he never leaves France for more than three months at a stretch to make sure that he remains eligible for French health benefits. As health and social policy research Alistair Hunter discovered, many elderly male migrants remain in France because they have access to better health care than they would have back home (Hunter 2018, 85).

In contrast, Mrs. Chin returned to Taiwan after three decades in the United States. Her health declined precipitously following a failed spinal surgery (Sun 2021). Hers was a practical, if painful, decision. She knew she would become almost entirely dependent on her children and grandchildren. The bright future she imagined for them would grow dimmer if they had to spend so much time taking care of her. She opted instead to move to an assisted-living facility in Taiwan. While, in the United States, she had too much savings to qualify for a government-supported facility, in Taiwan she could easily afford a spacious one-bedroom apartment in a high-end assisted-living facility. She speaks highly of Taiwan's National Health Insurance (NHI), a universal, single-payer health program established in 1996, which is cheaper and more comprehensive than Medicare in the United States. She also found communicating with doctors easier in her own language.

Because most migrants move in order to work, questions about where they belong come to the fore when they retire. They often make a clear distinction between the role of countries of origin and destination. For example, Ghanaian immigrants working as caregivers for aging Americans viewed the United States as "a place to work" instead of "a place to receive care" (Coe 2017a, 151). For them, "an elderhood at home could be enjoyed, but old age abroad was miserable" (Coe 2017a, 149). As soon as they reached the age of 55, many hopped on the next plane, banking on the expectation that the remittances they had sent their siblings, cousins, and even distant relatives over the years would translate into concrete help toward their reintegration.

Yet many of these individuals did not factor into their decision-making just how much their homelands had changed during their absence—changes that make it difficult to adjust, to achieve the social mobility they dreamed of, or to call upon social networks for support (Sun 2018). Some older Ghanaian returnees, for instance, were surprised to learn that their hard-earned savings were not enough to support the lifestyles they planned for. The cost of living in Ghana had risen remarkably during their absence. Nor would their relatives back home let them easily relinquish their role as dependable economic provider (Coe 2017a). African migrants in France gave up hope of depending on family members back home, whom they saw as having become too greedy and materialistic (Hunter 2018). Because migrants tend to dream of their homelands as places of plentiful resources rather than settings of constraint, the longer they stay away, the larger the disconnect between aspirations and reality grows (Levitt and Lamba-Nieves 2011).

As disillusionment with their social networks increases, return migrants look instead to the market and the state. With elder care a big business, senior-care residences and in-home services, including part-time and live-in caregivers, are on the rise in countries like Peru, Ghana, Taiwan, India, and mainland China (Coe 2017b; Leinaweaver 2010; Sun 2021). But elder return migrants' interactions with the state can be fraught with tensions and misunderstandings. To be eligible for health care or subsidized housing, they must show they have been residing in the country for a minimum period. As a result, even people who want to return home permanently cannot afford to do so because they risk losing access to the social protections they rely on in receiving countries (Gilbertson 2009).

When returnees lack savings or earn too little during their working lives, all too often they depend upon noncontributory income support that cannot be transferred abroad (Böcker and Hunter 2017, 355). Although some states, such as Spain, France, and the Netherlands, have tried schemes allowing return migrants to receive means-tested public benefits in their homelands, these programs are fairly uncommon and limited in scope. Spain provides a one-time lump sum payment rather than lifelong benefits for senior returnees. In the Netherlands, even senior migrants who are now Dutch citizens are ineligible to transfer benefits from abroad (Böcker and Hunter 2017).[7]

As countries of origin grow wealthier, they develop entitlements and welfare programs that strongly influence migrant decisions (Wang 2004). In fact, sociologist Ken Sun (2014b) found numerous Taiwanese migrants who returned to take advantage of the NHI. As their health declined, they saw these benefits as a windfall, especially given the rising cost of health care in the countries where they had settled. As in the case of John, with whom we began this chapter, the local population often criticizes returnees harshly for "milking" public benefits just as the NHI faced increasing deficits.

Migrants' ability to construct sufficiently robust transnational resource environments gets a boost when states collaborate across borders. While these are still relatively rare, a few bi- and multilateral efforts address seniors' needs. For example, senior citizens who worked most of their lives inside the United States but now live outside it can apply to receive their social security payments in their countries of residence (US Social Security Administration n.d.). The European Union's multilateral social security agreements, designed to enhance the portability of social protection rights within the European Union, allows older migrants to transfer their social security benefits across member states relatively easily (D'Addio and Cavalleri 2015). Indeed, depending upon where they worked and the nature of their entitlements based on their current residency, some migrants construct resource environments from sources based in multiple countries of destination.

Issues regarding transnational elder care do not end with death. Rather, death care—services regarding the transportation, cremation, or burial of the dead—is a concern that migrants and states also have to grapple with. While some long-term migrants wish to be buried in the countries where they settled, many more want to be buried back home (Sun 2021; Félix 2011). This final trip is relatively easy to arrange when families can pay. Less well-off families must depend on family and community networks to come up with the necessary financial support. The same hometown associations through which migrants channel money and supplies to support development back home also support transnational burials (Smith et al. 2004). Some municipal and national agencies, such as the Institute for Mexicans Living Abroad, also provide funding for families in need (Félix 2011).

Migrant Workers Who Care for the Elderly

Rita Sarpong moved halfway around the world to care for seniors in Massachusetts so she could make a better life for her family in Ghana. Most weeks, Rita works more than 100 hours (Matchan 2018). In the mornings, she cares for a 90-year-old retired insurance agent with severe arthritis before she drives nearly an hour for her evening shift caring for an infirm 80-year-old woman. Even after such long work days, Rita still comes up short once she sends money home. She, and the many other home health aides like her, frequently go underpaid. They are subject to harassment and abuse against which they have little or no legal recourse.

Rita is part of a migration flow set off when certain countries try to attract well-off elderly migrants by promising them a secure retirement. While they migrate to get affordable, readily available care, Rita migrates to provide it (Dodson and Zincavage 2007; Huang et al. 2012; Liang 2014). In many cases, these are 3-D jobs (dirty, dangerous, and demanding) that native-born workers reject as too difficult, poorly paid, and without prospects for advancement. Without migrant care workers like Rita, therefore, the rapidly growing population of seniors in East Asia, Northern Europe, and North America would not get the care they need.

In addition to home-based care, migrants also provide much of the direct health and companion care in formal institutional settings. As *Boston Globe* reporter Linda Matchan (2018) explained, nearly 50 percent of nursing home workers and home health aides in the New England area are foreign-born women from less-developed regions like West Africa and Latin America. Across the globe, these women make important contributions to the resource environments of others while their own resource environments remain painfully thin.

Governments, which need migrants to care for their elderly citizens, regulate the migrant domestic and health care worker sectors in different ways. To address large-scale labor shortfalls, Japan, Singapore, and Korea signed multilateral treaties to bring in enough elder care workers to staff their hospitals and facilities (Huang et al. 2012, 202). Japan, for example, signed the Economic Partnership Agreement (EPA) with Indonesia (effective in May 2008), the Philippines (October 2008), and Vietnam (October 2009) to recruit qualified nurses and certified health care workers (Lan 2018a; Toyota 2006). All EPA workers in Japan are employed by hospitals or care facilities, rather than in private homes.

As we have repeatedly seen, the same workers who care for the vulnerable are extremely vulnerable themselves (Coe 2019). They regularly face discrimination and harassment, as social norms about who should care for whom are strongly influenced by racial, class, and gender biases. One study found that agencies in Hong Kong, Singapore, and Taiwan sharply distinguished between migrant workers from Indonesia and the Philippines. They depicted Filipinas as better educated, English-speaking providers who could stimulate children's development. In contrast, Indonesian domestic workers embodied traditional Muslim values and therefore had a "natural" propensity to be patient, loyal, and hardworking—qualities needed for elder care (Lan 2006). By associating the elderly with "images of decay, disease and disgust" these agencies produce ethno-national and racialized femininities that differentiate the markets for elder care and childcare workers (Huang et al. 2012, 198).

In countries such as the United States, where nursing homes receive government funding through Medicare and Medicaid, the institutions and their workers are subject to greater regulation (Coe 2019). But different levels of workers are subject to different levels of regulation. Social policy scholars Lisa Dodson and Rebekah Zincavage (2007) found migrant and nonmigrant women who work as certified nursing assistants (CNAs), a fast-growing but only minimally regulated occupation, to be particularly at risk. They were more likely to be paid below minimum wage, forced to suffer abuse from employers and clients, and penalized for taking sick or personal leave. They were discouraged from expressing grief over the death of a client because it posed "a potential disruption to an orderly workflow" (Dodson and Zincavage 2007, 917). Sociologists Dan Clawson and Naomi Gerstel (2014, 10) found that CNAs "faced a highly punitive sick leave policy under which they could be fired even if they still had sick time available and even if they were taking an epileptic or asthmatic child to the hospital, a circumstance covered by the FMLA [Family and Medical Leave Act in the United States]." Very few of the CNAs these researchers encountered knew of the FMLA or their legal rights; instead, "the nursing home's records showed that over a six-month period only a single missed day was recorded as an FMLA day" (Clawson and Gerstel 2014, 10).

Conclusion

In a globalizing world, the rights of older persons to protection and care—as citizens, human beings, consumers, and kin or community members—are fulfilled transnationally through a hybridized mix of resources culled from countries of origin and destination. As states redefine social and legal citizenship—and, by so doing, extend, block, regulate, and outsource social protections for noncitizens and residents—market actors emerge as important purveyors of services for those who can afford them. These solutions work for a segment of the older population, especially in wealthier destination countries, who have many more choices about how to organize their care. Market-based care, however, leaves behind those who lack resources and exacerbates already stark inequalities. Among the most vulnerable are elder care workers themselves.

What, then, is unique about transnational social protection at this later stage of the life cycle? Notably, this is the population most in need. As demographer Donatella Lanari and political scientist Odoardo Bussini (2012, 936) write, immigrants with blue-collar backgrounds "are particularly at risk of health deterioration, since most changes in health occur in middle and old age." This concern applies especially to the growing numbers of "frail elderly" who suffer from several chronic conditions and are unable to live independently. Just as social welfare provisions are shrinking, ever more seniors who are living longer and longer find themselves far from family members who can care for them.

As we have seen, the portability of public benefits allows some retired migrants to bring their resources with them and retire wherever they would like. Many others, who depend on means-tested social welfare, face restrictions to their mobility because nation-states limit the eligibility for and timing of access to certain state-sponsored benefits (Gehring 2017; Hunter 2018). Even when returning migrants are legal citizens, their access to state-sponsored benefits still provokes controversy (Ho 2019; Newendorp 2020; Sun 2021).

The many individuals who worked for years in one country only to retire in another need access to the benefits they earned during their working years. Relying only on what the state provides in the countries they return to is to drain resources from those who support these systems as taxpayers. Public systems are stressed, even without large numbers of retirement migrants. Think, for example, what would happen if even a small fraction of Mexican Americans living in the United States moved back to Mexico after retirement. Their needs would overwhelm the Mexican health care system. Should they not be able to bring with them at least some of the benefits they earned during their many years of work in the United States? Don't governments bear some measure of responsibility for noncitizens who worked productively for many years inside their borders? Shouldn't we remind those who accuse elderly returnees of unfairly accessing health and social services that the remittances they sent back over decades provided essential support to their family members back home?

Interdependence is key to addressing elder care across borders, both for elders and for their caregivers. Elder care in the Global North depends upon the labor power of younger migrants from the Global South. This mutual need is evident across multiple cases that differ only in their details. As birth rates fall and the aging population grows across Europe and North America, it will only deepen. Working environments require proper regulation. A loosely regulated elder care market can result in protections for seniors at the expense of paid caregivers' well-being (Peng 2018). Social protections for elder-care workers, therefore, are just as important a part of our story as the need for social protections for the elderly.

6
Conclusion
Reimagining Communities and Reconfiguring the Safety Net

Our book challenges much of the conventional wisdom about how and where social welfare is provided across the life cycle. What has changed? We used to assume that people had access to social protections based on their citizenship and residence, but many people now study, live, work, and retire in countries other than the places where they are citizens. We expected states to provide some level of basic protection to their citizens, but now, even countries that offered generous protections in the past are dramatically cutting back on social welfare provision. We took for granted that some types of workers would get some benefits through their workplace, but many jobs no longer come with health insurance or pensions. People employed in temporary or informal jobs or in the gig economy are often left to fend for themselves. In these pages, we show how, in response, a new, hybrid transnational social protection (HTSP) regime has emerged that complements, supplements, or, in some cases, substitutes for national social welfare systems as we knew them.

What Have We Learned?

Social protection, therefore, is no longer solely organized around citizenship, geography, or social networks. Rather, individuals cobble together the protections they need to manage risk and enhance opportunities from multiple resources and multiple places from the time they are born until the time they die. HTSP is *transnational* because it is not bounded by a single nation-state. In fact, it operates between—and within—multiple states, at multiple levels, including the subnational, national, regional, and international. HTSP is *hybrid* in that it does not depend upon a single source but combines multiple sources of protection including the state, the market, nongovernmental

Transnational Social Protection. Peggy Levitt, Erica Dobbs, Ken Chih-Yan Sun, and Ruxandra Paul,
Oxford University Press. © Oxford University Press 2023. DOI: 10.1093/oso/9780197666821.003.0007

organizations (NGOs), and individual social networks. The combination of these resources across and within states makes up what we call a *resource environment*. Each component of the resource environment operates according to a distinct logic, based on whether social protections are primarily understood as *constitutional rights, human rights, commodities,* or *community.* While, in most cases, these are all at work to varying degrees, the dominant logic, and how it combines with its counterparts, affects how plentiful or restrictive the resulting resource environment is. This denationalizing, de-territorializing, and decoupling of social benefits from citizenship status creates multiple opportunities for some and exacerbates risk for many others.

The world we describe is one in which increasing numbers of people live for extended periods outside their countries of citizenship without full rights or voice (*long-term residents without membership*). Increasingly, people are also *long-term members without residence.* They live outside their country of citizenship but still participate in some way in its political and economic life. These individuals span the socioeconomic spectrum, from poor migrants who are forced to move because they cannot support their families back home to highly educated professionals who can easily take advantage of opportunities available to them anywhere. A new form of stratification results that distinguishes those who are fully politically integrated in two places from those who are not protected anywhere. Migration redistributes inequality rather than decreases it. Moreover, social protection policies are never just about protection. They also function to politically coopt by making people dependent and, therefore, easier to control, or to repel by denying people the care they need and thereby forcing them to go elsewhere.

In the sections that follow, we revisit the different logics upon which HTSP is based, and the different opportunities and costs it gives rise to, that we believe policymakers urgently need to consider.

The State and Its Logic

The state remains the most important source of social protection for many households, whether directly, through social spending and public benefits, or indirectly, through labor regulations and immigration policy. Nevertheless, guaranteeing rights based on a constitutional logic has its limits. First, the extent to which social rights are ensured in national constitutions varies considerably from one country to another. Second, seeing social protection as a constitutional right links access to formal membership in the national political community, thereby giving preference to members who are physically present in the national territory. Therefore, policymakers concerned about addressing the discrepancy between insiders and outsiders might focus on fast-tracking naturalization or on strengthening policies that bolster multiculturalism and define national solidarity and inclusion in diversity- and immigration-friendly terms. They can also encourage country-of-origin actors to rethink their obligations to their citizens abroad by extending public benefits across borders, making them more portable, negotiating labor protections in receiving states, and supporting family dependents who remain back home.

As these pages make clear, however, in the decades since T. H. Marshall laid out his framework for civil, political, and social citizenship, the social contract between citizen and state has radically changed. States are supersizing and downsizing. Many states that provided generous social protections to their citizens in the past are now reducing, restricting, or outsourcing service provision. At the same time, some—including several countries where social welfare was minimal in the past—now extend protections to emigrants who are citizens without residence. In some cases, they also include certain benefits to individuals living within their borders who are not legal residents or citizens. The rise of HTSP, then, raises complicated questions that policymakers must grapple with: Who should receive protection and what is the future role of states in providing basic care? How much inequality and exposure to risk should governments tolerate within their borders? To what extent should countries of origin be held accountable for protecting their citizens abroad? Should those who do not cross borders be prioritized over those who do?

The Market and Its Logic

While many states are downsizing, more and more people need and want reliable, high-quality, affordable care. In response, a flourishing market for social protection has emerged. Marketization allows for and expands choice, puts the power in the hands of individuals, and makes citizens into active consumers rather than passive recipients of care. It grants individuals greater control over deciding what they want and where to get it. For policymakers who seek to reduce state involvement in social protection and who see potential benefits in heightened competition over social protection provision, the market is an attractive option. Private providers just want customers who can pay. They do not distinguish between citizen and noncitizen, only between consumers with money in their pockets or those without it. Market solutions treat inequality as natural and expected. For that reason, they absolve the state of its responsibility to manage risk, thereby further linking social protection to individual planning and personal responsibility. It is up to individuals to make this work on their own.

As we have argued, however, the market faces severe limitations when it comes to ensuring social protection and mitigating risk. Its primary weakness is that access to even the most basic level of protection is limited to those with sufficient economic resources. Since only individuals with money can buy health insurance or hire nannies or home health care providers, the market as a source of social protection is highly stratified. When the market prevails, the state's ability or willingness to remediate inequality is legally and institutionally limited.

Moreover, in countries where the market is the primary source of health care, competition between insurers and providers does not lower prices enough so that most people can afford care, as the US example makes abundantly clear. In Europe, countries like the Netherlands and Switzerland also have private health care systems where insurers compete for patients, but the government heavily subsidizes costs and closely regulates markets to keep health care within reach. Much of Europe, in fact, operates with these kinds of hybrid public–private models that are just emerging in the United States.

Market-based models also have a second key weakness: The "market" for a particular good or service is often created—or limited—by the state. As we described in Chapter 4, Blue Cross Blue Shield's Baja California plan is a transnational health insurance program: participants get their emergency care in the United States and their primary care in Mexico. As people in border regions often move back and forth to work, shop, or socialize, so transnational medical insurance effectively institutionalizes a set of informal arrangements already in place. Similar schemes, however, did not take shape in Texas, another border state with significant patient traffic between the United States and Mexico. Its state legislature blocked a similar proposal, underscoring the enduring power of the state in the social protection marketplace.

To maximize choice and improve access to the global market, policymakers might encourage the development of care options that are "migrant friendly," customized to meet migrants' needs. States could also actively educate their citizens about available opportunities not only nationally but abroad. It is important to remember, however, that a perfect market does not exist. Information is never entirely available nor transparent, few consumers are able to make completely informed decisions, and the market rarely regulates itself or spontaneously addresses the negative spillover effects it produces. More importantly, market-based solutions are contingent upon individual resources and do little to address the collective problems people face nationally and transnationally. Too much reliance on the market, therefore, severely undermines the state's commitment to protect the public good.

Community: NGOs and Social Networks as Alternatives

In a world where the state often cannot or will not provide, and the market is out of reach, local and international NGOs become major providers of social services to vulnerable individuals. Hometown associations (HTAs), for example, bring together migrant and nonmigrant members of sending communities to support health care, education, and infrastructure projects. Religious organizations frequently provide direct social services at all stages of the life cycle: They support families, run schools and universities, operate health care institutions, and advocate for labor rights. They are particularly active in providing for refugees, a uniquely vulnerable population. However, much of what religious institutions (and sometimes HTAs, for that matter) provide comes through formal or informal partnerships with the state or through the market: Hospital chains run by religious orders often depend on government contracts and private insurance as sources of revenue. Religious orders run "public" schools only when they are accredited by the state. As with the market, the role of NGOs in the resource environment is therefore not completely independent of the state. Religious institutions sometimes only provide services to beneficiaries who subscribe to their beliefs, or restrict access to those who do not.

That said, there are important outliers. In the cases of humanitarian emergencies, international civil society organizations such as the Red Cross step in to assist countries of destination where migrants face risks. In some cases, transnational NGOs intervene when governments are ill-equipped to care for even their own citizens. When it comes to global public health, for example, the Bill and Melinda Gates Foundation is one of the largest funders of global health programs. It supports disease prevention, immunization, and vaccination programs around the world and provides major contributions to global health governance institutions, including the World Health Organization.

NGOs not only provide direct services, they are also important advocates for providing protections to migrants. Unions and other labor-related organizations play a key role in pushing states and employers to recognize the rights of vulnerable workers, regardless of their immigration status. As we have seen, though, the ability of unions to act as effective advocates is dependent on their recognition by the state: In places where their political status is tenuous, they have a harder time winning or maintaining social protection for migrants and citizens alike. In cases where national and transnational NGOs which support social protection for migrants are less entangled with the state, they may also be less able to move or maintain policy.

The role of family and community social networks is a consistent thread in state-, market-, and NGO-based approaches to social protection. Not only are they a source of direct care, they are also a source of funding and information about where to find it. As the state downsizes as a social protection provider and more people must purchase services from the market, those with limited resources become even more reliant on their social networks. It becomes their personal responsibility to identify and procure the protections they need and to navigate the often cumbersome and confusing bureaucracies that provide them. The problems with this are abundantly clear. Support from family and friends, especially those who have limited resources themselves, is unreliable, noncontractual, and unlikely to cover all of a family's needs. It is much more difficult for noncitizens who are not fluent in the local language and are unfamiliar with how local institutions work to navigate the system on their own. In many cases, even if individuals know where to go, they are afraid to use services because of their undocumented status. Recognizing this, policymakers and service providers have a big public education problem on their hands. They need to make sure that potential beneficiaries know where to find the services they need and are eligible for and that they feel safe enough to use them.

International Law, the State, and the Logic of Human Rights

Since the risks that migrants face are transnational, it might be tempting for policymakers to look to shifting social protection provision to supranational institutions as an answer to some of these challenges. After all, successful interventions involve adapting the scale of the solution to the scale of the problem. In addition, international conventions treat rights as endowed by personhood rather than on the basis of citizenship or on the individual's ability to purchase them. As such, they try to mitigate discrimination and prioritize vulnerable migrant categories that social welfare provision through employers or national insurance systems leave behind.

Nevertheless, progress has been slow to adopt this vision of social protection as a human right. First, governments traditionally prioritize citizens over noncitizens. Many countries lack the capacity to take care of their own nationals, let alone the noncitizens living within their borders. Second, international conventions and protocols are not enforceable. They rely on signatories to honor their commitments. Because, as we have repeatedly seen, signatories often implement their commitments selectively, migrants cannot depend upon them. Market considerations rather than a commitment to basic social protections for all are generally a much more effective regulatory "stick" (R. Paul 2017). Third, actually putting social protections as universal human rights into practice would require a significant supersizing of state provision to cover all the people physically present in a national territory, regardless of their legal status. This is because the institutions that currently promulgate these protocols and conventions lack the capacity to implement them. To achieve anything approximating this, policymakers in countries of both origin and destination would need to prioritize, expand, and actually create mechanisms to provide the social protections based on personhood that are codified in international law. Were social protection to move in this more humanitarian-based direction, policymakers would face the difficult challenge of convincing their electorates to accept an expanded social safety net for noncitizens at the same time that protections for citizens are decreasing.

Putting It Together

In the hybrid transnational social protection regime that we describe, partnerships between governments, international organizations, civil society, and the private sector blur the lines between state and nonstate provision. Even so, the state's role is central. Its priorities—for market-based solutions, remittance channeling, or return resettlement, for example—tend to dominate policy debates. We stress, however, the disjuncture between what states want and what individuals and families actually do. The resource environments migrants create from the diverse set of protections they can access is their way of fighting back. No matter what states do, individuals proactively respond to and manage risk in the best way they can for themselves and their families. The stories we tell throughout this book are of creativity and resilience, of even the most vulnerable people responding proactively when opportunities arise to make the most of little. We do not believe that states should be allowed to back away from their commitment to meeting the basic needs of the citizens and noncitizens that live within their borders. We are, however, filled with admiration for the everyday responses of ordinary individuals in their absence.

Why Should We Care: Emerging Policy Conundrums

The twenty-first century brings new paradoxes and dilemmas: as welfare states undergo retrenchment, governments extend protections to their diasporas and expect enduring financial and political commitments in return; markets celebrated for expanding choice price out citizens and target more affluent, foreign customers; and civil society organizations touted for intervening where governments fail to protect prove more corrupt and inscrutable than the state institutions they claim to outperform. The resulting hybrid transnational social protection regime clearly enhances opportunities for some and makes it more difficult for others to get even the most basic protections. It simultaneously gives rise to new solutions and new vulnerabilities. No matter how it is ultimately evaluated, the current hybrid transnational social protection regime sets the parameters for any conversation about policy reform to include managing risk at the local, regional, national, and international levels. Ignoring or misunderstanding the structure and functioning of this regime could result in failures to develop successful policies and interventions. As such, we highlight a few key conundrums of which policymakers and advocates should be mindful.

Policy vs. the Polity

Liberal democratic states must grapple with the tension between the social contract they have with their citizens, the social democratic policies that emerge from this contract, and the social cohesion needed to maintain it.

While countries of destination sometimes accept vulnerable migrants for humanitarian reasons or in response to international pressures, most of the time, they allow migrants in to be able to fulfill the state's explicit promise to taxpayers to provide day care, early childhood education, health services, and senior care. Even when states do not provide these services directly, they can facilitate household access to migrant workers through the market. For example, in countries where women enter the workforce without state-supported child- and/or elder care, lax enforcement of immigration laws or bilateral agreements with relatively poor countries allow citizens to directly buy the care services they need from immigrant women. Whether formally or informally, states need immigrants to fulfill the social contract.

Using migration to fulfill the social contract, however, clearly complicates state–society relations. Social scientists have long argued that the modern welfare state relies on some form of "kinship or fellow feeling" within a given political community (Freeman 1986, 52). We need to feel some affinity and solidarity with people to be willing to redistribute our hard-earned resources to them. When the political community is experienced as being in a constant state of flux vis-á-vis its membership, it becomes more difficult to consolidate those bonds. Political scientists have long argued that diversity inhibits the development of the welfare state (Alesina and Glaser 2004) and leads to distrust (Putnam 2007). While this latter claim has been widely disputed (Van der Meer and Tolsma 2014; Kesler and Bloemraad 2010), there is clear evidence that anti-immigrant sentiment fuels the rise of far-right populist parties (Arzheimer 2017; Norris and Inglehart 2019). While populists promise to greatly reduce migration, they do not commit as clearly to liberal democracy (Müller 2016; Mounk 2018). Indeed, some populist politicians, like Hungary's Viktor Orban, have promised to establish "illiberal democracies" in their countries. This leaves liberal democracies that are also immigrant-receiving states in a bind: fulfilling the promise of social democracy requires some level of immigration, but immigration gives rise to forces that threaten social democratic policies and liberal democracy itself.

Invisible Immigrants

The challenges of migration are not limited to liberal democracies. In countries where civil and political rights are limited for citizens and nonexistent for foreigners, migrants tend to be invisible in the public sphere and unable to demand social protections. Instead, they live parallel lives, separated not only by social and legal standing, but often by geography as well. However, circumstances may lay bare, despite government efforts to the contrary, just how connected immigrant and host societies actually are. Here, Singapore in the age of COVID-19 is a cautionary tale. In February 2020, as COVID-19 raged in China, Singapore implemented minimal restrictions. The government advised businesses to "maintain normalcy" (Ministry of Trade and Industry Singapore 2020). Good hygiene, contact tracing, and withdrawing from social contact if ill were the main lines of defense as schools, gyms, parks, and businesses remained open. Cases soon exploded, however; not among the general population, but among Singapore's migrant workers, who live in isolated and overcrowded dormitories at the margins of the city. By June 2020, more than 95 percent of the recorded COVID-19 cases were traced to low-wage migrant workers (Bengali and Jennings 2020). Excluding noncitizens from social protection presumes that the problems faced by these groups exist independently of society at large. As a *New York Times* correspondent noted, "It was as if the entire city had fallen so completely into the habit of regarding the laborers as some other kind of person that the basic fact of our corporeal interconnectedness never occurred to anybody" (Stack 2020). In times of crisis, the social safety net is only as strong as its weakest link.

Shaky Solutions

Countries of origin have also had to rethink state–society relations in the context of global migration. Many nations count on migrants to generate resources that support new risk-management strategies. The remittance payments that migrants send home allow their family members to purchase a level of services through the market that the state is unwilling or unable to provide. Collective remittances also fund basic social services and major upgrades in migrants' home communities. The education and professional training migrants acquire abroad, and the transnational networks they forge, transform realities, living standards, and lifestyle aspirations in countries of origin.

Traditionally, this system rested on two key assumptions. The first was that migrants would effectively exit without voice once they left. Increasingly, this is not the case—in fact, a new kind of social contract is emerging between states and their citizens who are not in residence. Migrants increasingly demand a greater say in the affairs of their country of origin, or at least a role that is commensurate with their economic contributions. More and more, countries of origin rely on their money, political sway, and intellectual and technical skills. To fulfill their part of the bargain, they must meet emigrants' demands for things like more extensive social supports or external voting rights. Doing so, however, requires a commitment of resources and political will that many states may be unable or unwilling to give.

Second, all of these strategies—importing workers and benefitting from emigration—rely on the underlying assumption that international migration flows will remain relatively open. But, again, the COVID-19 pandemic highlights the underlying weakness of this assumption. Within weeks of the pandemic being declared, 100 countries had partial or universal restrictions on entry for nonresidents or nonnationals, and an additional ninety-nine had suspended flights, effectively restricting entry for people living outside of the region (Brumfiel 2020). While it may be easy to dismiss the COVID-19 pandemic as a black swan event, there are multiple reasons to think that disruptions to international migration flows will continue—especially in countries where far-right nationalist parties are on the rise.

The Problem of Free Riding

These conundrums also point to the fact that countries of origin and destination have come to rely on migration not only as a form of social protection for some, but as a way to avoid or reorganize their responsibility for protecting others. When highly skilled doctors arrive from India, countries like the United States and the United Kingdom get the benefit of their expertise, while having paid little or nothing for their education. When noncitizens are ineligible for unemployment or disability payments, countries benefit from their labor in good times without assuming any of the fiscal commitments to them when times get tough. Collectively, this reads as a form of "free riding"—states reap the benefits from a motivated and often quite skilled workforce without assuming any of the fiscal or political risks of investing in social protection. While beneficial to states in the short term, free riding may be vulnerable to changes in immigration policy in the long run.

Protection and Precarity

Finally, many migrants are a source of social protection for their families and the people they work for but lead precarious lives themselves. This is especially true in the case of domestic workers, who are particularly vulnerable given that their work in the private sphere takes place away from the allegedly protective eye of the state. Domestic workers are also disproportionately female and more likely than other kinds of workers to be undocumented. Yet the presence of immigrant domestic workers in the labor market often frees other women to pursue careers outside of the home. This tension between the liberatory power of transnational systems of social protection and the precarity experienced by others who allow the HTSP system to operate is a particularly difficult conundrum to address. A positive step forward would be to further separate eligibility for social rights and protections from citizenship status.

COVID as a Mirror: What Does It Reveal?

As we complete this manuscript, COVID-19 is still ravaging the world. Pathogens develop nonrandomly: they take advantage of key vulnerabilities in polities, markets, and societies. Pandemics, in particular, hold up a mirror in which societies can see their true face, from penury to privilege, displaying the failures of adequate social protection and dangers of marginalization. COVID-19 exposed the disastrous consequences of worldwide systemic racism, exploitation, and unequal access to health care. In the United States alone, Black and Indigenous Americans experienced the highest death tolls—about 2.3 times as high as the rates for whites and Asians.[1] People who live in favelas cannot easily socially distance; as a result, COVID spread like wildfire in Brazil. In Germany, slaughterhouses that rely heavily on Polish, Romanian, and Bulgarian migrant workers became epicenters of illness after employers crammed workers together and failed to provide personal protective equipment and conditions for basic hygiene (Paul 2020).

COVID-19 illustrates the social patterning of health and disease. Around the world, the more affluent and educated could work remotely and rely on the market to reduce risk of exposure to the virus (by getting food delivered, shopping online, avoiding public transportation, etc.). With retirement homes, care centers, and schools closing, many people in Western Europe hired migrants as care workers and nannies to look after aging parents, disabled relatives, and children at home. Governments negotiated special agreements and organized special charter flights to facilitate the travel of Eastern European essential migrant workers despite international travel bans that forced everyone else to stay home (Paul 2020). Privileged migrants used their cross-border family and social networks to secure the care and resources they needed (Cao and Sun 2021). Some relocated to their homelands, where they could work remotely from a setting in which the pandemic was better contained (Sun forthcoming). For those families unable to secure care assistance during lockdowns, however, COVID-19 triggered a mental health pandemic. This was especially devastating for women, who assume the primary burden for caring for children, the sick, and the elderly. COVID-19 shows the skewed distribution of risks within and across societies, and the dramatic differences in individuals' ability to respond to them.

As we have argued throughout these pages, risk management, which is now largely perceived as an individual or community responsibility, involves weighing dangers and making tough choices. Even during these unprecedented times of lockdowns, quarantines, and travel bans, international migration continues because our world depends upon it. When former President Donald Trump signed an executive order banning new employment-based visas, including H-1B visas for highly skilled migrants, in June 2020, the administration waived restrictions for health care workers who could treat COVID patients, experts doing medical research, and people who could "facilitate the immediate and continued economic recovery of the United States."[2] While the administration continued to malign immigrants as threats to native-born communities, its actions reflected what an integral part of the social safety net that immigrants have become.

Next Steps

We return once again to what this book is meant to do and what it does not do. What we offer in these pages is a broad framework for understanding HTSP around the world, across sectors, at different stages of the life cycle. We weave together various theoretical and policy threads about aspects of social protection across borders that were previously considered in isolation. We do not and cannot provide a comprehensive, state-of-the-art analysis of each type of social protection in each region that we cover. Rather, we offer illustrative cases with the hope that researchers and policymakers will find our framework compelling enough to extend and deepen our analysis.

Indeed, many important issues remain. One topic of future study would be internal migration and social protection. Our focus here has been on the reconfiguration of hybrid social protection across borders. But boundaries and borders exist internally as well as internationally. For example, internal migrants in China need to secure a local *hukou* (personal and household registration) status to access social benefits, but many rural-to-urban migrants face great difficulties doing so. They become, in essence, residents without membership within their own country, forced to create very limited resource environments from the sources they are still eligible for. The Chinese case is not unique. These pages illustrate over and over again how subnational residence in a particular state, province, or region can enhance or limit an individual's resource environment. Therefore, the effect of internal as well as international migration on HTSP merits further study.

And, if hybrid transnational social protection is the wave of the future, what are the implications for a future world as it could be?

One possibility is that we will move toward a world of more multilateral and multi-scalar partnerships. But what could a truly multilateral partnership look like—that took the interests of individual states, the private sector, and the social needs of all members and citizens into account? To answer that question, we might look to the closest approximation of this that is already operational—the European Union.

The European Union exists as a supranational entity, a union of states that manage common problems together through a complex system of multilevel governance. Although it does not have a monopoly on the legitimate use of force, the European Union does have legislative, executive, and judicial branches, and it has some power to make policy and to sanction those individuals or member states that do not comply.

More importantly, for our purposes, it institutionalizes transnationalism in a few key ways. First, freedom of movement is a core principle, and as such, states cannot limit the movement of EU members as much as they can nonmembers. In addition, EU regulations allow for citizens of any given member state to access (or maintain) social benefits when living in other EU countries. Although this is quite messy and complicated to operationalize, and eligibility policies vary by country, the regulations and policies that make it possible are in place. Finally, member-state citizens generally have some political (voting) rights if they are residing in another member state. Thus, the European Union has de-territorialized social rights and, to some extent, denationalized political rights, through EU citizenship.

The evolution of other regional trade blocs into supranational states could help to codify existing patterns of movement across international borders and, along the way, help stabilize and expand resource environments for individuals and their families. The fragile emergence of this in the Association of Southeast Asian Nations and Union of South American Nations are examples of such developments, although they are very vulnerable to changes in the political winds. At the same time, however, the European Union's advantages come precisely from the fact that it is not a "superstate" and has never strived to become one by superseding the power of its member nations.

Another possibility for the world is that the role of the state as a provider of social protection may be re-evaluated. In the wake of the global pandemic, there are already signs of "bringing the state back in." In the United States, the Biden administration unveiled a budget plan that, although unsuccessful, included huge new social safety nets to benefit the poor and middle class (including guaranteed paid leave, child benefits, and universal prekindergarten education). In Europe, the European Union offered to provide funding for member states to transition from emergency measures taken to preserve jobs during the COVID-19 crisis to new measures that support a job-rich recovery. The pandemic has also helped citizens to fight back against retrenchment at the state level: France saw the unraveling of President Macron's attempt to push through pension system reform (one of his main campaign promises), under pressure from trade unions, strikers, and citizens affected by the pandemic-hit economy (Clercq 2021).

Reimagining (Transnational) Community

Our book grapples with how individuals and families gain access to social protections across borders that help them mitigate risk and take advantage of opportunities in a world on the move. The distinct logics upon which the various sources of social protection are based also reflect different ways in which we imagine communities across borders: as aggregations of citizens, human beings, consumers, or responsible communities and individuals. The conflicts between these different logics are at the core of the conflicts over how we should protect both migrants and nonmigrants from today's uncertainties and dangers.

International migration is both a cause and a consequence of this quest, and therefore, social protection is increasingly organized across borders. The changing dynamics we describe, and the myriad ways in which the state, the market, civil society, and social networks are mobilized in response, raise a set of more basic questions. What does it mean to be a community in this changing context? What obligations do a community's members have to each other? How do our responsibilities to one another change when they are not based solely on sharing the same space or nationality? Where do the rights and responsibilities of citizenship get fulfilled when so many people live for extended periods as residents without full membership? Do our obligations only extend to "contributors"—and if so, how do we measure so-called contributions? What does this mean for the poor, the disabled, the elderly, or the very young?

Since the modern welfare state emerged in the late nineteenth century, we have largely conceived of social protection as a national project, limited both geographically and politically by the state. In these pages, we have talked a lot about states, but in thinking about community, it is worth noting how the nation—as distinct from the state—functions within the frameworks we described. Benedict Anderson (1991) famously wrote that nations are "imagined" in three key ways. First, they are imagined as limited, with finite boundaries. They are not universalistic. Second, they are imagined as sovereign and capable of making their own decisions. Finally, nations are imagined as communities bound by a "deep horizontal comradeship" (7).

We write at a critical moment. The nationally bounded and rooted social protection regime that depends primarily on the state is being transformed. It is being challenged by or operates in tandem with a hybrid transnational social protection regime. Beneficiaries construct resource environments across borders, in often fragile, fleeting ways, to the best of their ability based on the strategies available to them. The conditions that drive forward these changes and the institutional arrangements that emerge in response left the station long ago. But the underlying philosophical and moral shift in who we are as a community and what our obligations are to one another has not kept pace. Can the idea of community be rethought such that ensuring basic protections for all of its members, regardless of differences in status or location, becomes not only plausible but optimal and the right thing to do?

Our analysis suggests that, under some conditions, reimagining the community is not only possible, but advantageous. Again, the clearest example is the European Union. It grew out of the deeply rooted idea that "Europe" constitutes a community with a shared history, commitment to liberal democracy, and level of interdependence that makes it good sense to pursue significant economic cooperation. Yet the idea of what Europe is and who gets to be European has changed dramatically over time. The European community is not alone in reimaging itself in broader ethnic and geographic terms in light of the lived transnational practices of its citizens. In Latin America, Bolivian and Ecuadorian political parties post campaign ads in Madrid metro stations, sending a strong signal that politicians in these countries of origin recognize that some of their constituents vote from outside their borders. Similarly, Dominican politicians campaign up and down the East Coast of the United States, where there are significant emigrant populations. If the polity itself can be reimagined, so can the policies that govern and protect it.

COVID-19 made clear the practical and moral limitations of the closed imagined community. It also drove home our need to fundamentally rethink who is "essential" and that who merits that designation may have little to do with nationality or citizenship. While frontline medical staff are clearly critical, those at the front line of keeping the economy going also tend to be the lowest paid and most vulnerable workers: housekeeping staff, warehouse and distribution workers, agricultural workers, and health aides for the elderly. But, as we have repeatedly shown, outsourcing means that these workers are often ineligible for benefits or are outside the purview of existing labor agreements that regulate workplace safety and wages. They are also disproportionately more likely to be ethnic minorities and/or of immigrant origin (Chaganti et al. 2020).

This adds up to the difficult moral bargain we have returned to over and over again in these pages—enhanced protections for some come at the expense of others. While the well-educated, well-off enjoy greater choice and opportunity, they come at the cost of greater risk and vulnerability for those providing the care. As Singapore learned the hard way, however, ignoring our "corporeal interconnectedness" is a form of magical thinking that is both medically imprudent and morally bankrupt. In our ever more globalized world, which we believe will endure despite periods of heightened nationalism and populism, our individual and collective destinies are inextricably intertwined. Whatever we, as citizens and policymakers, decide, we must recognize that a fundamental shift in the organization of social life is already well underway. Nations persist but many aspects of social, economic, and political experience transcend national borders. The way many people live and the way they protect and provide for their families is already transnational. It is up to us to reimagine the communities to which we belong and to which we are responsible and to redefine our rights and obligations accordingly.

Notes

Introduction

1. The Organisation for Economic Co-operation and Development broadly defines social protections as health care, senior care, services for families and small children, education starting from early childhood, and policies to protect active members of the labor market.
2. The definition of neoliberalism, in political and economic terms, that we use in these pages is a set of "economic ideas that aim at increasing the power of markets—and the corporations operating in them—in the allocation of goods and services and the reduction of discretionary government interventions to make them credible with market actors" (Madariaga 2020, 5). What this means for policy is that states are forced to step back from regulating firms and labor markets.
3. This is similar to what Bilecen and Barglowski (2015) call assemblages of social protection and what Ho et al. (2021) call care assemblages.

Chapter 1

1. All names are pseudonyms.
2. *Anak* is the Tagalog word for child.
3. *Tulay* means bridge in Tagalog.
4. As Parreñas (2005, 41) writes, "OWWA does not receive any funds from the government; rather, it funnels money from migrant workers and their families to the government. Membership in OWWA, which is required of overseas contract workers, costs migrants a nominal fee that covers the operational costs of the agency. However, OWWA does not reinvest its funds in programs that benefit its constituents." Furthermore, as one high-ranking OWWA official informed her, "most of these funds 'sit' in an emergency release fund reserved to cover the cost of sudden mass deportation of Filipinos from high-risk destinations—for example, to evacuate Filipino contract workers from Israel if war were to break out there" (Parreñas 2005, 41).
5. According to Mahdavi (2016, 188), "in cases where the citizenship of the mother can transfer to the child (as is the case for Filipina migrant women and their children), the expectant mother will be transferred to the care of the embassy of the sending country." This process becomes complicated and challenging, however, "for mothers who come from countries that do not have embassies on the ground (such as Madagascar)

or whose embassy officials may not wish to extend citizenship rights to children of women they see as 'unfit' mothers."

6. Lily is a student profiled by Shamus Khan in *Privilege: The Making of an Adolescent Elite at St. Paul's School* (2011).
7. "Wild geese" refers to the seasonal visits that South Korean parents make to their children living in English-speaking countries.
8. Some research estimates that 10–20 percent of the approximately 1,500 infants born in New York Chinatown Health Center might be sent back to the People's Republic of China; however, the accurate number of these "sent-back" children is difficult to obtain (Bohr and Tse 2009). In their survey of 210 Chinese mothers who relocated from Fujian Province to New York City, Kwong et al. (2009) found 57 percent separated from their infants because they needed to return to work and lacked access to childcare.
9. Tomorrow's Children is a pseudonym for the institution where Leslie Wang volunteered during her fieldwork in China.

Chapter 2

1. The equivalent of three years' salary in the Philippines.
2. He paid the recruitment fee to Petro-Fil Manpower Services, Inc., a company based in Manila, and Ligaya Avenida, a California-based consultant who recruits and screens teachers for the J-1 program. It covered his airfare and rent for his first few months in Arizona, a $2,500 fee for Avenida, and a fee of several thousand dollars to Alliance Abroad Group, a Texas-based company that is an official State Department sponsor for J-1 visa holders.
3. See, for instance, the websites of Fulbright Romania (Fulbright Romania n.d.) or the French Institute of Bucharest (Institut Français Bucarest 2020).

Chapter 3

1. The lower house of the national legislature.
2. The right to live and work in the territory without any restrictions of conditions to be able to stay (https://www.immd.gov.hk/eng/services/roa/eligible.html).

Chapter 4

1. During the tuberculosis epidemic of the eighteenth and nineteenth centuries, foreign patients traveled to sanatoria in the mountains (the Alps) or to Italy because people believed the climate fostered recovery (Snowden 2019). Pilgrimages to holy sites could also be considered a form of spiritual and medical tourism, because many pilgrims believed that physical and psychological healing came together (Jenkins 2021).

2. Highly specialized medical care that involves advanced and complex procedures and treatments over an extended period.
3. The federal government in the United States affords few protections to people in the country for short stays. Some see this policy as a way to dissuade potential migrants from coming to seek care. Tourists and visitors to the United States for extended periods do not qualify for public health insurance. They cannot be listed as dependents on their relatives' health insurance and therefore depend upon expensive emergency care. They can purchase international health insurance, which covers any health expenses they incur while abroad. A quick review of internet forums on the topic, however, reveals outrage expressed by Indian American families whose parents visited and required medical attention. The companies that promised to cover all of these expenses actually covered very little. Some families cited tactics to avoid paying claims, such as defining emergency surgery for appendicitis as treatment for a chronic condition that would therefore not be covered. Some families reported spending even more money trying to sue their insurers.
4. Many Western media outlets have portrayed SARS and the coronavirus that causes COVID-19 as threats to Western societies and blamed Asia for their spread. Reports of Asian Americans shunned and Asian businesses suffering present evidence of this misplaced prejudice.

Chapter 5

1. John Leung is a respondent whom Ken Sun (2021) interviewed for his book.
2. This chapter builds upon a number of recent review articles, anthologies, and special issues of academic journals in the subfields of transnational aging (e.g., Karl and Torres 2015; Horn and Schweppe 2015; Näre et al. 2017; Dossa and Coe 2017; Pickering et al. 2019).
3. For examples and information on how pensions are calculated and paid, see https://europa.eu/youreurope/citizens/work/retire-abroad/state-pensions-abroad/index_en.htm.
4. Expats with residency status who are employed full-time by an Instituto Mexicano del Seguro Social (IMSS; Mexican Institute of Social Security)-registered company are automatically enrolled in the IMSS. Foreigner residents in Mexico who are not working for an IMSS-enrolled company, or who are not working at all, can choose to purchase IMSS health insurance separately for a small monthly fee. See https://www.pacificprime.lat/blog/what-foreigners-should-know-about-the-mexican-healthcare-system/
5. For this reason, Japanese retirees also avoid interacting with their co-ethnics in receiving communities.
6. See http://ec.europa.eu/social/main.jsp?catId=849&langId=en.
7. The qualifying residence periods vary by areas and regions of France (Hunter 2018, 64–65).

Chapter 6

1. According to a recent American Public Media report, "If they had died of COVID-19 at the same actual rate as Whites, about 17,000 Black, 3,000 Latino, 500 Indigenous, and 50 Pacific Islander Americans would still be alive." See https://www.apmresearch lab.org/covid/deaths-by-race.
2. https://www.whitehouse.gov/presidential-actions/proclamation-suspending-entry-aliens-present-risk-u-s-labor-market-following-coronavirus-outbreak/.

References

Acedera, Kristel Anne, Brenda S. A. Yeoh, and Maruja M. B. Asis. 2018. "Migrant Mothers and Left-Behind Families: The Rituals of Communication and the Reconstitution of Familyhood Across Transnational Space and Time." In *Transnational Migrations in the Asia-Pacific: Transformative Experiences in the Age of Digital Media*, edited by Catherine Gomes and Brenda S. A. Yeoh, pp. 153–174. London: Rowman and Littlefield.

Ackers, Louise, and Peter Dwyer. 2004. "Fixed Laws, Fluid Lives: The Citizenship Status of Post-Retirement Migrants in the European Union." *Ageing and Society 24* (3): pp. 451–475.

AFL-CIO. 2021. "Executive Paywatch." Accessed July 11, 2021. https://aflcio.org/paywatch.

Agren, David. 2020. "Farewell Seguro Popular." *Lancet 395* (10224): pp. 549–550.

Aginam, Obijiofor. 2002. "International Law and Communicable Diseases." *Bulletin of the World Health Organization 80* (12): pp. 946–951.

Aguinas, Dovelyn Rannveig. 2009. *Committed to the Diaspora: More Developing Countries Setting Up Diaspora Institutions*. Washington, DC: Migration Policy Institute.

Alesina, Alberto, and Edward Glaeser. 2004. *Fighting Poverty in the US and Europe: A World of Difference*. New York: Oxford University Press.

Altstedter, Ari. 2019. "The World's Cheapest Hospital Has to Get Even Cheaper." *Bloomberg Businessweek*. March 26. https://www.bloomberg.com/news/features/2019-03-26/the-world-s-cheapest-hospital-has-to-get-even-cheaper.

Amengual, Matthew. 2010. "Complementary Labor Regulation: The Uncoordinated Combination of State and Private Regulators in the Dominican Republic." *World Development 38* (3): pp. 405–414.

Amin, Iftekhar, and Stan Ingman. 2014. "Elder Care in the Transnational Setting: Insights from Bangladeshi Transnational Families in the United States." *Journal of Cross-Cultural Gerontology 29* (3): pp. 315–328.

Amuedo-Dorantes, Catalina, and Susan Pozo. 2011. "New Evidence on the Role of Remittances on Healthcare Expenditures by Mexican Households." *Review of Economics of the Household 9* (1): pp. 69–98.

Anderson, Benedict. 1991. *Imagined Communities: Reflections on the Origin and Spread of Nationalism*. New York: Verso.

Anderson, Bridget. 2010. "Migration, Immigration Controls and the Fashioning of Precarious Workers." *Work, Employment and Society 24* (2): pp. 300–317.

Anderson, Stuart. 2018. "55% of America's Billion-Dollar Startups Have an Immigrant Founder." *Forbes*. October 25. https://www.forbes.com/sites/stuartanderson/2018/10/25/55-of-americas-billion-dollar-startups-have-immigrant-founder/.

Anderson, Vivienne. 2014. "'World-Travelling': A Framework for Re-Thinking Teaching and Learning in Internationalised Higher Education." *Higher Education 68* (5): pp. 637–652.

Anderson, Vivienne, Sharon Young, Keely Blanch, and Lee Smith. 2015. "Beginning Teachers as Policy Workers in Malaysia and New Zealand." *International Education Journal: Comparative Perspectives 14* (2): pp. 30–42.

Andersson, Hans E., and Susanna Nilsson. 2011. "Asylum Seekers and Undocumented Migrants' Increased Social Rights in Sweden." *International Migration 49* (4): pp. 167–188.

Andrews, Abigail, and Fátima Khayar-Cámara. 2022. "Forced out of Fatherhood: How Men Strive to Parent Post-Deportation." *Social Problems 69* (3): pp. 699–716. https://doi.org/10.1093/socpro/spaa061.

Anner, Mark. 2017. "Monitoring Workers' Rights: The Limits of Voluntary Social Compliance Initiatives in Labor Repressive Regimes." *Global Policy 8* (S3): pp. 56–65. https://doi.org/10.1111/1758-5899.12385.

Anzia, Sarah F., and Terry M. Moe. 2015. "Public Sector Unions and the Costs of Government." *The Journal of Politics 77* (1): pp. 114–127.

Apollo Hospitals. 2019. "Hospitals in Hyderabad." Accessed April 7, 2022. https://www.apollohospitals.com/locations/india/hyderabad.

Arah, Onyebuchi A., Uzor C. Ogbu, and Chukwudi E. Okeke. 2008. "Too Poor to Leave, Too Rich to Stay: Developmental and Global Health Correlates of Physician Migration to the United States, Canada, Australia, and the United Kingdom." *American Journal of Public Health 98* (1): pp. 148–154.

Arango, Joaquin. 2013. *Exceptional in Europe? Spain's Experience with Immigration and Integration*. Washington DC: Migration Policy Institute.

Arends-Kuenning, Mary, Kathy Baylis, and Rafael Garduño-Rivera. 2019. "The Effect of NAFTA on Internal Migration in Mexico: A Regional Economic Analysis." *Applied Economics 51* (10): pp. 1052–1068.

Arrighi, Jean-Thomas, and Rainer Bauböck. 2017. "A Multilevel Puzzle: Migrants' Voting Rights in National and Local Elections." *European Journal of Political Research 56* (3): pp. 619–639.

Arzheimer, Kai. 2017. "Electoral Sociology – Who Votes for the Extreme Right and Why – and When?" In *The Populist Radical Right: A Reader*, edited by Cas Mudde, pp. 277–289. New York: Routledge.

ASEAN. 2018. "ASEAN (Association of Southeast Asian Nations) Consensus on the Protection and Promotion of the Rights of Migrant Workers." Jakarta, ID: ASEAN Secretariat. https://asean.org/storage/2019/01/3.-March-2018-ASEAN-Consensus-on-the-Protection-and-Promotion-of-the-Rights-of-Migrant-Workers.pdf.

Asianet Newsable. n.d. *Why Are All Nurses from Kerala?* Accessed May 1, 2008. https://www.youtube.com/watch?v=Ct5ezPe3-fg.

Avato, Johanna, Johannes Koettl, and Rachel Sabates-Wheeler. 2010. "Social Security Regimes, Global Estimates, and Good Practices: The Status of Social Protection for International Migrants." *World Development 38* (4): pp. 455–466.

Azevedo, Mário Luiz Neves. 2014. "The Bologna Process and Higher Education in Mercosur: Regionalization or Europeanization?" *International Journal of Lifelong Education 33* (3): pp. 411–427.

Bada, Xóchitl. 2014. *Mexican Hometown Associations in Chicagoacán: From Local to Transnational Civic Engagement*. New Brunswick, NJ: Rutgers University Press.

Bada, Xóchitl, and Shannon Gleeson. 2015. "A New Approach to Migrant Labor Rights Enforcement: The Crisis of Undocumented Worker Abuse and Mexican Consular Advocacy in the United States." *Labor Studies Journal 40* (1): pp. 32–53.

Baldassar, Loretta. 2014. "Too Sick to Move: Distant 'Crisis' Care in Transnational Families." *International Review of Sociology 24* (3): pp. 391–405.
Baldassar, Loretta. 2016. "De-demonizing Distance in Mobile Family Lives: Co-presence, Care Circulation and Polymedia as Vibrant Matter." *Global Networks 16* (2): pp. 145–163.
Baldassar, Loretta, Cora Vellekoop Baldock, and Raelene Wilding. 2007. *Families Caring Across Borders: Migration, Ageing and Transnational Caregiving*. New York: Palgrave Macmillan.
Balkır, Canan, and Berna Kırkulak. 2009. "Turkey, the New Destination for International Retirement Migration." In *Migration and Mobility in Europe Trends, Patterns and Control*, edited by Heinz Fassmann, Max Haller, and David Lane, pp. 123–143. Cheltenham, UK: Edward Elgar Publishing.
Barberis, Eduardo, and Paolo Boccagni. 2014. "Blurred Rights, Local Practices: Social Work and Immigration in Italy." *British Journal of Social Work 44* (suppl 1): pp. i70–i87.
Barenberg, Mark. 2015. *Widening the Scope of Worker Organizing: Legal Reforms to Facilitate Multi-Employer Organizing, Bargaining, and Striking*. New York: Roosevelt Institute.
Barry, Ellen, and Katie Benner. 2022. "U.S. Drops Its Case Against M.I.T. Scientist Accused of Hiding China Links." *The New York Times*. January 20. https://www.nytimes.com/2022/01/20/science/gang-chen-mit-china-initiative.html.
Batay Ouvriye. 2006. "Press Release—Solidarity with U. Miami Workers." *Batay Ouvriye*. March 12. https://www.batayouvriye.org/English/Positions1/umiami.html.
BBC. 2017. "Non-EU Parents 'Have EU Residence Right.'" *BBC News*. May 10. https://www.bbc.com/news/world-europe-39868868.
Beaumont, Paul Reid, and Peter Eugene McEleavey. 1999. *The Hague Convention on International Child Abduction*. New York: Oxford University Press.
Beckfield, Jason. 2010. "The Social Structure of the World Polity." *American Journal of Sociology 115* (4): pp. 1018–1068.
Benedict, Olumide Henrie, and Wilfred Isioma Ukpere. 2012. "Brain Drain and African Development: Any Possible Gain from the Drain?" *African Journal of Business Management 6* (7): pp. 2421–2428.
Bengali, Shashank, and Ralph Jennings. 2020. "These Governments Tamed COVID-19. They're Keeping Social Distancing in Place." *Los Angeles Times*. June 17. https://www.latimes.com/world-nation/story/2020-06-17/social-distancing-remains-as-asia-eases-covid-19-lockdowns.
Benhabib, Seyla. 2004. *The Rights of Others: Aliens, Residents, and Citizens*. Cambridge, UK: Cambridge University Press.
Berckmoes, Lidewyde H., and Valentina Mazzucato. 2018. "Resilience among Nigerian Transnational Parents in the Netherland: A Strength-Based Approach to Migration and Transnational Parenting." *Global Networks 18* (4): pp. 589–607.
Bernhardt, Annette, Rosemary Batt, Susan Houseman, and Eileen Appelbaum. 2016. *Domestic Outsourcing in the United States: A Research Agenda to Assess Trends and Effects on Job Quality*. Kalamazoo, MI: W.E. Upjohn Institute.
Bilecen, Başak. 2020. "Asymmetries in Transnational Social Protection: Perspectives of Migrants and Nonmigrants." *The Annals of the American Academy of Political and Social Science 689* (1): pp. 168–191.
Bilecen, Başak, and Karolina Barglowski. 2015. "On the Assemblages of Informal and Formal Transnational Social Protection." *Population, Space, and Place 21* (3): pp. 203–214.

Block, Daniel. 2018. "India's Hospitals are Filling up with Desperate Americans." *Foreign Policy*. February 2. https://foreignpolicy.com/2018/01/02/indias-hospitals-are-filling-up-with-desperate-americans/.

Block, Miguel Ángel González, Arturo Vargas Bustamante, Luz Angélica de la Sierra, and Aresha Martínez Cardoso. 2012. "Redressing the Limitations of the Affordable Care Act for Mexican Immigrants Through Bi-National Health Insurance: A Willingness to Pay Study in Los Angeles." *Journal of Immigrant and Minority Health 16* (2): pp. 179–188.

Bloemraad, Irene, Fabiana Silva, and Kim Voss. 2016. "Rights, Economics, or Family? Frame Resonance, Political Ideology, and the Immigrant Rights Movement." *Social Forces 94* (4): pp. 1647–1674. https://doi.org/10.1093/sf/sov123.

Boccagni, Paolo. 2011. "Migrants' Social Protection as a Transnational Process: Public Policies and Emigrant Initiative in the Case of Ecuador." *International Journal of Social Welfare 20* (3): pp. 318–325.

Boccagni, Paolo. 2013. "Caring about Migrant Care Workers: From Private Obligations to Transnational Social Welfare." *Critical Social Policy 34* (2): pp. 221–240.

Boccagni, Paolo. 2015. "Burden, Blessing, or Both: On the Mixed Role of Transnational Ties in Migrant Informal Social Support." *International Sociology 30* (3): pp. 250–268.

Bochenek, Michael Garcia. 2016. *What is Happening to the Children of the Calais* "Jungle"? New York: Human Rights Watch.

Böcker, Anita, and Alistair Hunter. 2017. "Legislating for Transnational Ageing: A Challenge to the Logics of the Welfare State." *European Journal of Ageing 14* (4): pp. 353–363.

Bohr, Yvonne. 2010. "Transnational Infancy: A New Context for Attachment and the Need for Better Models." *Child Development Perspectives 4* (3): pp. 189–196.

Bohr, Yvonne, Cindy H. Liu, Stephen H. Chen, and Leslie K. Wang. 2018. "Satellite Babies: Costs and Benefits of Culturally Driven Parent-Infant Separations in North American Immigrant Families." In *Parenting from Afar and the Reconfiguration of Family Across Distance*, edited by Maria Rosario T. de Guzman, Jill Brown, and Carolyn Pope Edwards, pp. 304–320. New York: Oxford University Press.

Bohr, Yvonne, and Connie Tse. 2009. "Satellite Babies in Transnational Families: A Study of Parents' Decision to Separate from Their Families." *Infant Mental Health Journal 30* (3): pp. 265–286.

Boli, John. 2005. "Contemporary Developments in World Culture." *International Journal of Comparative Sociology 46* (5–6): pp. 383–404.

Boros, Lajos, and Gábor Hegedűs. 2016. "European National Policies Aimed at Stimulating Return Migration." In *Return Migration and Regional Development in Europe: Mobility Against the Stream*, edited by Robert Nadler, Zoltán Kovács, Birgit Glorius, and Thilo Lang, pp. 333–357. New Geographies of Europe. London: Palgrave Macmillan.

Botea, Razvan. 2018. "Guvernul de la Bucuresti aduce mai multi muncitori din Vietnam. Dar nu toti specialistii cred ca aceasta este solutia la criza de pe piata muncii." *Ziarul Financiar*. November 29. https://www.zf.ro/eveniment/guvernul-de-la-bucuresti-aduce-mai-multi-muncitori-din-vietnam-dar-nu-toti-specialistii-cred-ca-aceasta-este-solutia-la-criza-de-pe-piata-muncii-17721245.

Boyd, William, and Edmund J. King. 1994. *The History of Western Education*. Lanham, MD: Barnes and Noble Books.

Božić, Saša. 2006. "The Achievement and Potential of International Retirement Migration Research: The Need for Disciplinary Exchange." *Journal of Ethnic and Migration Studies 32* (8): pp. 1415–1427.

Brandhorst, Rosa-Maria, Loretta Baldassar, and Raelene Wilding. 2019. "The Need for a 'Migration Turn' in Aged Care Policy: A Comparative Study of Australian and German Migration Policies and Their Impact on Migrant Aged Care." *Journal of Ethnic and Migration Studies*. Online Edition. https://www.tandfonline.com/doi/full/10.1080/1369183X.2019.1629893.

Bronfenbrenner, Kate. 2000. *Uneasy Terrain: The Impact of Capital Mobility on Workers, Wages, and Union Organizing*. Ithaca, NY: Cornell University.

Brookes, Marissa, and Jamie K. McCallum. 2017. "The New Global Labour Studies: A Critical Review." *Global Labour Journal 8* (3): pp. 201–218.

Brooks, Jeffrey. 1985. *When Russia Learned to Read: Literacy and Popular Literature, 1861-1917*. Princeton, NJ: Princeton University Press.

Brown, Hana E. 2011. "Refugees, Rights, and Race: How Legal Status Shapes Liberian Immigrants' Relationship with the State." *Social Problems 58* (1): pp. 144–163.

Brown, Wendy. 2015. *Undoing the Demos: Neoliberalism's Stealth Revolution*. Cambridge, MA: MIT Press.

Brownell, Ginanne. 2013. "A Testing Time for Private Schools in Eastern Europe." *The New York Times*. December 15. https://www.nytimes.com/2013/12/16/world/europe/a-testing-time-for-private-schools-in-eastern-europe.html.

Brumfiel, Geoff. 2020. "Countries Slammed Their Borders Shut to Stop Coronavirus. But Is It Doing Any Good?" *NPR* (*National Public Radio*). May 15. https://www.northcountrypublicradio.org/news/npr/855669867/countries-slammed-their-borders-shut-to-stop-coronavirus-but-is-it-doing-any-good.

Bryceson, Deborah. 2019. "Transnational Families Negotiating Migration and Care Life Cycles Across Nation-state Borders." *Journal of Ethnic and Migration Studies 45* (16): pp. 3042–3064.

Budd, John W., and Brian P. McCall. 1997. "The Effect of Unions on the Receipt of Unemployment Insurance Benefits." *Industrial and Labor Relations Review 50* (3): pp. 478–492.

Bulman, May. 2018. "Fury as NHS Recruits 100 Doctors from India Only for Home Office to Deny Them All Visas." *The Independent*. April 27. https://www.independent.co.uk/news/uk/home-news/nhs-doctor-recruitment-india-home-office-visas-rejected-amber-rudd-windrush-a8324831.html.

Buzan, Barry, and Ole Wæver. 2003. *Regions and Powers: The Structure of International Security*. Cambridge, UK: Cambridge University Press.

Calarco, Jessica McCrory. 2018. *Negotiating Opportunities: How the Middle Class Secures Advantages in School*. New York: Oxford University Press.

Calavita, Kitty. 1998. "Immigration, Law, and Marginalization in a Global Economy: Notes from Spain" *Law and Society Review 32* (3): pp. 529–566.

Cano, Gustavo, and Alexandra Délano. 2007. "The Mexican Government and Organised Mexican Immigrants in The United States: A Historical Analysis of Political Transnationalism (1848–2005)." *Journal of Ethnic and Migration Studies 33* (5): pp. 695–725.

Cao, Xuemei, and Ken Chih-Yan Sun. 2021. "Seeking Transnational Social Protection during a Global Pandemic: The Case of Chinese Immigrants in the United States." *Social Sciences and Medicine 287* (October): 114378. https://doi.org/10.1016/j.socscimed.2021.114378.

Carling, Jørgen. 2008. "Toward a Demography of Immigrant Communities and Their Transnational Potential." *International Migration Review 42* (2): pp. 449–475.

Carling, Jørgen, Cecilia Menjivar, and Leah Schmalzbauer. 2012. "Central Themes in the Study of Transnational Parenthood." *Journal of Ethnic and Migration Studies 38* (2): pp. 191–217. https://doi.org/10.1080/1369183X.2012.646417.

Carrillo, Héctor. 2017. *Pathways of Desire: The Sexual Migration of Mexican Gay Men.* Chicago, IL: University of Chicago Press.

Casado-Díaz, María A. 2006. "Retiring to Spain: An Analysis of Differences Among North European Nationals." *Journal of Ethnic and Migration Studies 32* (8): pp. 1321–1339.

Casado-Díaz, María A., and Ana B. Casado-Díaz. 2014. "Linking Tourism, Retirement Migration and Social Capital." *Tourism Geographies 16* (1): pp. 124–140.

Cebotari, Victor, Valentina Mazzucato, and Ernest Appiah. 2017. "A Longitudinal Analysis of Well-being of Ghanaian Children in Transnational Families." *Child Development 89* (5): pp. 1768–1785.

Chadwick, Kay. 1997. "Education in Secular France: (Re)Defining Laïcité." *Modern and Contemporary France 5* (1): pp. 47–59.

Chaganti, Sara, Amy Higgins, and Marybeth J. Mattingly. 2020. *Health Insurance and Essential Service Workers in New England: Who Lacks Access to Care for COVID-19?* Boston, MA: Federal Reserve Bank of Boston.

Chan, Albert P. C., Arshad Ali Javed, Sainan Lyu, Carol K. H. Hon, and Francis K. W. Wong. 2016. "Strategies for Improving Safety and Health of Ethnic Minority Construction Workers." *Journal of Construction Engineering and Management 142* (9): 05016007.

Chang, Andy Scott. 2018. "Producing the Self-Regulating Subject: Liberal Protection in Indonesia's Migration Infrastructure." *Pacific Affairs 91* (4): pp. 695–716.

Chang, Andy Scott. 2021. "Selling a Resume and Buying a Job: Stratification of Gender and Occupation by States and Brokers in International Migration from Indonesia." *Social Problems 68* (4): pp. 903–924.

Chauvet, Lisa, Flore Gubert, and Sandrine Mesplé-Somps. 2013. "Aid, Remittances, Medical Brain Drain and Child Mortality: Evidence Using Inter and Intra-Country Data." *The Journal of Development Studies 49* (6): pp. 801–818.

Chee, Maria W. L. 2005. *Taiwanese American Transnational Families: Women and Kin Work.* New York: Routledge.

Chen, Lin H., and Mary E. Wilson. 2013. "The Globalization of Healthcare: Implications of Medical Tourism for the Infectious Disease Clinician." *Clinical Infectious Diseases 57* (12): pp. 1752–1759.

Chezum, Brian, Cynthia Bansak, and Animesh Giri. 2018. "Are Remittances Good for Your Health? Remittances and Nepal's National Healthcare Policy." *Eastern Economic Journal 44* (4): pp. 594–615.

Chishti, Muzaffar, Faye Hipsman, and Sarah Pierce. 2014. *Ebola Outbreak Rekindles Debate on Restricting Admissions to the United States on Health Grounds.* Washington, DC: Migration Policy Institute.

Chopra, Vidur, and Sarah Dryden-Peterson. 2020. "Borders and Belonging: Displaced Syrian Youth Navigating Symbolic Boundaries in Lebanon." *Globalisation, Societies and Education 18* (4): pp. 449–463.

Christou, Anastasia, and Russell King. 2015. *Counter-Diaspora: The Greek Second Generation Returns* "Home" *(Vol. 6).* Cambridge, MA: Harvard University Press.

Ciobanu, Ruxandra Oana, Tineke Fokkema, and Mihaela Nedelcu. 2017. "Ageing as a Migrant: Vulnerabilities, Agency and Policy Implications." *Journal of Ethnic and Migration Studies 43* (2): pp. 164–181.

Clack, Erin E. 2020. "Nike Is Reviewing Its Supply Chain After Reports of Uighur Labor Abuse in China." *Footwear News*. March 11. https://footwearnews.com/2020/business/manufacturing/nike-labor-abuse-china-uighur-supply-chain-1202946113/.

Clawson, Dan, and Naomi Gerstel. 2014. *Unequal Time: Gender, Class, and Family in Employment Schedules*. New York: Russel Sage Foundation.

CLEISS. 2019. *French Social Security System I—Health, Maternity, Paternity, Disability, and Death*. Paris: Centre des Liaisons Européennes et Internationales de Sécurité Sociale. https://www.cleiss.fr/docs/regimes/regime_france/an_1.html.

Clercq, Geert. 2021. "Macron Says France's Pension Reform Cannot Go Ahead as Planned." *Reuters*. June 4. https://www.reuters.com/world/europe/frances-pension-reform-cannot-go-ahead-planned-macron-2021-06-03/.

Coe, Cati. 2011. "What is Love? The Materiality of Care in Ghanaian Transnational Families." *International Migration 49* (6): pp. 7–24.

Coe, Cati. 2017a. "Returning Home: The Retirement Strategies of Aging Ghanaian Care Workers." In *Transnational Aging and Reconfiguration of Kin Work*, edited by Parin Dossa and Cati Coe, pp. 141–158. New Brunswick, NJ: Rutgers University Press.

Coe, Cati. 2017b. "Transnational Migration and the Commodification of Eldercare in Urban Ghana." *Identities: Global Studies in Culture and Power 24* (5): pp. 542–556.

Coe, Cati. 2019. *The New American Servitude Political Belonging among African Immigrant Home Care Workers*. New York: New York University Press.

Cohen, I. Glenn. 2015. *Patients With Passports: Medical Tourism, Law and Ethics*. New York: Oxford University Press.

Cohen, Jeffrey H. 2011. "Migration, Remittances, and Household Strategies." *Annual Review of Anthropology 40* (1): pp. 103–114.

Colectivo Migración para Las Américas. 2020. "Migración para Las Américas." Accessed April 2020. http://migracionparalasamericas.org/.

Connell, John. 2016. "Reducing the Scale? From Global Images to Border Crossings in Medical Tourism." *Global Networks 16* (4): pp. 531–550.

Connolly, Kate. 2012. "Germany 'Exporting' Old and Sick to Foreign Care Homes." *The Guardian*. December 26. http://www.theguardian.com/world/2012/dec/26/german-elderly-foreign-care-homes.

Connor, Phillip. 2017. *India Is a Top Source and Destination for World's Migrants*. Washington, DC: Pew Research Center.

Constable, Nicole. 2014. *Born Out of Place: Migrant Mothers and the Politics of International Labor*. Berkeley, CA: University of California Press. https://www.ucpress.edu/book/9780520282025/born-out-of-place.

Cook, Michael. 2015. "Surrogacy Business Shifts to Cambodia." *BioEdge*. November 7. https://www.bioedge.org/bioethics/surrogacy-business-shifts-to-cambodia/11638.

Cook-Martin, David. 2013. *The Scramble for Citizens: Dual Nationality and State Competition for Immigrants*. Stanford, CA: Stanford University Press.

Cordelli, Chiara. 2020. *The Privatized State*. Princeton, NJ: Princeton University Press.

Cortes, Patricia. 2015. "The Feminization of International Migration and Its Effects on the Children Left Behind: Evidence from the Philippines." *World Development, Migration and Development, 65* (January): pp. 62–78.

Cousins, Sophie. 2020. "In Qatar, Migrant Workers Cannot Afford a Lockdown." *Foreign Policy*. April 8. https://foreignpolicy.com/2020/04/08/qatar-south-asian-migrant-workers-cant-afford-coronavirus-lockdown-world-cup-2022/.

Craumer, Martha. 2002. "How to Think Strategically About Outsourcing." *HBS Working Knowledge*. July 22. https://hbswk.hbs.edu/archive/how-to-think-strategically-about-outsourcing.

Crawshaw, Marilyn, Eric Blyth, and Olga van den Akker. 2012. "The Changing Profile of Surrogacy in the UK—Implications for National and International Policy and Practice." *Journal of Social Welfare and Family Law 34* (3): pp. 267–277.

Cuadra, Carin Björngren. 2012. "Right of Access to Health Care for Undocumented Migrants in EU: A Comparative Study of National Policies." *European Journal of Public Health 22* (2): pp. 267–271.

Cuadra, Carin Björngren, and Sandro Cattacin. 2010. "Policies on Health Care for Undocumented Migrants in the EU27: Towards a Comparative Framework." *The European Journal of Public Health 22* (2): pp. 3–12. https://www.diva-portal.org/smash/get/diva2:1410077/FULLTEXT01.pdf.

Da, Wei. 2003. "Transnational Grandparenting: Child Care Arrangements Among Migrants from the People's Republic of China to Australia." *Journal of International Migration and Integration 4* (1): pp. 79–103.

D'Addio, Anna Cristina, and Maria Chiara Cavalleri. 2015. "Labour Mobility and the Portability of Social Rights in the EU." *CESifo Economic Studies 61* (2): pp. 346–376.

Dahl, Robert Alan. 1973. *Polyarchy: Participation and Opposition*. New Haven, CT: Yale University Press.

D'Arcy, Ciarán. 2015. "Gama Reaction: Turkish Workers Treated like 'Slaves', Says Solicitor." *The Irish Times*. August 1. https://www.irishtimes.com/news/crime-and-law/gama-reaction-turkish-workers-treated-like-slaves-says-solicitor-1.2303900.

Deacon, Bob. 2013. *Global Social Policy in the Making: The Foundations of the Social Protection Floor*. Bristol, UK: Policy Press.

Deacon, Bob, Michelle Hulse, and Paul Stubbs. 1997. *Global Social Policy: International Organizations and the Future of Welfare*. London: SAGE Publications.

De Haas, Hein. 2010. "Migration and Development: A Theoretical Perspective." *International Migration Review 44* (1): pp. 227–264.

Délano Alonso, Alexandra. 2018. *From Here and There: Diaspora Policies, Integration, and Social Rights Beyond Borders*. New York: Oxford University Press.

Deutsche Wirtschaftsnachrichten. 2014. "Deutsche Rentner Verdrängen Senioren in Osteuropa Aus Den Pflegeheimen (German Pensioneers Crowd out the Elderly from Nursing Homes in Eastern Europe)." *Deutsche Wirtschaftsnachrichten*, October 27. http://deutsche-wirtschafts-nachrichten.de/2014/10/27/deutsche-rentner-verdraengen-senioren-in-osteuropa-aus-den-pflegeheimen/.

Dobbs, Erica. 2017. "Bureaucrats and the Ballot Box: State-Led Political Incorporation in Ireland." In *The Politics of New Immigrant Destinations: Transatlantic Perspectives*, edited by Stefanie Chambers, Diana Evans, Anthony M. Messina, and Abigail Fisher Williamson, pp. 41–60. Philadelphia, PA: Temple University Press.

Dobbs, Erica, and Peggy Levitt. 2017. "The Missing Link? The Role of Sub-National Governance in Transnational Social Protections." *Oxford Development Studies 45* (1): pp. 47–63.

Dobbs, Erica, Peggy Levitt, Sonia Parella, and Alisa Petroff. 2018. "Social Welfare Grey Zones: How and Why Subnational Actors Provide When Nations Do Not?" *Journal of Ethnic and Migration Studies 45* (9): pp. 1595–1612.

Dodson, Lisa, and Rebekah M. Zincavage. 2007. "'It's like a Family': Caring Labor, Exploitation, and Race in Nursing Homes." *Gender and Society 21* (6): pp. 905–928.

Dossa, Parin, and Cati Coe, eds. 2017. *Transnational Aging and Reconfigurations of Kin Work*. New Brunswick, NJ: Rutgers University Press.

Doyle, David. 2015. "Remittances and Social Spending." *American Political Science Review 109* (4): pp. 785–802.

Doyle, Jim. 2014. "How a St. Louis-Based Health Care System Became One of the Nation's Biggest." *St. Louis Post-Dispatch*. February 23. https://www.stltoday.com/business/local/how-a-st-louis-based-health-care-system-became-one-of-the-nations-biggest/article_c07ada87-ab74-5175-a0b0-5219dd7b95f1.html.

Drabo, Alassane, and Christian Hubert Ebeke. 2010. *Remittances, Public Health Spending and Foreign Aid in the Access to Health Care Services in Developing Countries*. Working Papers. Clermont-Ferrand, FR: Le Centre d'études et de recherches sur le développement international (CERDI).

Dream in Mexico. 2020. "Education and Empowerment." Accessed April 2020. http://dreaminmexico.org/.

Dreby, Joanna. 2010. *Divided by Borders: Mexican Migrants and their Children*. Berkeley, CA: University of California Press.

Dreby, Joanna. 2015. *Everyday Illegal: When Policies Undermine Immigrant Families*. Oakland, CA: University of California Press.

Dromi, Shai M. 2020. *Above the Fray: The Red Cross and the Making of the Humanitarian NGO Sector*. Chicago: IL: University of Chicago Press.

Dubinsky, Karen. 2010. *Babies without Borders: Adoption and Migration Across the Americas*. Toronto: University of Toronto Press.

Ducanes, Geoffrey. 2015. "The Welfare Impact of Overseas Migration on Philippine Households: Analysis Using Panel Data." *Asian and Pacific Migration Journal 24* (1): pp. 79–106.

Duquette-Rury, Lauren. 2014. "Collective Remittances and Transnational Coproduction: The 3 × 1 Program for Migrants and Household Access to Public Goods in Mexico." *Studies in Comparative International Development 49* (1): pp. 112–139.

Duquette-Rury, Lauren. 2019. *Exit and Voice: The Paradox of Cross-Border Politics in Mexico*. Oakland, CA: University of California Press.

Duquette-Rury, Lauren, and Zhenxiang Chen. 2019. "Does International Migration Affect Political Participation? Evidence from Multiple Data Sources across Mexican Municipalities, 1990–2013." *International Migration Review 53* (3): pp. 798–830.

Eckstein, Susan Eva, and Giovanni Peri. 2018. "Immigrant Niches and Immigrant Networks in the U.S. Labor Market." *RSF: The Russell Sage Foundation Journal of the Social Sciences 4* (1): pp.1–17.

ECOWAS. 2019. "ECOWAS to Harmonise Labour laws in the region." *ECOWAS News*. May 22. https://www.ecowas.int/33826/.

Editor. 2017. "Canadian Citizenship Extends To Adopted Children." *Canadian Newcomer Magazine*. August 27. http://www.cnmag.ca/canadian-citizenship-extends-to-adopted-children/.

Escrivá, Ángeles. 2004. *Securing Care and Welfare of Dependants Transnationally: Peruvians and Spaniards in Spain*. Working Paper Number WP404. Oxford, UK: Oxford Institute of Population Ageing.

Ethics Committee of the American Society for Reproductive Medicine. 2013. "Cross-Border Reproductive Care: A Committee Opinion." *Fertility and Sterility 100* (3): pp. 645–650.

European Commission. n.d. "The Bologna Process and the European Higher Education Area." Accessed July 11, 2021. https://ec.europa.eu/education/policies/higher-education/bologna-process-and-european-higher-education-area_en.

European Commission. 2014. *The Erasmus Impact Study: Effects of mobility on the skills and employability of students and the internationalization of higher education institutions.* Luxembourg: Publications Office of the European Union. https://ec.europa.eu/assets/eac/education/library/study/2014/erasmus-impact-summary_en.pdf.

European Commission. 2017. *Communication from the Commission to the European Parliament and the Council—The Protection of Children in Migration.* COM/2017/0211 final. https://eur-lex.europa.eu/legal-content/en/TXT/?uri=CELEX%3A52017DC0211.

European Commission. 2021. *European employment strategy: Flexicurity.* Accessed July 11, 2021. https://ec.europa.eu/social/main.jsp?langId=en&catId=102.

Eyal, Nir, and Samia A. Hurst. 2008. "Physician Brain Drain: Can Nothing Be Done?" *Public Health Ethics 1* (2): pp. 180–192.

Fabbe, Kristin. 2019. *Disciples of the State? Religion and State-Building in the Former Ottoman World.* Cambridge, UK: Cambridge University Press.

Fairless, Tom. 2018. "Labor Shortage Lifts Wages on Europe's Eastern Flank." *The Wall Street Journal.* September 27. https://www.wsj.com/articles/labor-shortage-lifts-wages-on-europes-eastern-flank-1538049601.

Faist, Thomas. 2018. *The Transnationalized Social Question: Migration and the Politics of Social Inequalities in the Twenty-First Century.* New York: Oxford University Press.

Faist, Thomas, and Başak Bilecen. 2014. "Social Inequalities Through the Lens of Social Protection: Notes on the Transnational Social Question." *Population, Space and Place 21* (3): pp. 282–293.

Faist, Thomas, Başak Bilecen, Karolina Barglowski, and Joanna Jadwiga Sienkiewicz. 2015. "Transnational Social Protection: Migrants' Strategies and Patterns of Inequalities." *Population, Space and Place 21* (3): pp. 193–202.

Fassin, Didier. 2011. "Policing Borders, Producing Boundaries. The Governmentality of Immigration in Dark Times." *Annual Review of Anthropology 40* (October): pp. 213–226.

Félix, Adrián. 2011. "Posthumous Transnationalism: Postmortem Repatriation from the United States to México." *Latin American Research Review 46* (3): pp. 157–179.

Fenton, Estye. 2019. *The End of International Adoption: An Unraveling Reproductive Market and the Politics of Healthy Babies.* New Brunswick, NJ: Rutgers University Press.

Ferwerda, Jeremy. 2021. "Immigration, Voting Rights, and Redistribution: Evidence from Local Governments in Europe." *The Journal of Politics 83* (1): pp. 321–339.

Fine, Janice, and Jennifer Gordon. 2010. "Strengthening Labor Standards Enforcement through Partnerships with Workers' Organizations." *Politics and Society 38* (4): pp. 552–585.

Finn, Victoria. 2020. "Migrant Voting: Here, There, in Both Countries, or Nowhere." *Citizenship Studies 24* (6): pp. 730–750.

FitzGerald, David Scott. 2009. *A Nation of Emigrants: How Mexico Manages Its Migration.* Berkeley, CA: University of California Press.

FitzGerald, David Scott. 2019. *Refuge Beyond Reach: How Rich Democracies Repel Asylum Seekers.* New York: Oxford University Press.

Flores, Claudia, and Nicole Prchal Svajlenka. 2021. "Why DACA Matters." Center for American Progress. *NPR (National Public Radio)*, April 29. https://www.americanprogress.org/issues/immigration/news/2021/04/29/498944/why-daca-matters/.

Flynn, Michael A. 2014. "Safety and the Diverse Workforce: Lessons from NIOSH's Work with Latino Immigrants." *Professional Safety 59* (6): pp. 52–57.

Fonseca, Claudia. 2004. "The Circulation of Children in a Brazilian Working-Class Neighborhood: A Local Practice in a Globalized World." In *Cross Cultural Approaches to Adoption*, edited by Fiona Bowie, pp. 165–181. London: Routledge.

Ford, Michele. 2019. *From Migrant to Worker: Global Unions and Temporary Labor Migration in Asia*. Ithaca, NY: Cornell University Press.

Forney, Ben. 2017. "South Korea's Brain Drain." *The Diplomat*. July 6. https://thediplomat.com/2017/07/south-koreas-brain-drain/.

Fortuny, Karina and Ajay Chaudry. 2011. *A Comprehensive Review of Immigrant Access to Health and Human Services*. Washington DC: The Urban Institute.

Freeman, Gary P. 1986. "Migration and the Political Economy of the Welfare State." *The Annals of the American Academy of Political and Social Science 485* (1): pp. 51–63.

Freeman, Gary P. 1995. "Modes of Immigration Politics in Liberal Democratic States." *International Migration Review 29* (4): pp. 881–902.

Frekko, Susan E., Jessaca B. Leinaweaver, and Diana Marre. 2015. "How (not) to Talk about Adoption: On Communicative Vigilance in Spain." *American Ethnologist 42* (4): pp. 703–719.

Friedman, Milton. 1955. "The Role of Government in Education." In *Economics and the Public Interest*, edited by Robert Solo, pp. 123–144. New Brunswick, NJ: Rutgers University Press.

Friedman, Sara L., and Pardis Mahdavi, eds. 2015. *Migrant Encounters: Intimate Labor, the State, and Mobility Across Asia*. Philadelphia, PA: University of Pennsylvania Press.

Fuchs, Dale. 2007. "Norway Looks After Its Elderly—In Spain." *The Guardian*. June 26. https://www.theguardian.com/world/2007/jun/26/spain.international.

Fujiwara, Lynn. 2008. *Mothers Without Citizenship: Asian Immigrant Families and The Consequences of Welfare Reform*. Minneapolis: University of Minnesota Press.

Fulbright Romania. n.d. "The Fulbright Program." Accessed July 11, 2021. https://fulbright.ro/about/.

Gailey, Christine Ward. 2010. *Blue-Ribbon Babies and Labors of Love: Race, Class, and Gender in U.S. Adoption Practice*. Austin, TX: University of Texas Press.

Gaillard, Jacques, Anne-Marie Gaillard, and V.V. Krishna. 2015. "Return from Migration and Circulation of Highly Educated People: The Never-Ending Brain Drain." *Science, Technology, and Society 20* (3): pp. 269–278.

Galli, Chiara. 2020. "The Ambivalent U.S. Context of Reception and the Dichotomous Legal Consciousness of Unaccompanied Minors." *Social Problems 67* (4): pp. 763–781.

Gallotti, Maria. 2015. *Migrant Domestic Workers Around the World: Global and Regional Estimates*. Geneva: International Labour Organization.

Gamburd, Michele Ruth. 2000. *The Kitchen Spoon's Handle: Transnationalism and Sri Lanka's Migrant Housemaids*. Ithaca, NY: Cornell University Press.

Gamlen, Alan. 2019. *Human Geopolitics: States, Emigrants, and the Rise of Diaspora Institutions*. New York: Oxford University Press.

Gamlen, Alan, Michael E. Cummings, and Paul M. Vaaler. 2019. "Explaining the Rise of Diaspora Institutions," *Journal of Ethnic and Migration Studies 45* (4): pp. 492–516.

García, Ana Isabel López. 2020. "The 3×1 Programme and Criminal Violence in Mexico." *Global Networks 20* (4): pp. 625–655.

García, Ana Isabel López, and Pedro P. Orraca-Romano. 2019. "International Migration and Universal Healthcare Access: Evidence from Mexico's 'Seguro Popular.'" *Oxford Development Studies 47* (2): pp. 171–187.

Gavanas, Anna, and Inés Calzada. 2016. "Multiplex Migration and Aspects of Precarization: Swedish Retirement Migrants to Spain and Their Service Providers." *Critical Sociology 42* (7–8): pp. 1003–1016.

Geest, Sjaak Van Der, Anke Mul, and Hans Vermeulen. 2004. "Linkages between Migration and the Care of Frail Older People: Observations from Greece, Ghana and The Netherlands." *Ageing and Society 24* (3): pp. 431–450.

Gehring, Anoeshka. 2017. "Pensioners on the Move: A 'Legal Gate' Perspective on Retirement Migration to Spain." *Population, Space and Place 23* (5): pp. 1–12.

Gelatt, Julia. 2020. *Immigrant Workers: Vital to the U.S. COVID-19 Response, Disproportionately Vulnerable*. Washington, DC: Migration Policy Institute.

Gilbertson, Greta. 2009. "Caregiving across Generations: Aging, State Assistance, and Multigenerational Ties among Immigrants from Dominican Republic." In *Across Generations: Immigrant Families in America*, edited by Nancy Foner, pp. 135–159. New York: New York University Press.

Gingrich, Luann Good and Stefan Kongeter. 2017. *Transnational Social Policy: Social Welfare in a World on the Move*. New York: Taylor and Francis.

Glasgow, Godfrey F., and Janice Gouse-Sheese. 1995. "Themes of Rejection and Abandonment in Group Work with Caribbean Adolescents." *Social Work with Groups 17* (4): pp. 3–27.

Glennon, Theresa. 2016. "Legal Regulation of Family Creation through Gamete Donation: Access, Identity, and Parentage." In *Regulating Reproductive Donation*, edited by Susan Golombok, Rosamund Scott, John B. Appleby, Martin Richards, and Stephen Wilkinson, pp. 60–83. Cambridge, UK: Cambridge University Press.

Glick-Schiller, Nina and Thomas Faist. 2009. "Introduction: Migration, Development, and Social Transformation." *Social Analysis 53* (3): pp. 1–13.

Glick-Schiller, Nina, and Noel B. Salazar. 2013. "Regimes of Mobility Across the Globe." *Journal of Ethnic and Migration Studies 39* (2): pp. 183–200.

Glynn, Timothy P. 2011. "Taking Self-Regulation Seriously: High-Ranking Officer Sanctions for Work-Law Violations." *Berkeley Journal of Employment and Labor Law 32* (2): pp. 279–346.

Goldstein, Dana. 2018a. "Teacher Pay Is So Low in Some U.S. School Districts That They're Recruiting Overseas." *The New York Times*. May 2. https://www.nytimes.com/2018/05/02/us/arizona-teachers-philippines.html.

Goldstein, Dana. 2018b. "How a Times Education Reporter Discovered a Pipeline of Foreign Teachers." *The New York Times*. May 3. https://www.nytimes.com/2018/05/03/insider/arizona-teacher-walkout-foreign-recruitment.html.

Gomez, Maria Gudelia Rangel, Josana Tonda, G. Rogelio Zapata, Michael Flynn, Francesca Gany, Juanita Lara, Ilan Shapiro, and Cecilia Ballesteros Rosales. 2017. "Ventanillas de Salud: A Collaborative and Binational Health Access and Preventive Care Program." *Front Public Health 5* (151). Online Edition. https://doi.org/10.3389/fpubh.2017.00151.

Gonzales, Roberto G. 2015. *Lives in Limbo: Undocumented and Coming of Age in America*. Oakland, CA: University of California Press.

Goody, Esther N. 1982. *Parenthood and Social Reproduction: Fostering and Occupational Rules in West Africa*. Cambridge, UK: Cambridge University Press.

Gordon, Jennifer. 2005. "Law, Lawyers, and Labor: The United Farm Workers' Legal Strategy in the 1960s and 1970s and the Role of Law in Union Organizing Today." *University of Pennsylvania Journal of Labor and Employment Law 8* (1): pp. 1–72.

Gorodzeisky, Anastasia, and Andrew Richards. 2013. "Trade Unions and Migrant Workers in Western Europe." *European Journal of Industrial Relations 19* (3): pp. 239–254.

Gough, Ian, and Geof D. Wood. 2004. *Insecurity and Welfare Regimes in Asia, Africa, and Latin America: Social Policy in Development Contexts*. Cambridge, UK: Cambridge University Press.

Gov.UK. 2014. *Intercountry Adoption and British Citizenship*. https://www.gov.uk/government/publications/guidance-on-how-adopted-children-can-become-british/intercountry-adoption-and-british-citizenship.

Gowayed, Heba. 2018. "The Unnecessary Nudge: Education and Poverty Policy in a Cairo Slum." *Sociological Forum 33* (2): pp. 482–504.

Grace, Maggi. 2006. "United States Senate Special Committee on Aging Witness Testimony." Congressional Hearing. June 27. https://www.aging.senate.gov/hearings/the-globalization-of-health-care-can-medical-tourism-reduce-health-care-costs.

Grady, Denise. 2020. "Covid-19 Patient Gets Double Lung Transplant, Offering Hope for Others." *The New York Times*. June 11. https://www.nytimes.com/2020/06/11/health/coronavirus-lung-transplant.html.

Greenhouse, Steven. 2014. "Volkswagen Vote Is Defeat for Labor in South." *The New York Times*. February 14. https://www.nytimes.com/2014/02/15/business/volkswagen-workers-reject-forming-a-union.html.

Groenedijk, Kees. 2008. *Local Voting Rights for Non-Nationals in Europe: What We Know and What We Need to Learn*. Washington, DC: Migration Policy Institute.

Groll, Elias. 2013. "Cuba's Greatest Export? Medical Diplomacy." *Foreign Policy*. May 7. https://foreignpolicy.com/2013/05/07/cubas-greatest-export-medical-diplomacy/.

Gsir, Sonia, Jérémy Mandin, and Elsa Mescoli. 2017. "Countries of Origin as Organisers of Emigration: Moroccans and Turks in Belgium." In *Migrant Integration between Homeland and Host Society (Vol. 2)*, edited by Anna Di Bartolomeo, Sona Kalantaryan, Justyna Salamońska, and Philippe Fargues, pp. 61–79. Cham, CH: Springer.

Guerra, Valentina, and David Brindle. 2018. *Promoting the Social Inclusion of Migrant Children and Young People: The Duty of Social Services*. European Social Network—Social Services in Europe. https://ec.europa.eu/migrant-integration/librarydoc/promoting-the-social-inclusion-of-migrant-children-and-young-people---the-duty-of-social-services.

Guevarra, Anna Romina. 2010. *Marketing Dreams, Manufacturing Heroes: The Transnational Labor Brokering of Filipino Workers*. New Brunswick, NJ: Rutgers University Press.

Guo, Man, Jinyu Liu, Ling Xu, Weiyu Mao, and Iris Chi. 2016. "Intergenerational Relationships and Psychological Well-Being of Chinese Older Adults with Migrant Children: Does Internal or International Migration Make a Difference?" *Journal of Family Issues 36* (10): pp. 1351–1376.

Guo, Man, Meredith Stensland, Mengting Li, and Xinqi Dong. 2020. "Parent–Adult Child Relations of Chinese Older Immigrants in the United States: Is There an Optimal Type?" *Journal of Gerontology: Social Sciences 75* (4): pp. 889–898.

Guo, Man, Ling Xu, Jinyu Liu, Weiyu Mao, and Iris Chi. 2016. "Parent–Child Relationships Among Older Chinese Immigrants: The Influence of Co-residence, Frequent Contact, Intergenerational Support and Sense of Children's Deference." *Ageing and Society 36* (7): pp. 1459–1482.

Gustafson, Per. 2008. "Transnationalism in Retirement Migration: The Case of North European Retirees in Spain." *Ethnic and Racial Studies 31* (3): pp. 451–475.

Hagan, J. 2006. "Making Theological Sense of the Migration Journey from Latin America." *American Behavioral Scientist 49* (11): pp. 1554–1573.

Hahn, Karola, and Damtew Teferra. 2013. "Tuning as Instrument of Systematic Higher Education Reform and Quality Enhancement: The African Experience." *Tuning Journal for Higher Education 1* (1): pp. 127–163.

Han, Keunah. 2012. "Academic performance and cultural adaptation of South Korean Parachute Kids." Doctoral Dissertation. Temple University.

Hatos, Adrian. 2010. "The (Little) Effect that Parents' Labour Emigration has on their Children's School Performance: A Study of Secondary School Students in Oradea (Romania)." *The New Educational Review 20* (1): pp. 85–96.

Häusermann, Silja, and Hanna Schwander. 2012. "Varieties of Dualization? Labor Market Segmentation and Insider Outsider Divides across Regimes." In *The Age of Dualization: The Changing Face of Inequality in Deindustrializing Societies*, edited by Patrick Emmenegger, Silja Häusermann, Bruno Palier, and Martin Seeleib-Kaiser, pp. 27–51. New York: Oxford University Press.

Hertz, Rosanna, and Margaret K. Nelson. 2016. "Acceptance and Disclosure: Comparing Genetic Symmetry and Genetic Asymmetry in Heterosexual Couples Between Egg Recipients and Embryo Recipients." *Facts, Views and Vision in Obstetrics and Gynaecology 8* (1): pp. 11–22.

Hirschman, Albert O. 1970. *Exit, Voice, and Loyalty: Responses to Decline in Firms, Organizations, and States*. Cambridge, MA: Harvard University Press.

Ho, Elaine Lynn-Ee. 2019. *Citizens in Motion: Emigration, Immigration, and Re-Migration Across China's Borders*. Stanford, CA: Stanford University Press.

Ho, Elaine Lynn-Ee, Guo Zhou, Jian An Liew, Tuen Yi Chiu, Shirlena Huang, and Brenda S. A. Yeoh. 2021. "Webs of Care: Qualitative GIS Research on Aging, Mobility, and Care Relations in Singapore." *Annals of American Association of Geographers 111* (5): pp. 1462–1482. https://doi.org/10.1080/24694452.2020.1807900.

Hoang, Lan Anh. 2016. "Governmentality in Asian Migration Regimes: The Case of Labour Migration from Vietnam to Taiwan." *Population, Space and Place 23* (3): e2019.

Hoang, Lan Anh, and Brenda S. A. Yeoh. 2011. "Breadwinning Wives and 'Left-behind' Husbands: Men and Masculinities in the Vietnamese Transnational Family." *Gender and Society 25* (6): pp. 717–739.

Hoang, Lan Anh, and Brenda S. A. Yeoh, eds. 2015. *Transnational Labour Migration, Remittances and the Changing Family in Asia*. Basingstoke, UK: Palgrave Macmillan.

Hoare, Quintin, and Geoffrey Nowell Smith, eds. 1971. *Selections from the Prison Notebooks of Antonio Gramsci*. New York: International Publishers.

Hochschild, Arlie Russell. 2000. "The Nanny Chain." *The American Prospect 3* (December): pp. 32–36.

Holdaway, Jennifer, Peggy Levitt, Jing Fang, and Narasimhan Rajaram. 2015. "Mobility and Health Sector Development in China and India." *Social Science and Medicine 130* (April): pp. 268–276.

Hondagneu-Sotelo, Pierrette. 2007. *Doméstica: Immigrant Workers Cleaning and Caring in the Shadows of Affluence*. Second Edition. Oakland, CA: University of California Press.

Horn, Vincent, and Cornelia Schweppe, eds. 2015. *Transnational Aging: Current Insights and Future Challenges*. London: Routledge.

Hornbeck, Dustin. 2017. "Federal Role in Education Has a Long History." *The Conversation*. April 26. http://theconversation.com/federal-role-in-education-has-a-long-history-74807.

Horst, Cindy, Marta Bivand Erdal, Jørgen Carling, and Karin Afeef. 2014. "Private Money, Public Scrutiny? Contrasting Perspectives on Remittances." *Global Networks 14* (4): pp. 514–532.

Horton, Sarah, and Stephanie Cole. 2011. "Medical Returns: Seeking Health Care in Mexico." *Social Science and Medicine 72* (11): pp. 1846–1852.

HotNews. 2021. "Critici dure ale studentilor si elevilor pentru proiectul prin care Guvernul vrea sa ofere bani tinerilor sa invete in strainatate, pe care sa nu ii returneze daca se intorc in tara/Cum raspunde initiatorul." *HotNews*. April 5. https://www.hotnews.ro/stiri-educatie-24713031-organizatiile-studenti-elevi-critica-dur-proiectul-prin-care-guvernul-vrea-ofere-bani-tinerilor-invete-strainatate-care-nu-returneze-daca-intorc-romania.htm.

Hou, Angela Yung-Chi, Robert Morse, and Wayne Wang. 2017. "Recognition of Academic Qualifications in Transnational Higher Education and Challenges for Recognizing a Joint Degree in Europe and Asia." *Studies in Higher Education 42* (7): pp. 1211–1228.

Howard, Larry L., and Denise L. Stanley. 2017. "Remittances Channels and the Physical Growth of Honduran Children." *International Review of Applied Economics 31* (3): pp. 376–397.

Howard, Robert D. 2008. "Western Retirees in Thailand: Motives, Experiences, Wellbeing, Assimilation and Future Needs." *Ageing and Society 28* (2): pp. 145–163.

Huang, Futao. 2003. "Policy and Practice of the Internationalization of Higher Education in China." *Journal of Studies in International Education 7* (3): pp. 225–240.

Huang, Shirlena, and Brenda S. A. Yeoh. 2003. "The Difference Gender Makes: State Policy and Contract Migrant Workers in Singapore." *Asian and Pacific Migration Journal 12* (1-2): pp. 75–97.

Huang, Shirlena, and Brenda S. A. Yeoh. 2005. "Transnational Families and Their Children's Education: China's 'Study Mothers' in Singapore." *Global Networks 5* (4): pp. 379–400.

Huang, Shirlena, Brenda S. A. Yeoh, and Mika Toyota. 2012. "Caring for the Elderly: The Embodied Labour of Migrant Care Workers in Singapore." *Global Networks 12* (2): pp. 195–215.

Huber, Sarah, Sharvari Karandikar, and Lindsay Gezinski. 2018. "Exploring Indian Surrogates' Perceptions of the Ban on International Surrogacy." *Affilia: Journal of Women and Social Work 33* (1): pp. 69–84.

Huete, Cristina. 2015. "El informe que que vetó Sanidade pide a la Xunta el fin de la desigualdad sanitaria." *El País*. March 11. https://elpais.com/ccaa/2015/03/11/galicia/1426099502_544967.html.

Hunter, Alistair. 2018. *Retirement Home? Ageing Migrant Workers in France and the Question of Return*. New York: Springer Open. Online Edition. https://www.springer.com/us/book/9783319649757.

Hussmanns, Ralf. 2004. *Measuring the Informal Economy: From Employment in the Informal Sector to Informal Employment*. Working Paper No. 53. Geneva: International Labour Office.

IMTJ (International Medical Travel Journal). 2017. "Ascension Quits Partnership." *LaingBuisson*. December 28. https://www.laingbuissonnews.com/imtj/news-imtj/ascension-quits-partnership/.

InCont. 2011. "Poti sa studiezi la universitati renumite din strainatate, fara sa platesti taza de scolarizare!" *InCont*. February 1. https://incont.stirileprotv.ro/job-uri/poti-sa-studiezi-la-universitati-renumite-din-strainatate-fara-sa-platesti-taxa-de-scolarizare.html.

Institut Français Bucarest. 2020. "Home." Accessed July 3, 2020. http://www.institutfrancais.ro/Bucuresti/home.

Instituto de los Mexicanos en el Exterior. 2016. "Documento de Transferencia." *Gobierno de México*. August 22. https://www.gob.mx/ime/acciones-y-programas/documento-de-transferencia.

International Labour Office. 2018. *ILO Global Estimates of Migrant Workers and Migrant Domestic Workers: Results and Methodology: Special Focus on Migrant Domestic Workers*. Geneva: International Labour Organization.

International Labour Organization. 2015. *Good Practice—Wages Protection System (UAE)*. Geneva: International Labour Organization.

Irish Times. 2005. "Ictu to Consider Migrant Workers' Ombudsman." *Irish Times*. June 21. https://www.irishtimes.com/news/ictu-to-consider-migrant-workers-ombudsman-1.458152.

Iskander, Natasha. 2013. "Moroccan Migrants as Unlikely Captains of Industry: Remittances, Financial Intermediation, and La Banque Centrale Populaire." In *How Immigrants Impact Their Homelands,* edited by Susan Eva Eckstein and Adil Najam, pp. 156–190. Durham, NC: Duke University Press.

Iskander, Natasha. 2017. "The Right to have 'Society in the Bones': The Skill and Bodies of Male Workers in Qatar." *Women's Studies Quarterly 45* (3-4): pp. 234–244.

Jacobs, Harrison, and Annie Zheng. 2018. "Tens of Thousands of Chinese People Live at the Mercy of Apple's Factories — and They Don't Even Work There." *Business Insider*. May 15. https://www.businessinsider.sg/china-iphone-city-residents-foxconn-apple-effect-2018-5/.

Jenkins, Kathleen. 2021. *Walking the Way Together: How Families Connect on the Camino de Santiago*. New York: Oxford University Press.

Johnson, Martin. 2019. "US Detains Record 76,000 Minors Traveling Alone in 2019." *The Hill*. October 29. https://thehill.com/policy/national-security/department-of-homeland-security/468025-us-detains-record-75000-minors.

Johnston, Rory, Valorie A. Crooks, Jeremy Snyder, and Paul Kingsbury. 2010. "What is Known about the Effects of Medical Tourism in Destination and Departure Countries? A Scoping Review." *International Journal for Equity in Health 9* (24): pp. 1–13.

Jones, Maggie. 2015. "Why a Generation of Adoptees is Returning to South Korea." *The New York Times*. January 14. https://www.nytimes.com/2015/01/18/magazine/why-a-generation-of-adoptees-is-returning-to-south-korea.html.

Joppke, Christian. 1997. "Why Liberal States Accept Unwanted Immigration." *World Politics 50* (2): pp. 266–293.

Joseph, Tiffany D. 2015. *Race on the Move: Brazilian Migrants and the Global Reconstruction of Race*. Palo Alto, CA: Stanford University Press.

Joseph, Tiffany D. 2016. "What Health Care Reform Means for Immigrants: Comparing the Affordable Care Act and Massachusetts Health Reforms." *Journal of Health Politics, Policy, and Law 41* (1): pp. 101–116.

JuSoor. 2018. "About Our Organization." Accessed August 14, 2018. https://jusoorsyria.com/.

Kalaj, Ermira Hoxha. 2014. "Are Remittances Spent in a Healthy Way? Evidence from Albania." *SEER: Journal for Labour and Social Affairs in Eastern Europe 17* (2): pp. 237–266.

Kaltenborn, Markus. 2015. *Social Rights and International Development: Global Legal Standards for the Post-2015 Development Agenda*. New York: Springer.

Kang, Youbin. 2021. "The Rise, Demise, and Replacement of the Bangladesh Experiment in Transnational Labour Regulation." *International Labour Review 160* (3): pp. 407–430.

Karl, Ute, and Sandra Torres. 2015. *Ageing in Contexts of Migration*. New York: Routledge.

Kasper, Jennifer, and Francis Bajunirwe. 2012. "Brain Drain in Sub-Saharan Africa: Contributing Factors, Potential Remedies and the Role of Academic Medical Centres." *Archives of Disease in Childhood 97* (11): pp. 973–979.

Kaushik, Manas, Abhishek Jaiswal, Naseem Shah, and Ajay Mahal. 2008. "High-End Physician Migration from India." *Bulletin of the World Health Organization 86* (1): pp. 40–45.

Kino Border Initiative [KBI]. n.d. "Mission and Vision." Accessed July 11, 2021. https://www.kinoborderinitiative.org/mission-and-values/.

Kelly, Ann. 2018. "Ebola Vaccines, Evidentiary Charisma, and the Rise of Global Health Emergency Research." *Economy and Society 47* (1): pp. 135–161.

Kemp, Adriana, and Nelly Kfir. 2016. "Wanted Workers but Unwanted Mothers: Mobilizing Moral Claims on Migrant Care Workers' Families in Israel." *Social Problems 63* (3): pp. 373–394.

Kentish, Benjamin. 2018. "How Reliant Is the NHS on Foreign Doctors?" *The Independent*. June 4. https://www.independent.co.uk/news/uk/politics/nhs-foreign-doctors-how-many-reliant-immigration-theresa-may-brexit-explained-visa-a8383306.html.

Kesler, Christel, and Irene Bloemraad. 2010. "Does Immigration Erode Social Capital? The Conditional Effects of Immigration-Generated Diversity on Trust, Membership, and Participation across 19 Countries, 1981-2000." *Canadian Journal of Political Science / Revue Canadienne de Science Politique 43* (2): pp. 319–347.

Khan, Shamus Rahman. 2011. *Privilege: The Making of an Adolescent Elite at St. Paul's School*, Princeton, NJ: Princeton University Press. https://press.princeton.edu/books/paperback/9780691156231/privilege.

Kibria, Nazli. 2002. "Of Blood, Belonging, and Homeland Trips: Transnationalism and Identity among Second Generation Chinese and Korean Americans." In *the Changing Face of Home*, edited by Peggy Levitt and Mary Waters, pp. 295–311. New York: Russell Sage.

Kim, Eleana J. 2007. "Our Adoptee, Our Alien: Transnational Adoptees as Specters of Foreignness and Family in South Korea." *Anthropological Quarterly 80* (2): pp. 497–531.

Kim, Jeehum. 2012. "Remitting 'Filial Co-Habitation': 'Actual' and 'Virtual' Co-Residence between Korean Professional Migrant Adult Children Couples in Singapore and Their Elderly Parents." *Ageing and Society 32* (80): pp. 1337–1359.

Kim, Nadia Y. 2009. "Finding Our Way Home: Korean Americans, Homelands Trips, and Cultural Foreignness." In *Diasporic Homecomings: Ethnic Return Migrants in Comparative Perspective*, edited by Takeyuki Tsuda, pp. 305–324. Stanford, CA: Stanford University Press.

King, Russell. 2012. "Geography and Migration Studies: Retrospect and Prospect." *Population, Space and Place 18* (2): pp. 134–153.

King, Russell, Eralba Cela, Tineke Fokkema, and Julie Vullnetari. 2014. "The Migration and Well-Being of the Zero Generation: Transgenerational Care, Grandparenting, and Loneliness amongst Albanian Older People." *Population, Space and Place 20* (8): pp. 728–738.

King, Russell, Eralba Cela, Gabriele Morettini, and Tineke Fokkema. 2019. "The Marche: Italy's New Frontier for International Retirement Migration." *Population, Space, and Place 25* (5): pp. 1–12.

King, Russell, Aija Lulle, Dora Sampaio, and Julie Vullnetari. 2017. "Unpacking the Ageing–Migration Nexus and Challenging the Vulnerability Trope." *Journal of Ethnic and Migration Studies 43* (2): pp. 182–198.

Kingma, Mireille. 2018. *Nurses on the Move: Migration and the Global Health Care Economy*. Ithaca, NY: Cornell University Press.

Kitroeff, Natalie. 2017. "Construction Workers in L.A. Make Less Now than 40 Years Ago. Here's Why." *Los Angeles Times*. April 22. http://www.latimes.com/projects/la-fi-construction-trump/.

Kneebone, Susan. 2012. "Migrant Workers Between States in Search of Exit and Integration Strategies in Southeast Asia." *Asian Journal of Social Science 40* (4): pp. 367–391.

Knowles, Caroline. 2017. "Reframing sociologies of ethnicity and migration in encounters with Chinese London." *British Journal of Sociology 68* (3): pp. 454–473.

Kollar, Eszter, and Alena Buyx. 2013. "Ethics and Policy of Medical Brain Drain: A Review." *Swiss Medical Weekly 143* (October): w13845.

Kopinak, Kathryn. 2017. *The Relationship Between Employment in Maquiladora Industries in Mexico and Labor Migration to the United States*. Working Paper 120. San Diego, CA: The Center for Comparative Immigration Studies, University of California.

Kroløkke, Charlotte. 2014. "Eggs and Euros: A Feminist Perspective on Reproductive Travel from Denmark to Spain." *International Journal of Feminist Approaches to Bioethics 7* (2): pp. 144–163.

Kubalčíková, Kateřina, and Jana Havlíková. 2016. "Current Developments in Social Care Services for Older Adults in the Czech Republic: Trends Towards Deinstitutionalization and Marketization." *Journal of Social Service Research 42* (2): pp. 180–198.

Kwong, Kenny, Henry Chung, Loretta Sun, Jolene Chou, and Anna Taylor-Shih. 2009. "Factors Associated with Reverse-Migration Separation Among a Cohort of Low-Income Chinese Immigrant Families in New York City." *Social Work in Health Care 48* (3): pp. 348–359.

Lafleur, Jean-Michel, and Olivier Lizin. 2015. *Transnational Health Insurance Schemes: A New Avenue for Congolese Immigrants in Belgium to Care for Their Relatives' Health from abroad?* Transnational Studies Initiatives—Working Paper Series *3* (24). Cambridge, MA: Harvard University. https://orbi.uliege.be/handle/2268/172046.

Lafleur, Jean-Michel, and Maria Vivas Romero. 2018. "Combining Transnational and Intersectional Approaches to Immigrants' Social Protection: The Case of Andean Families' Access to Health." *Comparative Migration Studies 6* (14). Online Edition. https://comparativemigrationstudies.springeropen.com/articles/10.1186/s40878-018-0073-7.

Lafleur, Jean-Michel, and Daniela Vintila, eds. 2020. *Migration and Social Protection in Europe and Beyond (Vol. 3): A Focus on Non-EU Sending States*. IMISCOE. Rotterdam, NL: International Migration Research Network.

Lam, Theodora, Miriam Ee, Lan Anh Hoang, and Brenda S. A. Yeoh. 2013. "Securing a Better Living Environment for Left-Behind Children: Implications and Challenges for Policies." *Asian Pacific Migration Journal 22* (3): pp. 421–446.

Lamb, Sarah. 2009. *Aging and Indian Diaspora: Cosmopolitan Families in India and Abroad*. Bloomington, IN: Indiana University Press.

Lamba-Nieves, Deepak. 2017. "Hometown Associations and the Micropolitics of Transnational Community Development." *Journal of Ethnic and Migration Studies 44* (2): pp. 1–19.

Lan, Pei-chia. 2006. *Global Cinderella: Migrant Domestics and Newly Rich Employers in Taiwan*. Durham, NC: Duke University Press.

Lan, Pei-chia. 2018a. "Bridging Ethnic Differences for Cultural Intimacy: Production of Migrant Care Workers in Japan." *Critical Sociology 44* (7–8): pp. 1029–1043.

Lan, Pei-chia. 2018b. *Raising Global Families: Parenting, Immigration, and Class in Taiwan and the US*. Stanford, CA: Stanford University Press.

Lanari, Donatella, and Odoardo Bussini. 2012. "International Migration and Health Inequalities in Later Life." *Ageing and Society 32* (6): pp. 935–962.

Lansworth, Tom. 2012. *Recruiting Firm That Brought Filipino Teachers to Louisiana Ordered to Pay $4.5 Million in Damages for Exploitive Practices*. Washington, DC: American Federation for Teachers.

Lareau, Annette. 2011. *Unequal Childhoods: Class, Race, and Family Life*. Second Edition. Berkeley, CA: University of California Press.

Larmer, Brook. 2017. "The Parachute Generation." *The New York Times*. February 2. https://www.nytimes.com/2017/02/02/magazine/the-parachute-generation.html.

Lee, Jane Yeonjae, Robin A. Kearns, and Wardlow Friesen. 2010. "Seeking Affective Health Care: Korean Immigrants' Use of Homeland Medical Services." *Health and Place 16* (1): pp. 108–115.

Lee, Jennifer, and Min Zhou. 2015. *The Asian American Achievement Paradox*. New York: Russell Sage Foundation.

Lee, Sang E. 2010. "Unpacking the Packing Plant: Nicaraguan Migrant Women's Work in Costa Rica's Evolving Export Agriculture Sector." *Signs 35* (2): pp. 317–342.

Lee, Yean-Ju, and Hagen Koo. 2006. "'Wild Geese Fathers' and a Globalised Family Strategy for Education in Korea." *International Development Planning Review 28* (4): pp. 533–553.

Leinaweaver, Jessaca B. 2007. "On Moving Children: The Social Implications of Andean Child Circulation." *American Ethnologist 34* (1): pp. 163–180.

Leinaweaver, Jessaca B. 2010. "Outsourcing Care: How Peruvian Migrants Meet Transnational Family Obligations." *Latin American Perspectives 37* (5): pp. 67–87.

Leinaweaver, Jessaca B. 2012. "Little Strangers: International Adoption and American Kinship. A Review Essay." *Comparative Studies in Society and History 54* (1): pp. 206–216.

Leinaweaver, Jessaca B. 2013. *Adoptive Migration: Raising Latinos in Spain*. Durham, NC: Duke University Press.

Leinaweaver, Jessaca B. 2014. "Informal Kinship Fostering around the World: Anthropological Findings." *Child Development Perspectives 8* (3): pp. 131–136.

Leiter, Valarie, Jennifer Lutzy McDonald, and Heather Jacobson. 2006. "Challenging Children's Independent Citizenship: Immigration, Family, and the State." *Childhood 13* (1): pp. 11–27.

Lerner, Stephen. 2007. "Global Corporations, Global Unions." *Contexts 6* (3): pp. 16–22.

Levitsky, Steven, and Lucan A. Way. 2010. *Competitive Authoritarianism: Hybrid Regimes after the Cold War*. Cambridge, UK: Cambridge University Press.

Levitt, Peggy. 2001. *The Transnational Villagers*. Berkeley, CA: University of California Press.

Levitt, Peggy. 2007. *God Needs No Passport: Immigrants and the Changing American Religious Landscape*. New York: The New Press.

Levitt, Peggy 2009. "Routes and Roots: Understanding the Lives of the Second Generation Transnationally." *Journal of Ethnic and Migration Studies 35* (7): pp. 1225–1242.

Levitt, Peggy. 2012. "What's Wrong with Migration Scholarship? A Critique and a Way Forward." *Identities: Global Studies in Culture and Power 19* (4): pp. 493–500.

Levitt, Peggy, and Deepak Lamba-Nieves. 2011. "Social Remittances Revisited." *Journal of Ethnic and Migration Studies 37* (1): pp. 1–22.

Levitt, Peggy, and Sally Merry. 2009. "Vernacularization on the Ground: Local Uses of Global Women's Rights in Peru, China, India, and the United States." *Global Networks 9* (4): pp. 441–461.

Levitt, Peggy, and Narasimhan Rajaram. 2013a. "Moving toward Reform? Mobility, Health, and Development in the Context of Neoliberalism." *Migration Studies 1* (3): pp. 338–362.

Levitt, Peggy, and Narasimhan Rajaram. 2013b. "The Migration-Development Nexus and Organizational Time." *International Migration Review 47* (3): pp. 483–507.

Levitt, Peggy, Jocelyn Viterna, Armin Mueller, and Charlotte Lloyd. 2017. "Transnational Social Protection: Setting the Agenda." *Oxford Development Studies 45* (1): pp. 2–19.

Li, Yao-Tai. 2017. "Constituting Co-Ethnic Exploitation: The Economic and Cultural Meanings of Cash-in-Hand Jobs for Ethnic Chinese Migrants in Australia." *Critical Sociology 43* (6): pp. 919–932.

Liang, Li-Fang. 2014. "Live-in Migrant Care Workers in Taiwan: The Debates on the Household Service." *Asian and Pacific Migration Journal 23* (2): pp. 229–241.

Light, Donald W. 2012. "Categorical Inequality, Institutional Ambivalence, and Permanently Failing Institutions: The Case of Immigrants and Barriers to Health Care in America." *Ethnic and Racial Studies 35* (1): pp. 23–39.

Lijphart, Arend. 2012. *Patterns of Democracy*. New Haven, CT: Yale University Press.

Lim, Adelyn. 2016. "Transnational Organizing and Feminist Politics of Difference: The Mobilization of Domestic Workers in Hong Kong." *Asian Studies Review 40* (1): pp.70–88.

Liu, Cindy H., Stephen H. Chen, Yvonne Bohr, Leslie K. Wang, and Ed Tronick. 2017. "Exploring the Assumptions of Attachment Theory across Cultures: The Practice of Transnational Separation among Chinese Immigrant Parents and Children." In *The Cultural Nature of Attachment: Contextualizing Relationships and Development*, edited by Heidi Keller and Kim A. Bard, pp. 171–192. Cambridge, MA: MIT Press.

Liu, Hong. 2014. "Beyond Co-Ethnicity: The Politics of Differentiating and Integrating New Immigrants in Singapore." *Ethnic and Racial Studies 37* (7): pp. 1225–1238.

Locke, Richard M., Fei Qin, and Alberto Brause. 2007. "Does Monitoring Improve Labor Standards? Lessons from Nike." *ILR Review 61* (1): pp. 319–351.

Locke, Richard M., Ben A. Rissing, and Timea Pal. 2013. "Complements or Substitutes? Private Codes, State Regulation and the Enforcement of Labour Standards in Global Supply Chains." *British Journal of Industrial Relations 51* (3): pp. 519–552.

Lopez, Sarah Lynn. 2015. *The Remittance Landscape: Spaces of Migration in Rural Mexico and Urban USA*. Chicago, IL: University of Chicago Press.

Louie, Andrea. 2015. *How Chinese Are You? Adopted Chinese Youth and their Families Negotiate Identity and Culture*. New York: New York University Press.

Lund, Susan, Toos Daruvala, Richard Dobbs, Philipp Härle, Ju-Hon Kwek, and Ricardo Falcón. 2013. *Financial Globalization: Retreat or Reset? Global Capital Markets 2013*. New York: McKinsey Global Institute.

Lutz, Helma. 2008. *Migration and Domestic Work. A European Perspective on a Global Theme*. Aldershot, UK: Ashgate.

Madariaga, Aldo. 2020. *Neoliberal Resilience: Lessons in Democracy and Development from Latin America and Eastern Europe*. Princeton, NJ: Princeton University Press.

Madianou, Mirca. 2016. "Polymedia Communication Among Transnational Families: What Are the Long-Term Consequences for Migration." In *Family Life in an Age of Migration and Mobility: Global Perspectives through the Life Course*, edited by Majella Kilkey and Ewa Palenga-Möllenbeck, pp. 71–93. London: Palgrave Macmillan.

Madianou, Mirca, and Daniel Miller. 2011. "Mobile Phone Parenting: Reconfiguring Relationships Between Filipina Migrant Mothers and Their Left-Behind Children." *New Media and Society 13* (3): pp. 457–470.

Magda, Iga, Aneta Kiełczewska, and Nicola Brandt. 2018. *The 'Family 500+': Child Allowance and Female Labor Supply in Poland*. IBS Working Paper. Warsaw, PL: Institute for Structural Research.

Mahapatro, Sandhya, Ajay Bailey, K. S. James, and Inge Hutter. 2017. "Remittances and Household Expenditure Patterns in India and Selected States." *Migration and Development 6* (1): pp. 83–101.

Mahdavi, Pardis. 2016. *Crossing the Gulf: Love and Family in Migrant Lives*. Stanford, CA: Stanford University Press.

Mahlathi, Percy, and Jabu Dlamini. 2017. *From Brain Drain to Brain Gain: Understanding and Managing the Movement of Medical Doctors in the South Africa Health Care System*. Geneva: World Health Organization.

Margheritis, Ana. 2007. "State-Led Transnationalism and Migration: Reaching out to the Argentine Community in Spain." *Global Networks 7* (1): 87–106.

Marrow, Helen B. 2009. "Immigrant Bureaucratic Incorporation: The Dual Roles of Professional Missions and Government Policies." *American Sociological Review 74* (5): pp. 756–776.

Marrow, Helen B. 2011. *New Destination Dreaming: Immigration, Race, and Legal Status in the Rural American South*. Stanford, CA: Stanford University Press.

Marrow, Helen B. 2012a. "The Power of Local Autonomy: Expanding Health Care to Unauthorized Immigrants in San Francisco." *Ethnic and Racial Studies 35* (1): pp. 72–87.

Marrow, Helen B. 2012b. "Deserving to a Point: Unauthorized Immigrants in San Francisco's Universal Access Healthcare Model." *Social Science and Medicine 74* (6): pp. 846–854.

Marrow, Helen B., and Tiffany D. Joseph. 2015. "Excluded and Frozen Out: Unauthorised Immigrants' (Non)Access to Care after US Health Care Reform." *Journal of Ethnic and Migration Studies 41* (4): pp. 2253–2273.

Marshall, Thomas Humphrey. 1950. *Citizenship and Social Class*. Cambridge, UK: Cambridge University Press. https://www.jstor.org/stable/j.ctt18mvns1.

Masanjala, Winford H. 2018. "Brain Drain in Africa: The Case of Tackling Capacity Issues in Malawi's Medical Migration." *Africa Portal*. May 31. https://www.africaportal.org/publications/brain-drain-africa-case-tackling-capacity-issues-malawis-medical-migration/.

Masselink, Leah E., and Shoou-Yih Daniel Lee. 2013. "Government Officials' Representation of Nurses and Migration in the Philippines." *Health Policy and Planning 28* (1): pp. 90–99.

Matchan, Linda. 2018. "The US Has a Huge Need for Home Health Care, and Many from Ghana Do the Hard Work." *Globe Correspondent*. September 16. https://www.bostonglobe.com/metro/2018/09/16/pipeline-from-africa-recent-immigrants-much-success-paying-back-breaking-work-caring-stories-frail-americans-home-back-home-they-seen/kosI4rnpckOHnAUDBLfhcO/story.html.

Mathai, Kamini. 2015. "Brain Drain in Reverse." *The Times of India*. December 20. https://timesofindia.indiatimes.com/city/chennai/Brain-drain-in-reverse/articleshow/50251723.cms.

Mathijsen, Aneta, and François Pierre Mathijsen. 2020. "Diasporic Medical Tourism: A Scoping Review of Quantitative and Qualitative Evidence." *Globalization and Health 16* (27): pp. 1–15.

Mauk, Ben. 2014. "Abu Dhabi's High Cost of Culture." *The New Yorker*. January 28. https://www.newyorker.com/business/currency/abu-dhabis-high-cost-of-culture.

Mazzucato, Valentina. 2007. "Transnational Reciprocity: Ghanaian Migrants and the Care of Their Parents Back Home." In *Generations in Africa: Connections and Conflicts*, edited by Erdmute Alber, Sjaak van der Geest, and Susan R. Whyte, pp. 91–109. Münster, DE: LIT Verlag.

Mazzucato, Valentina. 2011 "Reverse Remittances in the Migration–Development Nexus: Two-way Flows Between Ghana and the Netherlands." *Population, Space, and Place 17* (5): pp. 454–468.

Mazzucato, Valentina, Victor Cebotari, Angela Veale, Allen White, Marzia Grassi, and Jeanne Vivet. 2015. "International Parental Migration and the Psychological Well-being of Children in Ghana, Nigeria, and Angola." *Social Science and Medicine 132* (May): pp. 215–224.

McCarthy, Niall. 2017. "Which Countries Have the Highest Levels of Labor Union Membership? [Infographic]." *Forbes*. June 20. https://www.forbes.com/sites/niallmccarthy/2017/06/20/which-countries-have-the-highest-levels-of-labor-union-membership-infographic/.

McDaniels, Andrea K. 2017. "'They Were the Secret:' Johns Hopkins Takes Mission to Lebanon, Around the World." *The Baltimore Sun*. October 25. https://www.baltimoresun.com/health/bs-hs-hopkins-international-20170808-story.html.

McKinsey Global Institute. 2003. *Offshoring: Is It a Win-Win Game?* New York: McKinsey & Company.

Meseguer, Covadonga, Sebastián Lavezzolo, and Javier Aparicio. 2016. "Financial Remittances, Trans-Border Conversations, and the State." *Comparative Migration Studies 4* (1): 13.

Meyer, J. John Boli, Francisco Ramirez, and George Thomas. 1997. "World Polity and the Nation State." *American Journal of Sociology 103* (1): pp. 144–181.

Millard, Adele, Loretta Baldassar, and Raelene Wilding. 2018. "The Significance of Digital Citizenship in the Well-Being of Older Migrants." *Public Health 158* (May): pp. 144–148.

Mingot, Ester Serra, and Valentina Mazzucato. 2018a. "Moving for a 'Better' Welfare? The Case of Transnational Sudanese Families." *Global Networks 19* (1): pp. 139–157.

Mingot, Ester Serra, and Valentina Mazzucato. 2018b. "Providing Social Protection to Mobile Population: Symbiotic Relationships between Migrants and Welfare Institutions." *Journal of Ethnic and Migration Studies 44* (13): pp. 2127–2143. Online Edition. https://www.tandfonline.com/doi/full/10.1080/1369183X.2018.1429900.

Ministerium für Bildung und Forschung [German ministry of education and research]. n.d. "Bildung Und Forschung: Türkei [Research and Education: Turkey]." Kooperation International. Accessed July 3, 2020. https://www.kooperation-international.de/laender/asien/tuerkei/.

Ministerul pentru Românii de Pretutindeni. 2020. "Departamentul Pentru Românii de Pretutindeni." Accessed July 4, 2020. http://www.mprp.gov.ro/web/.

Ministry of External Affairs. 2020. "Overseas Indian Affairs." Accessed July 4, 2020. https://www.mea.gov.in/overseas-indian-affairs.htm.

Ministry of Trade and Industry Singapore. 2020. "Advisory for Businesses on Large-Scale Events amidst the COVID-19 (Coronavirus Disease 2019) Situation." Singapore: MTI. https://www.mti.gov.sg/-/media/MTI/Newsroom/COVID-19/v2/Advisory-for-businesses-on-largescale-events15-Feb.pdf.

Mishra, Prachi. 2006. *Emigration and Brain Drain: Evidence from the Caribbean*. Working Paper No. 06/25. Washington DC: International Monetary Fund.

Mogaka, John J. O., Joyce M. Tsoka-Gwegweni, Lucia M. Mupara, and Tivani Mashamba-Thompson. 2017. "Role, Structure and Effects of Medical Tourism in Africa: A Systematic Scoping Review Protocol." *BMJ Open 7*: e013021.

Mok, Ka Ho. 2008. "Singapore's Global Education Hub Ambitions: University Governance Change and Transnational Higher Education." *International Journal of Educational Management 22* (6): pp. 527–546.

Mok, Ka Ho, and Xiao Han. 2016. "The Rise of Transnational Higher Education and Changing Educational Governance in China." *International Journal of Comparative Education and Development 18* (1): pp. 19–39.

Morantz, Alison D. 2013. "Coal Mine Safety: Do Unions Make a Difference?" *ILR Review 66* (1): pp. 88–116.

Mounk, Yascha. 2018. *The People Vs. Democracy: Why Our Freedom Is in Danger and How to Save It*. Cambridge, MA: Harvard University Press.

Moyce, Sally C., and Marc Schenker. 2018. "Migrant Workers and Their Occupational Health and Safety." *Annual Review of Public Health 39* (1): pp. 351–365.

Muchowiecka, Laura. 2013. "The End of Multiculturalism? Immigration and Integration in Germany and the United Kingdom." *Inquiries Journal 5* (6). Online Edition. http://www.inquiriesjournal.com/articles/735/the-end-of-multiculturalism-immigration-and-integration-in-germany-and-the-united-kingdom.

Mudambi, Ram, and Markus Venzin. 2010. "The Strategic Nexus of Offshoring and Outsourcing Decisions." *Journal of Management Studies 47* (8): pp. 1510–1533.

Mui, Ada C., and Tazuko Shibusawa. 2008. *Asian American Elders in the Twenty-First Century: Key Indicators of Well-Being*. New York: Columbia University Press.

Müller, Jan-Werner. 2016. *What Is Populism?* Philadelphia, PA: University of Pennsylvania Press.

Näre, Lena, Katie Walsh, and Loretta Baldassar. 2017. "Ageing in Transnational Contexts: Transforming Everyday Practices and Identities in Later Life." *Identities: Global Studies in Culture and Power 24* (5): pp. 515–523.

Newendorp, Nicole. 2020. *Chinese Senior Migrants and the Globalization of Retirement*. Palo Alto, CA: Stanford University Press.

Ní Ghráinne, Bríd, and Aisling McMahon. 2017. "A Public International Law Approach to Safeguard Nationality for Surrogate-Born Children." *Legal Studies 37* (2): pp. 324–342.

NIH. 2019. *Medical Education Partnership Initiative (MEPI)*. Bethesda, MD: Fogarty International Center of National Institute of Health.

Nolan, Eimear. 2018. "Foreign Doctors No Longer Want to Work in Irish Hospitals." *The Irish Times*. October 18. https://www.irishtimes.com/opinion/foreign-doctors-no-longer-want-to-work-in-irish-hospitals-1.3666637.

Norris, Pippa, and Ronald Inglehart. 2019. *Cultural Backlash: Trump, Brexit, and Authoritarian Populism*. Cambridge, UK: Cambridge University Press.

NPR. 2007. "India's Doctors Returning Home." *NPR (National Public Radio)*, November 30. https://www.npr.org/templates/story/story.php?storyId=16774871.

NPR. 2009. "La. Teacher Union Files Complaint Against Recruiter." *NPR (National Public Radio)*, October 2. https://www.npr.org/templates/story/story.php?storyId=113423285.

Nussbaum, Martha C. 2013. *Creating Capabilities: The Human Development Approach*. Cambridge, MA: Harvard University Press.

Nyiri, Pal. 2018. "Educating World Citizens: The Rise of International Education in the Twenty-First Century." In *Navigating History: Economy, Society, Knowledge, and Nature: Essays in Honour of Prof. Dr. C.A. Davids*, edited by Pepijn Brandon, Sabine Go, and Wybren Verstegen, pp. 64–80. Library of Economic History. Leiden, NL: Brill.

Nykanen, Eeva. 2001. "Protecting Children? The European Convention on Human Rights and Child Asylum Seekers." *European Journal of Migration and Law 3* (3–4): pp. 315–345.

Obucina, Vedran. 2019. "Will Romania Accommodate Asian Workers and Change Its Labor Market?" *Central European Financial Observer*. June 3. https://www.obserwatorfinansowy.pl/in-english/macroeconomics/will-romania-accommodate-asian-workers-and-change-its-labor-market/.

OECD. n.d. *Health at a Glance 2017: OECD Indicators*. Paris: OECD Publishing. https://www.oecd.org/els/health-systems/Health-at-a-Glance-2017-Chartset.pdf.

O'Halloran, Marie. 2005. "Higgins Says 'Bonded Labour' Used to Build Roads." *The Irish Times*. February 9. https://www.irishtimes.com/news/higgins-says-bonded-labour-used-to-build-roads-1.413379.

Øien, Cecilie. 2006. "Transnational Networks of Care: Angolan Children in Fosterage in Portugal." *Ethnic and Racial Studies 29* (6): pp. 1104–1117.

Olds, Kris. 2008. "Analysing Australia's Global Higher Ed Export Industry." *GlobalHigherEd*. June 24. https://globalhighered.wordpress.com/category/brisbane-communique/.

Oliver, Caroline. 2013. *Retirement Migration: Paradoxes of Ageing*. New York: Routledge.

Olivier, Marius, and Avinash Govindjee. 2013. "Labour Rights and Social Protection of Migrant Workers: In Search of a Co-Ordinated Legal Response," Paper presented at the inaugural conference of the Labour Law Research Network (LLRN), Barcelona, Spain, 13–15 June. https://www.upf.edu/documents/3298481/3410076/2013-LLRNConf_OlivierxGovind.pdf/fd58864e-aa42-4400-b854-5767063ffb8d.

Ong, Aihwa. 1999. *Flexible Citizenship: The Cultural Logics of Transnationality*. Durham, NC: Duke University Press.

Ono, Mayumi. 2008. "Long-Stay Tourism and International Retirement Migration: Japanese Retirees in Malaysia." In *Transnational Migration in East Asia*, edited by Shinji Yamashita, Makito Minami, David W. Haines, and Jerry S. Eades, pp. 151–162. Osaka, JP: National Museum of Ethnology.

Ono, Mayumi. 2015. "Commoditization of Lifestyle Migration: Japanese Retirees in Malaysia." *Mobilities 10* (4): pp. 609–627.

Orellana, Majorie Faulstich, Barrie Thorne, Anna Chee, and Wan Shun Eva Lam. 2001. "Transnational Childhoods: The Participation of Children in Processes of Family Migration." *Social Problems 48* (4): pp. 572–591.

Orme, Nicholas. 2006. *Medieval Schools: From Roman Britain to Renaissance England*. New Haven, CT: Yale University Press.

Osnos, Evan. 2014. *Age of Ambition: Chasing Fortune, Truth, and Faith in the New China*. New York: Alfred Knopf.

Papademetriou, Demetrios, and Madeleine Sumption. 2011. *Rethinking Points Systems and Employer-Selected Immigration*. Brussels, BE: Migration Policy Institute.

Paraskou, Anastasia, and Babu P. George. 2017. "The Market for Reproductive Tourism: An Analysis with Special Reference to Greece." *Global Health Research Policy 1* (1): pp. 2–16.

Parella Rubio, Sonia, Alisa Petroff and Thales Speroni. 2019. "Oportunidades y tensiones de la protección social más allá del marco nacional: la asistencia sanitaria transfronteriza en el contexto español." In *Mondo Migrante-Special Issue: Global and Transanational Social Protection: diritti sociali al di là delle frontier*, edited by Simone Castellani and Francesca Lagomarsino, pp. 85–105. Milán, IT: Franco Angeli.

Parreñas, Rhacel Salazar. 2000. "Migrant Filipina Domestic Workers and the International Division of Reproductive Labor." *Gender and Society 14* (4): pp. 560–581.

Parreñas, Rhacel Salazar. 2005. *Children of Globalization: Transnational Families and Gendered Woes*. Stanford, CA: Stanford University Press.

Parreñas, Rhacel Salazar. 2008. *The Forces of Domesticity: Filipina Migrants and Globalization*. New York, NY: New York University Press.

Parreñas, Rhacel Salazar. 2015. *Servants of Globalization: Migration and Domestic Work*. Second Edition. Stanford, CA: Stanford University Press.

Parreñas, Rhacel Salazar, Krittiya Kantachote, and Rachel Silvey. 2020. "Soft Violence: Migrant Domestic Worker Precarity and the Management of Unfree Labour in Singapore." *Journal of Ethnic and Migration Studies 47*(20): 4671–4687. https://doi.org/10.1080/1369183X.2020.1732614.

Parreñas, Rhacel Salazar, Rachel Silvey, Maria Cecilia Hwang, and Carolyn Areum Choi. 2019. "Serial Labor Migration: Precarity and Itinerancy among Filipino and Indonesian Domestic Workers." *International Migration Review 53* (4): pp. 1230–1258.

Paul, Anju Mary. 2015. "Negotiating Migration, Performing Gender." *Social Forces 94* (1): pp. 271–293.

Paul, Anju Mary. 2017. *Multinational Maids: Stepwise Migration in a Global Labor Market*. Cambridge, UK: Cambridge University Press.

Paul, Ruxandra. 2017. "Welfare Without Borders: Unpacking the Bases of Transnational Social Protection for International Migrants." *Oxford Development Studies 45* (1): pp. 33–46.

Paul, Ruxandra. 2020. *Citizens of the Market*. Unpublished manuscript.

PBS. 2017. "A Look at Hagwons in South Korea." *PBS* (Public Broadcasting Services)—School Inc.—A Personal Journey with Andrew Coulson. April 3. https://www.pbs.org/wnet/school-inc/video/look-hagwons-south-korea/.

Pelsue, Brendan. 2017. "When It Comes to Education, the Federal Government Is in Charge of ... Um, What?" *Harvard Ed. Magazine*. Fall 2017. https://www.gse.harvard.edu/news/ed/17/08/when-it-comes-education-federal-government-charge-um-what.

Peng, Ito. 2018. "Shaping and Reshaping Care and Migration in East and Southeast Asia." *Critical Sociology 44* (7–8): pp. 1117–1132.

Peng, Yinni, and Odalia M. H. Wong. 2013. "Diversified Transnational Mothering via Telecommunication: Intensive, Collaborative, and Passive." *Gender and Society 27* (4): pp. 491–513.

Pérez, Elena Ronda, Fernando G. Benavides, Katia Levecque, John G. Love, Emily Felt, and Ronan Van Rossem. 2012. "Differences in Working Conditions and Employment Arrangements Among Migrant and Non-Migrant Workers in Europe." *Ethnicity and Health 17* (6): pp. 563–577.

Pew Research Center. 2016. *Record 1.3 Million Sought Asylum in Europe in 2015*. Washington, DC: Pew Research Center.

Pickering, John, Valorie A. Crooks, Jeremy Snyder, and Jeffery Morgan. 2019. "What Is Known about the Factors Motivating Short-Term International Retirement Migration? A Scoping Review." *Population Ageing 12* (3): pp. 379–395.

Piore, Michael J. 1979. *Birds of Passage: Migrant Labor and Industrial Societies*. Cambridge, UK: Cambridge University Press. https://www.popline.org/node/497102.

Piore, Michael J., and Andrew Schrank. 2008. "Toward Managed Flexibility: The Revival of Labour Inspection in the Latin World." *International Labour Review 147* (1): pp. 1–23. https://doi.org/10.1111/j.1564-913X.2008.00021.x.

Piper, Nicola. 2017. "Global Governance of Labour Migration: from 'Management' of Migration to an Integrated Rights-Based Approach." In *Regulatory Theory: Foundations and Applications*, edited by Peter Drahos, pp. 377–394. Canberra: Australia National University Press.

Piper, Nicola, and Michele Ford, eds. 2006. "Migrant NGOs and Labor Unions: A Partnership in Progress?" *Asian and Pacific Migration Journal 14* (9): 299-430.

Piper, Nicola, and Keiko Yamanaka. 2005. *Feminized Migration in East and Southeast Asia: Policies, Actions and Empowerment*. Geneva: UNRISD (United Nations Research Institute for Social Development).

Pison, Gilles. 2013. "France 2012: Stable Fertility, Declining Infant Mortality." *Population and Societies 498* (3): pp. 1–4.

Piven, Frances Fox, and Richard Cloward. 2012. *Poor People's Movements: Why They Succeed, How They Fail*. New York: Knopf Doubleday Publishing Group.

Plimmer, Gill. 2013. "The Unstoppable Rise of Outsourcing." *Financial Times*. June 12. https://www.ft.com/content/ee63a82c-d353-11e2-b3ff-00144feab7de.

Ponce, Juan, Iliana Olivié, and Mercedes Onofa. 2011. "The Role of International Remittances in Health Outcomes in Ecuador: Prevention and Response to Shocks." *International Migration Review 45* (3): pp. 727–745.

Portes, Alejandro, Patricia Fernández-Kelly, and Donald Light. 2012. "Life on the Edge: Immigrants Confront the American Health System." *Ethnic and Racial Studies 35* (1): pp. 3–22.

Pun, Ngai, and Anita Koo. 2015. "A 'World-Class' (Labor) Camp/us: Foxconn and China's New Generation of Labor Migrants" *Positions: Asia Critique 23* (3): pp. 411–436.

Purdy, Matthew. 2001. "The Making of a Suspect: The Case of Wen Ho Lee." *The New York Times*. February 4. https://www.nytimes.com/2001/02/04/us/the-making-of-a-suspect-the-case-of-wen-ho-lee.html.

Purkayastha, Bandana, Miho Iwata, Shweta Majumdar, Ranita Ray, and Trisha Tiamzon. 2012. *As the Leaves Turn Gold: Asian Americans and Experiences of Aging*. Lanham, MD: Rowman & Littlefield Publishers.

Putnam, Robert D. 2007. "E Pluribus Unum: Diversity and Community in the Twenty-First Century The 2006 Johan Skytte Prize Lecture." *Scandinavian Political Studies 30* (2): pp. 137–174.

Pytel, Sławomir, and Oimahmad Rahmonov. 2019. "Migration Processes and the Underlying Reasons: A Study on Pensioner Migrants in Poland." *Population, Space and Place 25* (3): e2197. https://doi.org/10.1002/psp.2197.

Quandt, Sara A., Joseph G. Grzywacz, Antonio Marín, Lourdes Carrillo, Michael L. Coates, Bless Burke, and Thomas A. Arcury. 2006. "Illnesses and Injuries Reported by Latino Poultry Workers in Western North Carolina." *American Journal of Industrial Medicine 49* (5): pp. 343–351.

Raghuram, Parvati. 2009. "Which Migration, What Development? Unsettling the Edifice of Migration and Development." *Population, Space and Place 15* (2): pp. 103–117.

Rajan, S. Irudaya, and K.C. Zachariah. 2010. *Remittances to Kerala: Impact on the Economy*. Washington, DC: Middle East Institute.

Raudenbush, Danielle T. 2020. *Health Care Off the Books: Poverty, Illness, and Strategies for Survival in Urban America*. Oakland, CA: University of California Press.

Recchi, Ettore. 2015. *Mobile Europe: The Theory and Practice of Free Movement in the EU*. London: Palgrave Macmillan.

Record, Richard, and Abdu Mohiddin. 2006. "An Economic Perspective on Malawi's Medical 'Brain Drain.'" *Globalization and Health 2* (12). Online Edition. https://pubmed.ncbi.nlm.nih.gov/17176457/.

Redden, Elizabeth. 2019. "Stealing Information." Inside Higher Ed blog. April 29. https://www.insidehighered.com/news/2019/04/29/fbi-director-discusses-chinese-espionage-threat-us-academic-research.

Reuters. 2017. "'Dubai Is Danger': Death Brings Home Reality of Indian Workers' Life in Gulf." *Hindustan Times*. October 30. https://www.hindustantimes.com/india-news/dubai-is-danger-death-brings-home-reality-of-indian-workers-life-in-gulf/story-MvQBb0qskWZQLjTotOkODK.html.

Robinson, Mary, and Peggy Clark. 2008. "Forging Solutions to Health Worker Migration." *The Lancet 371* (9613): pp. 691–693.

Rodriguez, Robyn Magalit. 2010. *Migrants for Export: How the Philippine State Brokers Labor to the World*. Minneapolis, MN: University of Minnesota Press.

Rogers, Rosemarie. 1985. *Guests Come to Stay*. New York: Routledge.

Romo, Vanessa, and Joel Rose. 2019. "Administration Cuts Education and Legal Services for Unaccompanied Minors." *NPR (National Public Radio)*. June 5. https://www.npr.org/2019/06/05/730082911/administration-cuts-education-and-legal-services-for-unaccompanied-minors.

Roth, Wendy. 2012. *Race Migrations: Latinos and the Cultural Transformation of Race*. Stanford, CA: Stanford University Press.

Rubagumya, Fidel, Michael Hrdy, M. A. Uwase, B. Kamanzi, P. Kyamanywa, R. Petroze, and J. F. Calland. 2016. "Physician Brain Drain in Sub-Saharan Africa: The Career Plans of Rwanda's Future Doctors." *Rwanda Medical Journal 73* (1): pp. 5–10.

Rueda, David. 2014. "Dualization, Crisis, and the Welfare State." *Socio-Economic Review 12* (2): pp. 381–407.

Sabates-Wheeler, Rachel, Johannes Koettl, and Johanna Avato. 2011. "Social Security for Migrants: A Global Overview of Portability Arrangements." In *Migration and Social Protection: Claiming Social Rights Beyond Borders*, edited by Rachel Sabates-Wheeler and Rayah Feldman, pp. 91–116. Basingstoke, UK: Palgrave Macmillan.

Sainsbury, Diane. 2012. *Welfare States and Immigrant Rights: The Politics of Inclusion and Exclusion*. New York: Oxford University Press.

Sampaio, Dora, Russell King, and Katie Walsh. 2018. "Geographies of the Ageing-Migration Nexus: An Introduction." *Area 50* (4): pp. 440–443.

Sánchez, Brenda. 2017. "Deportados Unidos en la Lucha: Un grupo de apoyo a los mexicanos expulsados de EU." Conexión Migrante. March 24. https://conexionmigrante.com/2017-/03-/24/deportados-unidos-en-la-lucha-grupo-apoyo-a-los-mexicanos-repatriados/.

Sassen, Saskia. 1996. *Losing Control? Sovereignty in the Age of Globalization*. New York: Columbia University Press.

Sassen, Saskia. 2001. *The Global City: New York, London Tokyo*. Second Edition. Princeton, NJ: Princeton University Press.

Sassen, Saskia. 2006. *Territory, Authority, Rights: From Medieval to Global Assemblages*. Princeton, NJ: Princeton University Press.

Scheiber, Noam. 2019. "Volkswagen Factory Workers in Tennessee Reject Union." *The New York Times*. June 14. https://www.nytimes.com/2019/06/14/business/economy/volkswagen-chattanooga-uaw-union.html.

Scherman, Rhoda, Gabriela Misca, Karen Rotab, and Peter Selman. 2016. "Global Commercial Surrogacy and International Adoption: Parallels and Differences." *Adoption and Fostering 40* (1): pp. 20–35.

Schierup, Carl-Ulrik, Peo Hansen, and Stephen Castles. 2006. *Migration, Citizenship, and the European Welfare State: A European Dilemma*. New York: Oxford University Press.

Schmalzbauer, Leah. 2005. *Striving and Surviving: A Daily Life Analysis of Honduran Transnational Families*. New York: Routledge.

Schmalzbauer, Leah. 2008. "Family Divided: The Class Formation of Honduran Transnational Families." *Global Networks 8* (3): pp. 329–346.

Schmalzbauer, Leah. 2014. *The Last Best Place? Gender, Family, and Migration in the New West*. Stanford, CA: Stanford University Press.

Schmitter, Philippe C., and Terry Lynn Karl. 1991. "What Democracy Is . . . and Is Not." *Journal of Democracy 2* (3): pp. 75–88.

Schölgens, Gesa. 2013. "Renter-Traum Thailand: Tipps Für Pflege Im Ausland (Thailand – A Pensioneers' Dream: Tips for Long Term Care Abroad)." *Frankfurter Rundschau*. April 13. http://www.fr-online.de/vorsorge/-ausland-pflege-thailand-demenzkranke-alzheimer-auswandern-rente,21157290,22353290.html.

Scott, James. 1998. *Seeing Like a State: How Certain Schemes to Improve the Human Condition Have Failed*. New Haven, CT: Yale University Press.

Scribner, Todd. 2013. "Immigration as a 'Sign of the Times': From the Nineteenth Century to the Present." In *On "Strangers No Longer": Perspectives on the Historic U.S.-Mexican Catholic Bishops' Pastoral Letter on Migration*, edited by Todd Scribner and J. Kevin Appleby, pp. 3–35. New York: Paulist Press.

Séchet, Raymonde, and Despina Vasilcu. 2015. "Physicians' Migration from Romania to France: A Brain Drain into Europe?" *Cybergeo: European Journal of Geography 743* (October), Online Edition. https://doi.org/10.4000/cybergeo.27249.

Secretaría de Educación Pública. n.d.a. "Mexterior." Accessed April 2020. https://www.mexterior.sep.gob.mx/.

Secretaría de Educación Pública. n.d.b. "Programa Bincional De Educación Migrante. Accessed August 12: https://www.sep.gob.mx/es/sep1/sep1_Programa_Binacional_de_Educacion_Migrante.

Selman, Peter. 2012. "The Global Decline of Intercountry Adoption: What Lies Ahead?" *Social Policy and Society 11* (3): pp. 381–397.

Sen, Amartya. 1997. "Human Capital and Human Capability." *World Development 25* (2): pp. 1959–1961.

Sexsmith, Kathleen. 2015. "'But We Can't Call 9-1-1': Socially Unprotected Dairy Farmworkers in the New York Borderlands." Paper Presented at Global Social Protections Workshop (February). Harvard University.

Sexsmith, Kathleen. 2017. "'But We Can't Call 9-1-1': Undocumented Migrant Farmworkers and Access to Social Protection on New York Dairies." *Oxford Development Studies 45* (1): pp. 96–111.

Shams, Tahseen. 2020. *Here, There, and Elsewhere: The Making of Immigrant Identities in a Globalized World.* Palo Alto, CA: Stanford University Press.

Siddiqi, Arjumand, Daniyal Zuberi, and Quynh C. Nguyen. 2009. "The Role of Health Insurance in Explaining Immigrant versus Non-Immigrant Disparities in Access to Health Care: Comparing the United States to Canada." *Social Science and Medicine 69* (10): pp. 1452–1459.

Silver, Beverly. 2005. *Forces of Labor: Workers' Movements and Globalization Since 1870.* Second Edition. Cambridge, UK: Cambridge University Press.

Silvey, Rachel. 2006. "Consuming the Transnational Family: Indonesian Migrant Workers to Saudi Arabia." *Global Networks 6* (1): pp. 23–40.

Sklarow, Mark. 2011. "Ethical Guideposts for Independent Educational Consultants." *Journal of College Admission 210* (Winter): p.7.

Smales, Philippa. 2020. "The Use of ICTs by Domestic Workers and Domestic Worker Organisations." *Women in Action 1* (1): pp. 39–42.

Smith, Andrea, Richard N. Lalonde, and Simone Johnson. 2004. "Serial Migration and Its Implications for the Parent-Child Relationship: A Retrospective Analysis of the Experiences of the Children of Caribbean Immigrants." *Cultural Diversity and Ethnic Minority Psychology 10* (2): pp. 107–122.

Smith, Robert C. 2006. *Mexican New York: Transnational Lives of New Immigrants.* Berkeley, CA: University of California Press.

Smith, Robert C., Don J. Waisanen, and Guillermo Yrizar Barbosa. 2020. *Immigration and Strategic Public Health Communication: Lessons from the Transnational Seguro Popular Project.* New York: Taylor and Francis.

Snowden, Frank. 2019. *Epidemics and Society: From the Black Death to the Present.* New Haven, CT: Yale University Press.

Solari, Cinzia D. 2018. *On the Shoulders of Grandmothers: Gender, Migration, and Post-Soviet Nation Building.* New York: Routledge.

Soysal, Yasemin Nuhoglu, and David Strang. 1989. "Construction of the First Mass Education Systems in Nineteenth-Century Europe." *Sociology of Education 62* (4): pp. 277–288.

Spalding, Ana K. 2013. "Lifestyle Migration to Bocas Del Toro, Panama: Exploring Migration Strategies and Introducing Local Implications of the Search for Paradise." *International Review of Social Research 3* (1): pp. 67–86.

Spicer, Neil. 2008. "Places of Exclusion and Inclusion: Asylum-Seeker and Refugee Experiences of Neighbourhoods in the UK." *Journal of Ethnic and Migration Studies 34* (4): pp. 491–510.

Stack, Megan K. 2020. "A Sudden Coronavirus Surge Brought Out Singapore's Dark Side." *The New York Times.* May 20. https://www.nytimes.com/2020/05/20/magazine/singapore-coronavirus.html.

Steer, Liesbet, Julia Gillard, Emily Gustafsson-Wright, and Michael Lantham. 2015. *Non-State Actors in Education in Developing Countries*. Washington, DC: Center for Universal Education at Brookings Institution.

Storrow, Richard F. 2010. "The Pluralism Problem in Cross-border Reproductive Care." *Human Reproduction 25* (12): pp. 2939–2943.

Strasser, Sabine, and Eda Elif Tibet. 2019. "The Border Event in the Everyday: Hope and Constraints in the Lives of Young Unaccompanied Asylum Seekers in Turkey." *Journal of Ethnic and Migration Studies*. Online Edition. https://doi.org/10.1080/1369183X.2019.1584699.

Sullivan, Eileen and Zolan Kanno-Youngs. 2021. "U.S. Shows Progress in Moving Migrant Children from Border Jails." *The New York Times*. April 30. https://www.nytimes.com/2021/04/30/us/politics/biden-border-children.html?searchResultPosition=2.

Sun, Ken Chih-Yan. 2012. "Fashioning Reciprocal Norms of Elder Care: A Case of Immigrants in the U.S. and Their Parents in Taiwan." *Journal of Family Issues 33* (9): pp. 1240–1271.

Sun, Ken Chih-Yan. 2013. "Rethinking Migrant Families from a Transnational Perspective: Experiences of Parents and Their Children." *Sociology Compass 7* (6): pp. 445–458.

Sun, Ken Chih-Yan. 2014a. "Transnational Kinscription: A Case of Parachute Kids and Their Parents in Taiwan." *Journal of Ethnic and Migration Studies 40* (9): pp. 1431–1449.

Sun, Ken Chih-Yan. 2014b. "Transnational Healthcare Seeking: How Aging Taiwanese Return Migrants Think About Homeland Public Benefits." *Global Networks 14* (4): pp. 533–550.

Sun, Ken Chih-Yan. 2017. "Managing Transnational Ambivalence: How Stay-behind Parents Grapple with Family Separation Across Time." *Identities: Global Studies in Culture and Power 24* (5): pp. 509–605.

Sun, Ken Chih-Yan. 2018. "Negotiating the Boundaries of Social Membership: The Case of Aging Return Migrants to Taiwan." *Current Sociology 66* (2): pp. 286–302.

Sun, Ken Chih-Yan. 2021. *Time and Migration: How Long-Term Taiwanese Migrants Negotiate Later-Life*. Ithaca, NY: Cornell University Press.

Sun, Ken Chih-Yan. forthcoming. "Transnational Family Caregiving During a Global Pandemic." In *Confronting the Global Care Crisis during COVID-19: Past Problems, New Issues, and Pathways to Change*, edited by Mignon Duffy, Amy Armenia, and Kim Price-Glynn. New Brunswick, NJ: Rutgers University Press.

Sun, Ken Chih-Yan, and Xuemei Cao. 2022. "Intimacies Compared: How Caregivers for Left-behind Parents Respond to Multi-Local Family Separation." *American Behavioral Scientist 66* (2): pp. 699–716. https://doi.org/10.1177/00027642221075266.

Sun, Ken Chih-Yan, and Nazli Kibria. 2022. "The Micro-Politics of Recognition and Care: How Adult Children in Urban China Negotiate Relationships with Emigrant Siblings." *Social Problems 69* (4): pp. 952–967. https://doi.org/10.1093/socpro/spab021.

Sunil, Thankam S., Viviana Rojas, and Don E. Bradley. 2007. "United States' International Retirement Migration: The Reasons for Retiring to the Environs of Lake Chapala, Mexico." *Ageing and Society 27* (4): pp. 489–510.

Sussman, Anna Louie. 2019. "The Poland Model—Promoting 'Family Values' With Cash Handouts." *The Atlantic*. October 14. https://www.theatlantic.com/international/archive/2019/10/poland-family-values-cash-handouts/599968/.

Thai, Hung Cam. 2014. *Insufficient Funds: The Culture of Money in Low-Wage Transnational Families*. Stanford, CA: Stanford University Press.

Thang, Leng, Sachiko Sone, and Mika Toyota. 2012. "Freedom Found? The Later-Life Transnational Migration of Japanese Women to Western Australia and Thailand." *Asian and Pacific Migration Journal 21* (2): pp. 239–262.

The United Nations. 2021. "International Migration 2020 Highlights." *United Nations.* January 15. https://www.un.org/development/desa/pd/sites/www.un.org.development.desa.pd/files/international_migration_2020_highlights_ten_key_messages.pdf.

Thelen, Kathleen. 2019. "The American Precariat: U.S. Capitalism in Comparative Perspective." *Perspectives on Politics 17* (1): pp. 5–27.

Thieme, Susan. 2017. "Educational Consultants in Nepal: Professionalization of Services for Students Who Want to Study Abroad." *Mobilities 12* (2): pp. 243–258.

Thomas, Susan. 2017. "The Precarious Path of Student Migrants: Education, Debt, and Transnational Migration among Indian Youth." *Journal of Ethnic and Migration Studies 43* (11): pp. 1873–1889.

Titzmann, Peter F., and Richard M. Lee. 2018. "Adaptation of Young Immigrants: A Developmental Perspective on Acculturation Research." *European Psychologist 23* (1): pp. 72–82.

Toyota, Mika. 2006. "Ageing and Transnational Householding: Japanese Retirees in Southeast Asia." *International Development Planning Review 28* (4): pp. 515–531.

Toyota, Mika, and Leng Thang. 2012. "Reverse Marriage Migration: A Case Study of Japanese Brides in Bali." *Asian and Pacific Migration Journal 21* (3): pp. 345–364.

Tribune News Service. 2016. "Why China's 'Parachute Kids' Risk Loneliness, Alienation to Study in the United States." *South China Morning Post.* November 24. https://www.scmp.com/news/china/society/article/2048887/why-chinas-parachute-kids-risk-loneliness-alienation-study-united.

Trooboff, Stevan, Michael Vande Berg, and Jack Rayman. 2007. "Employer Attitudes toward Study Abroad." *Frontiers: The Interdisciplinary Journal of Study Abroad 15* (1): pp. 17–34.

Tsogas, George. 2018. "Transnational Labor Regulation, Reification, and Commodification: A Critical Review." *Journal of Labor and Society 21* (4): pp. 517–532.

Tsourapas, Gerasimos. 2021. *Migration Diplomacy in the Middle East and North Africa: Power, Mobility, and the State.* Manchester, UK: Manchester University Press.

Turner, David, and Hüseyin Yolcu, eds. 2014. *Neo-Liberal Educational Reforms: A Critical Analysis.* New York: Routledge.

UNHCR [United Nations High Commissioner for Refugees]. 2018. "Official Version – Draft 3 of the Global Compact on Refugees." June 4. https://www.unhcr.org/events/conferences/5b1579427/official-version-draft-3-global-compact-refugees-4-june-2018.html.

United States Conference of Catholic Bishops. 2003. "Strangers No Longer Together on the Journey of Hope." January 22. https://www.usccb.org/issues-and-action/human-life-and-dignity/immigration/strangers-no-longer-together-on-the-journey-of-hope.

U.S. Citizenship and Immigration Services. 2017. "Hague Process." Accessed July 11, 2021. https://www.uscis.gov/adoption/immigration-through-adoption/hague-process.

U.S. Department of Justice. 2021. "MIT Professor Arrested and Charged with Grant Fraud." U.S. Attorney's Office-District Massachusetts. January 14. https://www.justice.gov/usao-ma/pr/mit-professor-arrested-and-charged-grant-fraud.

U.S. Social Security Administration. n.d. "Payments to Beneficiaries Outside the U.S." Accessed May 21, 2020. https://www.ssa.gov/deposit/foreign.htm.

Valle, Eunice Vargas. 2017. Email message to Peggy Levitt. April 5, 2017.

Van der Meer, Tom, and Jochem Tolsma. 2014. "Ethnic Diversity and Its Effects on Social Cohesion." *Annual Review of Sociology 40* (July): pp. 459–478.

Van Walsum, Sarah. 2011. "Regulating Migrant Domestic Work in the Netherlands: Opportunities and Pitfalls." *Canada Journal of Women and the Law 23* (1): pp. 141–165.

Vega, Alma, and Karen Hirschman. 2019. "The Reasons Older Immigrants in the United States of America Report for Returning to Mexico." *Ageing and Society 39* (4): pp. 722–748.

Vertovec, Steven. 2007. "Super Diversity and Its Implications." *Ethnic and Racial Studies 30* (6): pp. 1024–1054.

Vezzoli, Simona, and Thomas Lacroix. 2010. *Building Bonds for Migration and Development: Diaspora Engagement Policies of Ghana, India and Serbia.* Eschborn, GE: International Migration Institute.

Victor, Christina R., Wendy Martin, and Maria Zubair. 2012. "Families and Caring amongst Older People in South Asian Communities in the UK: A Pilot Study." *European Journal of Social Work 15* (1): pp. 81–96.

Villa-Torres, Laura, Tonatiuh González-Vázquez, Paul J. Fleming, Edgar Leonel González-González, César Infante-Xibille, Rebecca Chavez, and Clare Barrington. 2017. "Transnationalism and Health: A Systematic Literature Review on the Use of Transnationalism in the Study of the Health Practices and Behaviors of Migrants." *Social Science and Medicine 183* (June): pp. 70–79.

Vitarelli Batista, M. 2021. "Higher Education Regionalization in South America." *Higher Education Policy 34* (May): pp. 474–498.

Vittin-Balima, Cécile. 2002. "Migrant workers: The ILO standards." *Labour Education 4* (129): pp. 5–12.

Vögtle, Eva Maria, and Kerstin Martens. 2014. "The Bologna Process as a Template for Transnational Policy Coordination." *Policy Studies 35* (3): pp. 246–263.

Vullnetari, Julie, and Russell King. 2008. "'Does Your Granny Eat Grass?' On Mass Migration, Care Drain and the Fate of Older People in Rural Albania." *Global Networks 8* (2): pp. 139–171.

Waldinger, Roger D., Chris Erickson, Ruth Milkman, Daniel Mitchell, Abel Valenzuela, Kent Wong, and Maurice Zeitlan. 1996. *Helots No More: A Case Study of the Justice for Janitors Campaign in Los Angeles.* Working Paper #15 in the Series. Los Angeles: The Lewis Center for Regional Policy Studies.

Walsh, Katie, and Lena Näre, eds. 2016. *Transnational Migration and Home in Older Age.* New York: Routledge.

Wang, Joseph. 2004. *Healthy Democracies: Welfare Politics in Taiwan and South Korea.* Ithaca, NY: Cornell University Press.

Wang, Leslie K. 2016. *Outsourced Children: Orphanage Care and Adoption in Globalizing China.* Stanford, CA: Stanford University Press.

Wang, Leslie K. 2018. "Chinese American 'Satellite Babies,' Raised Between Two Cultures." *Contexts 17* (4): pp. 24–29.

Wang, Sean H. 2017. "Fetal Citizens? Birthright Citizenship, Reproductive Futurism, and the 'Panic' over Chinese Birth Tourism in Southern California." *Environment and Planning D: Society and Space 35* (2): pp. 263–280.

Wang, Zhiyuan. 2020. "The Mixed Strategy of Authoritarian Labor Rights Repression." *Journal of Human Rights 19* (3): pp. 344–362.

Wassink, Joshua T. 2016. "Implications of Mexican Health Care Reform on the Health Coverage of Nonmigrants and Returning Migrants." *Public Health Policy 106* (5): pp. 848–850.

Waters, Johanna L. 2005. "Transnational Family Strategies and Education in the Contemporary Chinese Diaspora." *Global Networks 5* (4): pp. 359–377.

Waters, Johanna L. 2011. "Time and Transnationalism: A Longitudinal Study of Immigration, Endurance and Settlement in Canada." *Journal of Ethnic and Migration Studies 37* (7): pp. 1119–1135.

Waters, Mary C. 1999. *Black Identities: West Indian Immigrant Dreams and American Realities* Cambridge, MA: Harvard University Press.

Weil, David. 1991. "Enforcing OSHA: The Role of Labor Unions." *Industrial Relations: A Journal of Economy and Society 30* (1): pp. 20–36.

Weil, David. 2008. "A Strategic Approach to Labour Inspection." *International Labour Review 147* (4): pp. 349–375.

Weil, David. 2014. *The Fissured Workplace*. Cambridge, MA: Harvard University Press.

Weil, David, and Amanda Pyles. 2005. "Why Complain-Complaints, Compliance, and the Problem of Enforcement in the U.S. Workplace United States." *Comparative Labor Law and Policy Journal 27* (1): pp. 59–92.

Werf, Martin Van Der. 2001. "How Much Should Colleges Pay Their Janitors?" *The Chronicle of Higher Education*. August 3. https://www.chronicle.com/article/How-Much-Should-Colleges-Pay/14771.

Wessendorf, Suzanne. 2014. "'Being Open, but Sometimes Closed'. Conviviality in a Super-Diverse London Neighbourhood." *European Journal of Cultural Studies 17* (4): pp. 392–405.

Wibulpolprasert, Suwit, and Cha-Aim Pachanee. 2008. "Addressing the Internal Brain Drain of Medical Doctors in Thailand: The Story and Lesson Learned." *Global Social Policy 8* (1): pp. 12–15.

Wills, Jane. 2008. "Making Class Politics Possible: Organizing Contract Cleaners in London." *International Journal of Urban and Regional Research 32* (2): pp. 305–323.

Wiśniewska, Agnieszka, Marta Musiał, and Beata Świecka. 2017. "The Program 'Family 500 plus'—Implications for Household Finance in Poland." *CBU International Conference Proceedings 5*: pp. 490–494.

Woldegiorgis, Emnet Tadesse, Petronella Jonck, and Anne Goujon. 2015. "Regional Higher Education Reform Initiatives in Africa: A Comparative Analysis with the Bologna Process." *International Journal of Higher Education 4* (1): pp. 241–253.

Wolszczak-Derlacz, Joanna, and Aleksandra Parteka. 2018. "The Effects of Offshoring to Low-Wage Countries on Domestic Wages: A Worldwide Industrial Analysis." *Empirica 45* (1): pp. 129–163.

Wong, Kee Mun, and Ghazali Musa. 2015. "International Second Home Retirement Motives in Malaysia: Comparing British and Japanese Retirees." *Asia Pacific Journal of Tourism Research 20* (9): pp. 1041–1062.

World Bank. 2016. Migration and Remittances Factbook 2016. Washington, DC: World Bank.

World Bank. 2020. "World Bank Predicts Sharpest Decline of Remittances in Recent History." April 22. https://www.worldbank.org/en/news/press-release/2020/04/22/world-bank-predicts-sharpest-decline-of-remittances-in-recent-history.

World Bank Group. 2019. *Leveraging Economic Migration for Development: A Briefing for the World Bank Board*. Washington, DC: World Bank.

WRC [Worker Rights Consortium]. n.d. "The WRC Method." Accessed July 11, 2021. https://www.workersrights.org/our-work/.

Yarris, Kristin Elizabeth. 2017. *Care Across Generations: Solidarity and Sacrifice in Transnational Families*. Stanford, CA: Stanford University Press.

Yea, Sallie. 2019. "Secondary Precarity in Asia: Family Vulnerability in an Age of Unfree Labour." *Journal of Contemporary Asia 49* (4): pp. 552–567.

Yeates, Nicola. 2006. "GSP Forum: New (?) Directions in Global Social Policy." *Global Social Policy 6* (1): pp. 16–20.

Yeates, Padraig. 2001. "Turkish Company Expected to Win Bypass Contract after Undercutting Irish Firms." *The Irish Times*. August 16. https://www.irishtimes.com/news/turkish-company-expected-to-win-bypass-contract-after-undercutting-irish-firms-1.322739.

Yeoh, Brenda S. A., Shirlena Huang, and Theodora Lam. 2005. "Transnationalizing the 'Asian' Family: Imaginaries, Intimacies and Strategic Intents." *Global Networks 5* (4): pp. 307–315.

Yılmaz, Volkan, and Puren Aktas. 2020. "The Making of a Global Medical Tourism Destination: From State-Supported Privatisation to State Entrepreneurialism in Healthcare in Turkey." *Global Social Policy 21* (2): p. 18. https://doi.org/10.1177%2F1468018120981423.

Your Europe. n.d. "Recognition of Academic Diplomas." Accessed July 11, 2021. https://europa.eu/youreurope/citizens/education/university/recognition/index_en.htm.

Zechner, Minna. 2008. "Care of Older Persons in Transnational Settings." *Journal of Aging Studies 22* (1): pp. 32–44.

Zechner, Minna. 2017. "Transnational Habitus at the Time of Retirement." *Identities: Global Studies in Culture and Power 24* (5): pp. 573–589.

Zhang, Gehui, and Heying Jenny Zhan. 2009. "Beyond the Bible and the Cross: A Social and Cultural Analysis of Chinese Elders' Participation in Christian Congregations in the United States." *Sociological Spectrum 29* (2): pp. 295–317.

Zhou, Min. 1998. "'Parachute Kids' in Southern California: The Educational Experience of Chinese Children in Transnational Families." *Educational Policy 12* (6): pp. 682–704.

Zhou, Min, and Hon Liu. 2016. "Homeland Engagement and Host-Society Integration: A Comparative Study of New Chinese Immigrants in the United States and Singapore." *International Journal of Comparative Sociology 57* (1–2): pp. 30–52.

Zhou, Yanqiu Rachel. 2012. "Space, Time, and Self: Rethinking Aging in the Contexts of Immigration and Transnationalism." *Journal of Aging Studies 26* (3): pp. 232–242.

Index

For the benefit of digital users, indexed terms that span two pages (e.g., 52–53) may, on occasion, appear on only one of those pages.

Tables and figures are indicated by *t* and *f* following the page number